W9-AUI-424

"I have long appreciated Herb Sendek's ability to unite and inspire his players to perform at a higher level. That degree of selflessness is only possible when true leadership is present. Herb and Buddy have taken these concepts and applied them to business strategy. *Gen Y Now* provides leaders with real-world tools to build a winning plan."
> — Jeff Van Gundy, former head basketball coach, Houston Rockets

"Buddy Hobart and Coach Sendek have delivered a slam dunk. By providing such keen insights into this all-important generation they have developed a leadership guide for everyone looking to build a team in the new economy."
> — Tom Booth, Schering-Plough Consumer HealthCare, VP of International Marketing

"If we look back across the generations that came before us, we recognize that each confronted unique challenges and, for better or worse, shaped the world. As a university president now welcoming freshman classes that have never known a time when the Internet was not ubiquitous or when an unlimited scope of information was not at their fingertips, I can attest to the fact that Generation Y operates in a different modality. Buddy Hobart and Herb Sendek offer astute commentary on the implications and potential of this generational sea change for those who seek to operationalize leadership."
> — Dr. Michael M. Crow, president, Arizona State University

"Gen Y is who will replace our leadership in the coming years. This book should be on every leader's list."
— Bradley D. Penrod, AAE, Executive Director, CEO, Pittsburgh International Airport

"Competitive companies and lean nonprofit organizations need to attract and retain the best talent, especially in tough economic times. Hobart and Sendek provide a clear message: don't confuse Generation Y employees' desire for progress, need for feedback, and insistence on meaningful work and work/life balance for self-centeredness, slacking, or disloyalty. Read this book and you will recognize the value Generation Y brings to the workplace. Learn how to engage Generation Y. Their talent will bring you technological expertise and continuous innovation."
— Manuel London, College of Business, State University of New York at Stony Brook, author, *Job Feedback*

"*Gen Y Now* is a compelling account of the demographic trends facing the organizations of tomorrow, coupled with strategies for the managers and leaders of today."
— Michael McQueen, author, *The New Rules of Engagement*

"*Gen Y Now* provides important insights into the realities of tomorrow's workforce; realities that dispel some of the common myths about this generation and guide you to understand their real value and importance."
— Bette Price, CMC, coauthor, *GenBlending: Ten Surprising Trends about Generation Y that Will Make or Break Your Business*

"Gen Yers are potential champions for any business. I've had great success with giving people goals and letting them go at them. With this book, you can, too."
— Andrew Wood, author, *Traits of Champions*

"It is natural to push back against the habits of Gen Y, but *Gen Y Now* presents a compelling motive to do just the opposite. Read this book to tap into the advantages of Gen Y — ahead of your competition."
— Jeff Taylor, MillennialMarketer.com

"*Gen Y Now* is like a great mentor in a business culture that requires every manager to step up to the plate and oversee Generation Y employees. Those who succeed will earn the strategic, competitive advantage. Hobart and Sendek offer practical insight and dozens of ideas for turning Gen Y employees into world-class performers!"
— Carol A. Hacker, author, *Hiring Top Performers — 350 Great Interview Questions for People Who Need People*

"This book is right on target. It not only helps leaders gain an awareness of the challenges, it also provides real-world strategies for success."
— Doug Collins, four-time NBA all-star, head basketball coach, and sports analyst

Buddy Hobart & Herb Sendek

Select Press

Solutions 21
www.Solutions-21.com
1.866.765.2121

© 2009 Solutions 21

Price: $29.95

Published by Select Press
Novato, California

Cover design by Albert B. Ciuksza, Jr.

ISBN 978-189077726-5

Printed in Korea

Dedication

This book is dedicated to our heroes, the Greatest Generation, and to the many coaches who touched us along the way. Both of these groups are represented by Francis E. "McGee" Mannion (1925–2008).

The Greatest Generation sacrificed their youth and their lives to save the world. Because of their sacrifice, we enjoy the freedom we have today.

To the coaches in our lives — thank you for sacrificing your time and energy to help us and so many others along the way. We are deeply grateful.

P.S. McGee, you are a true hero. Eaten bread is not so soon forgotten.

We would like to thank the *Gen Y Now* team for all of their ideas, help, and contributions. Throughout the course of writing this book, our team has provided invaluable guidance and support. We have truly appreciated every idea, suggestion, and contribution.

Chris Caprio

Jim Caprio

Rick Crandall, PhD

Marino DeFilippo

Vanessa Urch Druskat, PhD

Donna Germeyer

Karen Muraco

Alison Northrop

Dave Phelps

Cathy Plese

Dr. Joseph Rudman and his Carnegie Mellon University class "Writing for Economists"

Mark Vay

Lynne Ventress

Contents

Chapter 1

A Tidal Wave of Change for Organizations

The ACM Company recruited Ben, age 24, from a top university. He had great credentials and hit the ground running at ACM. He had a combination of computer skills, emotional intelligence, sales skills, and drive that put him in the top 20% of company sales performance shortly after his training period.

He continued to be a top performer for about a year, then he quit unexpectedly. His boss was shocked. Ben didn't bother to explain to his boss his reasons for leaving but told us he wasn't getting enough feedback or appreciation at ACM. The money was great because he got a draw and commissions, but he wasn't being given chances to develop or advance.

ACM lost a top performer and never knew why. Ben considered going back to school, touring Europe, or going with a competitor of ACM. He's still making up his mind and meanwhile is waiting tables at a local restaurant.

1

Do you recognize Ben in your company or have you heard a similar story? We have heard many such stories.

Ben is your future!

The most dramatic changes in the workplace are happening now. Like any major change that occurs over the course of several years, you may not see the full effects until it is too late. To paraphrase Peter Drucker, author of more than 30 books on management and leadership, the one thing we can predict with certainty is demographic changes. And it's your job as a leader to deal with these changes.

> **"Management is about coping with complexity. Leadership is about coping with change."**
> —JOHN KOTTER, HARVARD UNIVERSITY, AUTHOR, *LEADING CHANGE*

Simply put, your workforce is completely changing. Your experienced workers are retiring and younger workers will be taking over. These younger workers — whom we're calling Generation Y (Gen Y) — will dominate for decades. They are an even bigger group than the Baby Boomers.

You Can Predict the Future Now!

To encapsulate the entire book, younger workers bring important new skills, ideas, and energy to your workplace. However, they are also harder to hire, harder to motivate, demand

> **"Prediction is very difficult, especially about the future."**
> —NIELS BOHR, PHYSICIST

more of you and your organization, want bigger rewards sooner, and are more likely to leave you. In general, they see the world differently and will be demanding change whether you're ready for it or not. In order to succeed in the future, you need to embrace Gen Y and make changes now!

Control Your Own Future

Imagine if you'd known in 1995 how important the Internet was going to be. Or about the dot-com bubble through 2001 or the real estate bust of 2007. You would have made changes and either profited or avoided major downturns.

Today we know that Baby Boomers are aging and retiring and that younger workers (Gen Yers) will dominate the workforce for the next 30 years or more.

Like any major change that takes years, you may not see the full effects of this generational transformation until it is too late. More to the point, you may see it and dismiss it as "this, too, shall pass." For example, when times are tough, even Gen Y may have to scramble for jobs, and conform to currently accepted norms. This *temporary conformity* may lull leaders into believing Gen Y can be treated just like previous generations were treated. But the long-term trend is set, despite any blips.

KEY POINT

Demographics prove that Generation Y will dominate the future with sheer numbers.

Whether it affects you now or later, your workforce is completely changing. It's up to the Baby Boomers and Generation X — the current managers and leaders — to manage this change for your organization. This book is designed to help you integrate Gen Yers into your organization now.

Consultant's Corner

We Can Help

Working as a consultant is a unique learning opportunity. Solutions 21 has partnered with firms around the world, ranging from start-ups to *Fortune* 500s. We have worked in manufacturing plants, law firms, executive boardrooms, and nearly everything in between. While there are similar issues in every industry, seldom are the challenges identical across the board.

Until Generation Y!

The one universal issue we hear, regardless of the industry or location is, "We can't seem to find and keep new talent." Every organization we talk to says the same thing. "These folks are different. They're not loyal and will quit in a minute. They expect things they haven't earned yet. They think they're special and they expect big rewards without working for them."

Why Can't They Be Like We Were, Perfect in Every Way...?

For the sake of full disclosure, I, too, believed "these kids" were spoiled. Having been born in 1959, the youngest of six children to Greatest Generation parents, I did not think very highly of the attitudes Generation Y was bringing to the workforce. I am a product of my generation — a Baby Boomer. I must confess, when we set out to write this book I viewed it as another business challenge to be solved. Solutions 21 had worked successfully many times for organizations to develop recruiting and retention strategies, and I thought, "What could be so different this time?"

This is where my coauthor, Coach Herb Sendek, stepped in to coach me...and completely change my perspective. Coach helped me to see my prejudices and how I could never be successful consulting about Generation Y (let alone coauthoring a book) without an attitude adjustment.

YOU Have the Same Challenge

As a lifelong student of leaders and leadership who works with Gen Y every day, Coach Sendek challenged me the same way we will challenge you in this book. The problem businesses face attracting and retaining Gen Y is not about Gen Y. It is about *leadership.*

This book is, purely and simply, about leadership and how to operationalize your leadership to produce a winning game plan for working with Gen Y. Everyone knows that whoever has the best talent and develops a solid game plan usually wins. We will show you how to build a plan and a *system that both attracts and keeps the best talent.*

To further anticipate the point of this book, I've now come farther than just eliminating my prejudice against Gen Y. I now consider myself — like Coach Sendek — an *advocate for* Gen Y.

Gen Y Is a Blessing in Disguise

It won't be long before Gen Y is in charge of the workplace — and we'll be better off for it. We Boomers and Gen Xers need to help Gen Yers develop into the next generation of leaders. With the right mentoring and guidance, Gen Y is poised to make lasting and constructive changes in the workplace. Then we will all be better off than continuing the status quo.

> "When we are no longer able to change a situation, we are challenged to change ourselves."
> —Victor Frankl, author, *Man's Search for Meaning*

Leading Change

Let us also tell you what this book is *not* about. We will *never* ask you to compromise your values and ethics or settle for less than the best. This book is about leadership and how to attract and retain the talent you need to succeed.

Gen Y IS Change

Whether you're prepared or not, Gen Y will be your workforce, and they are different. You have the choice of getting on the train or ignoring it and being run over.

Several years ago the staff at Solutions 21 had the good fortune of working with a gentleman, Mark Taylor, who is a great business leader and was a captain in the Army Reserves. Mark could always be counted on to "walk the talk." He led by example and lived the saying, "If it's to be, it's up to me."

All good leaders know that *action* is required to bring about positive results. Nothing can be solved or changed by wishing it away. Mark also believed in a saying that you've heard in one form or another: "There are two kinds of people in this world; those who effect change and those who are affected by change." Which one are you?

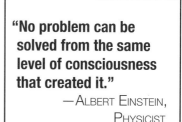

> "No problem can be solved from the same level of consciousness that created it."
> —Albert Einstein, Physicist

If you are not ready and willing to support change in your organization, make no mistake, Gen Y will see that you and your business are affected by it. If you are willing to be proactive about change, then the first advice we have for you is that it starts at the top.

Consult for Your Own Team

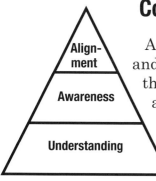

As we (the not-so-odd couple of Coach and Consultant) began to work on this book, we realized that tackling a consulting project is not much different from tackling change in an organization or the challenge of creating a winning basketball program. There are three key steps every leader must take, regardless of the challenge: *understanding, awareness,* and *alignment.*

Families Want to Understand Gen Y Too

As we have worked with leaders around the country and lectured on this topic, both of us have been amazed at the side benefits our work has produced. While we set out to help business leaders create better recruiting and retention strategies, we found we were accomplishing much more — we were also helping family leaders understand their children better.

After our talks we have been approached by senior executives from every industry imaginable to thank us for the insights — not just as business leaders, but as *parents!* We did not set out to write a book for parents. And this book will only address Generation Y from a business perspective. However, if gaining a deep awareness of Gen Y helps even one person improve relationships with their children, we will feel deeply honored and grateful.

Once leaders reach the third step, it is their responsibility to drive the desired change throughout their organizations' culture. We call this *operationalizing leadership*.

This book is structured to follow this model and to provide you with real strategies and ideas to operationalize your leadership.

Conclusion

Every generation is different and the established generations typically bemoan the fact that the new ones are not like they are. Generation Y is here and will be your employees for the next 30 or more years — if you can keep them. Rather than their differences being a problem, Gen Y's attitudes and expectations can make us all better leaders and managers. Take advantage of this opportunity to get ahead of the curve now and celebrate Gen Y!

At the end of the first fourteen chapters, following the traditional conclusion, we will include a brief biography of a real Gen Y individual that describes his or her work situation. These bios are designed to provide you with an additional perspective on the points described in this book.

Name: Matthew
Location: Midwest
Age: 23

Matthew's background:

- was in charge of all video production and hosted a TV show at his high school

- known for being extremely personable

- completed his undergraduate degree at a large state university with a major in supply chain management

- just started his first job with a nationwide chain

- currently based out of the corporate headquarters, going through training

Straight out of college, Matthew joined his company because of its 28-week training program. Matthew had other options after leaving college, and he specifically chose this company because he wanted thorough training. It offered less money than other companies, but he thought the learning experience was invaluable, and that working with peers was a nice perk.

He is receiving exposure to many different parts of the company and investigating jobs within the company that suit him best. He and the other 20 people in the program will spend 10 weeks focusing on specific product lines, 8 weeks in local stores, doing all the jobs that a typical employee and manager would do, and 10 weeks in the planning and allocation division. He is learning what it takes to succeed as a buyer, how the systems work, and what a typical day is like. At the end of his training, he will state his preference for where he'd like to work, and his preference will be weighed with his performance evaluations. Hopefully, he will end up with a job that is a good fit for his abilities and his desires.

Matthew says that is it is important for him to understand his goals and continuously work toward that end game. He will jump at any opportunity and use his network to better his situation. In his mind, the key is never to be satisfied or complacent. He supposes this way of thinking is different than older generations due to the low unemployment rate: He knew getting a job was inevitable. Gen Y does not feel lucky just to have a job because everyone eventually gets one.

Matthew's biggest gripe with older generations is their lack of innovation in the workplace. The older people he has worked with have taken a "this is how we've always done it" type of approach. Their way has worked in the past, so they assume that it will work in the future. Matthew would like to encourage them to take a minute to step back and evaluate the best way to do something. He feels that his fresh set of eyes is often able to see a better, more efficient way of accomplishing a task.

What makes Matthew take a job?

- great training program

- working with people his age

- location – is currently saving money by living with his parents

Chapter 2

Who Is Gen Y? The Data

At 31, Carlos is a Gen Y "elder." An entrepreneur from the age of 16, he owned businesses, managed sports teams, and invested in real estate.

When he decided he wanted to be an agent for athletes going into major league sports, he spent a year building a relationship with an established sports agency that was certified by the NFL and others. They wanted to hire him in a "normal" way, but he wanted to be an independent contractor. They'd never represented any of the first or second round football draft choices that got snapped up by the bigger agencies so, of course, Carlos made that his goal!

Within a month of signing an agreement with the agency, he was flying across the country on his own dime and was a favorite of two potential first-round picks. Perhaps his youthful energy appealed to them compared to the average "stuffy" agent.

There are a number of ways to slice the generations and they vary by a few years here and there. The way we're using it, "Generation Y" or "Gen Y" is the term used to describe all people born in the years 1977 through 1995. They make up over 25% of our country's total population. Gen Yers are the children of the population groups known as the Baby Boomers and Gen Xers. There are 79.5 million young people in Gen Y. They are now the largest population subgroup, surpassing the huge Baby Boom generation which totaled 77.7 million (Generation X accounts for about 48 million according to *Time* magazine).

Table of the Generations

Generation	Dates of Birth	Number
Baby Boomers	1945-1964	77.7 million
Generation X	1965-1976	48 million
Generation Y	1977-1995	79.5 million

Why Should You Care About Gen Y?

You should care about Gen Y first and foremost because they are your *current* employees born in 1977 and after. If they are dissatisfied with your organization and you are unable to retain them, it will be extremely expensive and difficult to replace them. Second, Gen Y will also be your *future* employees for the next thirty years or more. As your Baby Boomer and Gen X employees retire, Gen Yers will be their replacements and there will be stiff competition for these new workers due to changes in demographics.

The Labor Pool Is Shrinking

There is a looming crisis in the labor supply because 77.7 million Baby Boomers will be retiring. The Bureau of Labor Statistics predicts that by 2012, the American labor force will experience a 33% shortage of four-year degree candidates (a shortfall of 6 million graduates). According to The Future of Work Institute, between 1990 and 2025, the labor force growth rate will plummet from 11.9% a year to .2% due to fewer entrants and Baby Boomers retiring.

According to David Campeas, president and CEO of the recruiting firm PrincetonOne, back in the 1970s, there were two Baby Boomers to replace every retiree. This is no longer the case. For the first time in American history, the number of younger workers entering the labor market will not replace all those who are leaving. The Generation X workers born to the Boomers are not numerous enough to replace them.

Data from the US Bureau of Labor Statistics says:

• Every day, 10,000 Baby Boomers turn 55 years old.

• For every two experienced workers leaving the workforce, only one will enter.

• As of 2006, one in six workers was over age 55 (that number is now higher, of course).

• By 2030, American businesses will face a labor shortage of more than 35 million.

Losing Employees Is Costly

You must have a strategy to retain your current Gen Y employees because it is extremely expensive to replace an employee. Estimates vary widely and depend on your industry, but employee turnover costs a lot of money. Whether turnover is due to retirement, resignation, or terminations, it is expensive. For example, according to the US Department of Labor Statistics, the cost to replace an employee, at a minimum, is 25% of an employee's annual compensation. It can cost thousands to hire and train a new hourly employee. It can cost much more to replace a manager. At the high end, one Silicon Valley company estimates the cost of replacing an employee is over $125,000.

> **"Of the approximately 2,000 organizations participating in the study, only half had solid financial data reflecting the true cost of hiring one employee."**
> —Human Capital Metrics Consortium survey

In addition to all the finanacial and time costs of turnover, new employees may not be up to speed for months. This costs you in lower productivity.

The Need to Retain Knowledge Capital

In addition to the high cost of replacing a worker, there is the problem of losing the experience and information uniquely possessed by that person. When you

Turnover Has Very Real Costs

Here are some estimates of turnover costs per employee by industry from the Employment Policy Foundation:

- construction $14,500
- manufacturing $14,500
- trade & transportation $12,500
- information $19,500
- financial activities $18,000
- professional & business $15,500
- education & health $14,000
- leisure & hospitality $7,000
- other services $12,750

are replacing retiring, experienced workers with younger, inexperienced ones, you are losing an incredible amount of knowledge and experience known as knowledge capital. Experienced employees have inside knowledge of how your organization works, including how to deal with the internal, institutional bureaucracy. They have leadership skills. They have detailed knowledge of customers and prospects. Experienced employees have contacts and relationships they have developed and built over the course of their careers. They have product familiarity and knowledge. To some degree Gen X employees will bridge the gap to Gen Y, but there aren't enough of them to do it fully.

This is another reason you need to have a strategy to recruit and hire Gen Yers as well as a strategy to successfully integrate them into your organization. The new Gen Y employees you hire must be capable of accepting the transfer of knowledge capital from the workers they will eventually replace. You must create an environment where this cooperative sharing can exist. This means making sure your current workers are comfortable with Gen Yers and vice versa.

Negative Feelings About Gen Y

prejudice (n., pre•ju•dice) An adverse judgment or opinion formed beforehand or without knowledge or examination of the facts.

There are a lot of negative attitudes about Gen Y. Most people know someone from Gen Y and have some sort of opinion about that generation. Some people are uncomfortable with Gen Yers because they seem so "different." Some just have a gut feeling that Gen Y is "trouble." In the business world, many employers honestly consider hiring and working with Gen Yers as a problem.

It is human nature to fear or feel uncomfortable about something we don't really understand, and our research and experience show that Gen Y is, indeed, something people "don't really understand."

In speaking before business groups, and even in casual conversations, we have found that most Baby Boomers and

Gen Xers not only do not understand Gen Y, but they have a very poor opinion of that group. It seems that most of us are, in the true sense, prejudiced against Gen Yers. That is, we are prejudging them and attributing overwhelmingly negative characteristics to them without knowing all the facts.

Stereotypes of Generation Y

We have conducted leadership seminars around the country for business leaders (mostly Baby Boomers and Gen Xers) on Gen Y. The senior managers and executives in attendance represented a broad spectrum of industry. At the start of each session we asked everyone to write down five adjectives that best described Gen Y. There were always a few positive traits identified such as "well-educated" and "tech savvy" but the overwhelming majority of adjectives were negative. Over and over the same sentiments were expressed — and expressed vehemently. The top five adjectives used by older generations to describe Gen Y were:

- slackers/lazy
- need instant gratification
- self-centered/selfish
- disloyal/"job jumpers"
- pampered/spoiled

Similarly, we also spoke on a radio program about recruiting and retaining Gen Y employees, and invited listeners to email us their comments. Again, the majority of comments we received about Gen Y were negative. This email from a listener perhaps best exemplifies the broad anti-Gen Y animus that exists in the business populace at large:

I'm sure some snot-nosed kid right out of liberal arts college knows more than someone who has been working for 20 years. Puh-leese! God help us if this is the mindset of these pampered babies!

urban legend (n., ur•ban le•gend) an often lurid story or anecdote that is based on hearsay and widely circulated as true. For instance, the urban legend of alligators living in the sewers. — also called, *urban myth*

We believe many negative feelings that have developed about Gen Y are, in some ways, "urban legends." Sure, you may know a 25 year old who quit a great job and decided to go on the "professional" Frisbee circuit. Or a 28 year old who quit a $90K job because he did not have an executive parking space. Or a successful MA in social work who decided she could make more money, meet more interesting people, and have a more flexible schedule as a waitress than at her job in the social work field. Or the young couple who worked for one year after college and then quit to travel in South America for a year.

It also seems everyone has a story about a new Gen Y employee or prospective employee who has made outrageous demands. Many of the descriptions we have heard are so outrageous they are humorous.

Some of the stories about Gen Yers we have heard from their Gen X and Baby Boomer managers are:

• The new employee who "demanded" an indoor parking place because his car was brand new. There was only one indoor parking place, and it was used for wheel chair accessibility!

• An employee who quit after her extremely positive quarterly review. Since every area wasn't perfect, her manager provided some feedback and the employee quit on the spot saying, "No one has ever talked to me like that!"

• The employee who wanted to only work 6-hour days and take off between 10am and noon. Seems he found an "awesome Pilates [exercise] class."

• The new employee who was hired for his writing skills and then refused to write. He told his boss, "I've known how to write since first grade; I want to try something else now."

The Stereotypes Are Misleading

As these anecdotes are repeated, Gen Xers and Boomers start to believe that all prospective Gen Y employees are the same. Examples like these are exaggerated in the retelling, and become the image of Gen Y.

Are there Gen Yers who are spoiled, lazy, disloyal, and pampered? Absolutely — and you do not want them as employees. But we cannot paint the entire generation with so broad a brush. In fact, if we examine these negative traits closely, we will find one of two things. Either they are misconceptions and exaggerations or they are traits that can actually lead to positive and productive Gen Y performance in the workplace. In any case, Gen Y does not deserve the bad rap it gets.

Conclusion

Due to the shrinking labor pool, the high cost of replacing workers, and the negative impact of losing knowledge capital, it is imperative that you have a strategy to keep the talented Gen Y employees you already have on staff as well as a strategy to effectively compete for every new Gen Y employee that you will need to bring on board.

As we will explain in the next few chapters, keeping your existing Gen Y staff happy, and attracting the best and the brightest new Gen Y employees, is not easy. Boomer and Gen Xer managers grew up in eras that were much different from today. Gen Yers are a new breed of worker with different needs and expectations. Working with Gen Y is different than anything you've done before. It is most certainly not the same as working with employees from previous generations. As a leader, you must understand, accommodate, and even change yourself and your company for Gen Y. They are your future.

 Name: Elizabeth
Location: Northeast
Age: 28

Elizabeth's background:

- graduated from a college that is ranked in the top 60 of national universities

- earned her masters from a top-25 university

- spent two years working with the competitive Teach for America

- currently the executive director of a new initiative at a learning policy center

After a lifetime spent in school, Elizabeth is used to immediate results. With four years in college, two years getting her masters degree, and two years teaching with Teach for America, she has spent at least 20 years in the classroom, where grades are handed back within days or weeks and, as a teacher, she could watch her students making progress over the course of the year. Immediate feedback like this made Elizabeth feel that a difference was made as a result of her efforts. Her current job is a continual struggle for her because it works to effect large-scale, long-term change, whose outcomes will not be obvious until years in the future. She is forced to find other ways to receive the motivating feedback that she needs, such as through volunteering.

More than just the lack of feedback, Elizabeth has realized that she is not happy on a day-to-day basis at her job because it is not as collaborative as she would like. She and her coworkers spend their days in solitary academic pursuits, and it has shown her that she does not thrive in this type of environment. She feels isolated, and while she realizes she could try harder to talk with her coworkers, she also sees that socializing at work is not a big part of the culture.

She feels responsible for the success of the newly started project, so Elizabeth is going to stick it out and do what it takes to get it off the ground. However, she has given herself an end date and is working hard to make her position unnecessary. In general, she has a hard time seeing herself at this one job for a long time. She is concerned, because she doesn't know how future employers will view her job-hopping.

To be content at work, Elizabeth needs something that will hold her attention, which she can see is a part of her own creation and vision. She'd like to be in an organization that views her professional development as good for the entire organization, and she therefore will be given opportunities to learn and grow. She would like to build new skills and experience, and make connections with leaders and organizations in the community. Elizabeth sees the endless possibilities that are available for Generation Y, like the fact that she can live anywhere and do anything she wants, and she knows she isn't going to be pushed into a career that she hates for the rest of her life.

To Elizabeth, the characteristics of a good job are:

- flexibility, both in terms of time and selection of projects

- the opportunity to learn and grow professionally

- the organization realizing that her development is good for their overall success

- the opportunity to make connections with other leaders and organizations

Elizabeth is professionally motivated by:

- immediate feedback

- feeling that she made a difference

- the ability to effect long-term change

- social contact at work

Chapter 3

Major Myths About Gen Y

Twenty-five-year-old Korey earned a degree in computer sciences and got a programming job with a company in his hometown. He worked for two years and lived at home in his old room. However, the work was boring so he quit. He was offered related work on websites for another company but, while he could have done the work, it wasn't what he wanted to do. He moved to Silicon Valley to room with friends who worked for Google and similar companies. Meanwhile he did freelance work for his old company while he waited for just the right job.

There is a logical reason Gen Y is the way it is and it is helpful to understand it. More important, whatever Gen Y's characteristics may be, if we are good leaders, we will be able to work with them and bring out the best in them. *There are no attributes possessed by Gen Y that cannot be successfully managed, nurtured, and channeled in a beneficial way by a good leader.*

> ### KEY POINT
>
> Leaders need to see the talent and potential that lies within Gen Y without being distracted by what seem to be their flaws, faults, or shortcomings. That's one thing this book can do for you.

Let's look more closely at the five major myths about Gen Y that have developed over time.

Myth 1 — Gen Yers Are Slackers or Lazy

It is true that Gen Y puts a high value on family, friends, and leisure and does not give work priority over all other things. However, Gen Y has a surprisingly good work ethic.

According to a monstertrack.com survey of 2004 graduates entering the workforce, one of the top goals of Gen Y was to "work faster and better than their coworkers." They do want to contribute at work. They want to excel. We conducted a national survey asking all generations — Baby Boomers, Gen Xers, Gen Yers, and others — what qualities make someone successful. Those surveyed had to rank virtues like superior communication skills, efficiency, good time management, leadership ability, and so on. The top virtue chosen by Gen Xers and Baby Boomers was "hardworking." This is not surprising considering these generations' outstanding work ethic. What was surprising was that the Gen Yers also picked "hardworking" as their number one quality. They understand the direct connection between hard work and success. They believe in a work ethic just as other generations do.

KEY POINT
Gen Y loves to work at *meaningful* tasks.

What *is* different is Gen Y's requirement that their work be meaningful and interesting. Gen Y will not devote long hours to something they don't consider valuable or motivating. If you assign Gen Y a task that lacks substance, you will see a nonchalant, "slacker" approach to that task. If you give them boring, endless administrative work that is not linked to a more meaningful, important project, they are not going to work up to their potential. They will live down to your "lazy" expectations.

How to Inspire Gen Y

Many managers assume all new employees only want easy, fun, and exciting work. The prejudices we discussed take over and there is a tendency to jump to unfair conclusions. Let us be clear: we are not saying Gen Y will only do easy and fun work. They want *meaningful* work. When needed, Gen Y will do mundane tasks. The key is linking these work assignments to a more important goal. Put another way, Gen Y wants to know *why* they are doing a task and *how* it contributes.

We understand two key realities. First, in any job there are tasks and assignments that are not exciting. Many times these tasks are downright difficult, boring, time consuming, and mindless.

The second reality is that this work absolutely needs to be done. Any manager worth his paycheck will not assign work just to assign work. There is always a reason for the task needing to be completed.

There are two minor adjustments that all leaders must make if they are to successfully motivate Gen Y. The first adjustment is not new, but it is often overlooked or forgotten by leaders. Leaders must *explain the why* of these mundane assignments. Why is this task necessary, and how does it link to the bigger strategy?

KEY POINT

Leaders and managers have different responsibilities.

This might be a good time to mention the important distinction between a manager and a leader made by Peter Drucker and others.

Managers get things done through other people. Their weakness tends to be trying to do the work themselves rather than training and supervising others. *Leaders* not only get things done through others, but they *inspire* others. Their weakness tends to be forgetting to inspire. They must set the vision for the task. Gen Y responds better to leaders than to managers. They want to be inspired.

Communicate the Big Picture

Traditional managers tend to overlook the important step of explaining the why. They think it a waste of time to explain the bigger picture. They think the fact that they say something needs to be done is reason enough to cheerfully accept boring assignments. By taking just a few minutes to explain the bigger picture, managers will not only experience a more productive result, they will exhibit more leadership traits and will keep their employees engaged and motivated.

The second adjustment that needs to be made is to be open to suggestions about the task. As Gen Y employees tackle new tasks, they are constantly thinking about how to do them better and faster. Gen Y is not at all locked into the mentality of "it has always been done this way." If there is a more productive solution, they will find it and they expect to both share their findings and help implement the improvement. Leaders take time and listen to these suggestions. If Gen Y reinvents the wheel with their suggestions, the leader explains why this is and encourages their initiative. If Gen Y invents a better way to get something accomplished, the leader embraces the idea and celebrates the success.

If you assign Gen Yers jobs of substance and significance, you will see dedicated, hard-working performers. You just have to know what motivates them. They will put in long hours but they have to care about what they're doing. They can be very productive if they are treated like independent contractors (or actually used as them), given a clear goal that they buy into, and paid incentives for great performance. As a leader, you need to enlist their interest and commitment. You have to learn about their values and personal goals, then incorporate them in some way into their assignments. Offer them challenges, teach them new skills, and enlist their fresh perspectives.

The Leadership Difference

Gen Y will work as hard, if not harder, than any other generation. Already you can see how Gen Y can remind us about the importance of leadership practices that have always been important, but are often overlooked. Here's an example that illustrates exactly how Gen Y will respond to "boring" work when handled by two different managers.

A client of ours had a major sales opportunity that required them to act quickly. They developed a mail piece that needed to be sent, along with other details of the offer, to thousands of prospects. These pieces needed to be stuffed into a special envelope, sorted, and mailed. In order to maximize the financial opportunity, time was of the essence.

Two groups of college interns were assigned this task by two different supervisors. Each group had four participants who had been

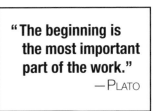

"The beginning is the most important part of the work."
— Plato

with the organization the same amount of time. On the surface, there were no variables that would have allowed one group to be more productive than the other.

The important variable turned out to be the upfront communication by the supervisor. One of the supervisors chose to be a leader. She took a few minutes and explained to her group (Group 1) the *why* of this task. She explained the opportunity, the strategic link, and the time-sensitive nature of the materials. She offered to stop back later in the day to help and wrote her cell phone number on the whiteboard, should there be any questions.

The other supervisor chose to be a manager in the worst of the "old-school" tradition. He assigned the task, explained what needed to be done, and left, leaving Group 2 to stuff envelopes.

The supervisor who offered to join them in the afternoon was thanked for the offer, but told, "We have it handled." Group 1 worked until late in the evening and finished the task.

Group 2 went home at 5:00 PM on the dot with the task less than half finished. The next day they started on it again. Group 1 volunteered to join them and helped to complete the task.

When senior management first described the above scenario, we were told how unmotivated Group 2 was and how the members of Group 1 were real winners. Words like "old fashioned" and "work ethic" were used to describe Group 1, and "lazy," "slacker," and "spoiled" for Group 2.

As we dug deeper with senior management, they began to realize the real issue — leadership. Group 1 was no more "old fashioned" than Group 2; they were just provided with a leader who displayed *timeless* leadership skills.

KEY POINT

Have you allowed your prejudices to take over when appraising a Gen Y employee? Have you taken time to examine your organizational leadership first before condemning Gen Y employees?

Coach's Corner

Explain the Why

I was coaching at North Carolina State and I decided on the starting lineup for our exhibition game. A particular player was not in the line up and arguably could have been, or even should have been. I had good, valid reasons for not having him in the starting line up although a reasonable person easily could have come to the opposite conclusion.

Where I made my mistake was, I didn't take the time to explain why to him. So the next day at practice the player doesn't show up. Eventually we got together and talked about the situation and, sure enough, he was upset that he wasn't in the starting line up for this exhibition game. I didn't spend a great deal of time explaining the reasons I didn't have him in the starting line up, but most certainly admitted that I was wrong for not having told him ahead of time. I didn't take time defending my position with him; I simply said I was wrong. I should have let him know the reasons for my decision. I could have avoided his missing practice, his being disenfranchised from our team, just by doing a better job of explaining why.

Myth 2 — Gen Y Needs Instant Gratification and Feedback

The second myth is that all new Gen Y employees want everything now and do not want to pay their dues. We have heard literally hundreds of times from executives and managers, "They want it all without working for it. They want to be the president after six months."

Do not fall for this myth. Certainly Gen Y has grown up in a world where "fast" is not only a virtue but a way of life. From *fast* food and *Instant* Messenger™ to *high-speed* Internet, and *fast-forward*, Gen Y is used to things happening quickly. They use email not "snail mail." They do not drive to the mall and visit multiple stores in order to comparison shop. They go online, visit multiple websites, and often make their purchases in the time it takes to back the car out of the garage. They have information instantly at their fingertips via the Internet. Cable and satellite TV have made hundreds of television stations available. Cell phones have connected them instantly to an array of friends. The large number of shopping centers available, combined with online shopping, has shown Gen Y that if they can't get what they want from one source, they can immediately go to another. Technology has made Generation Y accustomed to getting what they need easily and quickly.

QUESTION: You graduated from college in two years. You joined the Illinois legislature at 23. Why the hurry?

ANSWER: I'm a big believer that when opportunity presents itself, you've got to seize it. I've been very fortunate that the doors of opportunity have been opened, and I've walked through them.
—FROM A *TIME* MAGAZINE INTERVIEW WITH AARON SCHOCK, THE YOUNGEST MEMBER OF UNITED STATES CONGRESS AND THE FIRST TO BE BORN IN THE 1980s

Does Gen Y really need things to be instant or immediate on the job? Does Gen Y really expect to become a senior manager in their first year? The quick answer to both of these questions is a resounding NO.

The full answer is twofold. First, you may be able to use Gen Y's propensity for speed to your advantage. Second, some things like performance feedback *do need to happen more quickly* than you or your culture might be used to. For years most organizations have used a performance management system that has a 30-day, 90-day, and one-year review point for new employees. After that, a one-year review is the norm. The fact of the matter is, these review timelines do not work for Gen Y. And even if the timelines did work, rare is the organization that provides timely annual appraisals.

Gen Y Loves More Feedback

You cannot wait for the one-year anniversary to evaluate Gen Y, give them a raise, or ask for their input. They want feedback sooner. Gen Y *does not* believe they must be president in six months. They *do believe* they should get feedback regularly and be financially rewarded for their contributions.

To more fully understand this issue, let's look at a typical culture and performance management system.

- new-hire training
- 30-day evaluation
- 90-day evaluation
- one-year performance appraisal

• annual raise

• regularly scheduled annual reviews

Gen Y wants and needs feedback on a regular basis. They want to know how they are doing and if they are progressing. Gen Y wants to progress as quickly as they deserve from their abilities to contribute and they want to see steady progress to the next level. The standard performance management system, in many ways, creates an artificial and arbitrary time constraint. To be successful, leaders must challenge the performance management status quo and make time for regular feedback.

> **"My second job I work for a bunch of Boomers who don't get any part of pay for performance...They cannot see why a bunch of Gen Y and X are walking away in droves (over 20% turnover)."**
> —FROM A POST ON GENXFINANCE.COM

If you're not willing to give Gen Y timely feedback, they are willing to just put in their time until they jump to a situation that looks better. They are also willing to quit and go back to school, to train for a marathon, to travel, or to live at home for a while. They are not motivated to work just for the sake of working. They want to be in a "good" situation.

Leaders must also challenge the traditional idea that compensation is linked to tenure. Annual raises, based upon simply surviving for another year versus making significant contributions along the way, must be examined. Gen Y wants to be recognized for their contributions, not their tenure. We'll cover this point more in later chapters on issues like alignment. In order to recruit top talent, it is critical for your top candidates to know that *you* reward contribution, not tenure.

> ### KEY POINT
> **How are you recognizing and rewarding your workers (not just Gen Yers)? Do you have a mechanism in place to provide timely feedback and recognition?**

Myth 3 — Gen Yers Are Disloyal and Job Jumpers

Gen Y has a reputation for leaving jobs after one or two years and moving around from job to job. As we will discuss shortly in Chapter 4, Gen Yers have the freedom to move from job to job because they are delaying the responsibilities of marriage and parenting and have a strong financial safety-net in the form of parental support. They are also keenly aware of their other options.

However, Gen Yers will not be disloyal or job jump *if you give them the incentive to stay*. According to a monstertrack. com survey, 74% of graduating college seniors felt that having a relevant work experience was the most important part of a job. Accordingly, if a job is relevant, they will stay. As discussed above, Gen Y employees also want to care about their work, have frequent communication, and experience career progression. When these requirements are met, Gen Yers can be loyal, stable, long-term employees.

Gen Y makes managers face the fact that loyalty isn't given, it has to be earned. That's really true of all workers;

however, past workers have given you the benefit of the doubt and been more willing to just put in time. Gen Y is willing to work hard and loyally, but these individuals expect to learn new skills, be part of something worthwhile, and be appreciated. While it takes a bit more of your attention, it can work out better for the organization too. It's like the old argument about investing in training, the question being: "What if they leave after I pay to train them?" The answer is "Would you rather have a bunch of untrained workers who stay?"

> **"Only 32 percent of employees report being asked for input and a dismal 30 percent believe they are rewarded for accomplishments."**
>
> —FROM AN ONLINE SURVEY OF MORE THAN 2,000 ADULTS CONDUCTED IN AUGUST AND SEPTEMBER, 2008; CITED IN ALLBUSINESS.COM

As author Tom Peters has suggested, each person should act like they are in business for themselves even when they work for a company. More recently, Chris Martin, vice president for University Relations at West Virginia University, said that the reason younger people change jobs is that they are being loyal to themselves by learning and growing.

Remember, employment is always a two-way street. It is not just what Gen Y can do for you. You must now think about what you can do for Gen Y employees. Give Gen Yers interesting work, lots of feedback, chances to learn and advance, and rewards for good performance, and they can become your best and most loyal employees. Give them meaningless work that is going nowhere and watch them jump.

Myth 4 — Gen Y Is Self-Centered and Selfish

Certainly some members of Gen Y have been convinced by their parents, schools, and friends that they are the center of the universe. However, the majority of Gen Y is not as selfish as we imagine. Most are not "all about themselves." They place a high priority on family and friends. The Families and Work Institute describes Generation Y as more family-centric or dual-centric (with equal priorities on both career and family) and less work-only-centric than other generations. They support and believe in social causes and want their employers to as well. In a 2006 Institute survey, 79% of full-time Gen Y employees said they wanted to work for a company that cared about how it affected or contributed to society.

KEY POINT
Gen Y wants to contribute.

Gen Y is not simply looking for their companies to show they care. They are walking the talk and volunteering at record rates. The trends are overwhelming. Ever since Generation Y entered the teen years, the rate of volunteerism has increased significantly and has doubled in the 16–19 and 20–24 demographic.

Gen Y's goal is not simply to earn money. They want to contribute — at work, in the community, and in the world at large. If this generation were truly selfish, why would they give up their nights, weekends, and vacation time to volunteer?

Gen Y Likes Teamwork

As for being self-centered, our research reveals that the majority of this generation wants good relationships with their coworkers and employers. They want to be part of a team (61% of the respondents preferred to work in teams). These folks feel that a better work product is produced by collaborating. A sample comment from the survey highlights the point that Gen Y is focused on results, not just on themselves:

> As a team, you have to compromise, which I am not always a fan of, but you also build off one another's ideas. Generally you come up with something better together than either one of you would have come up with separately.

When we dug into the responses of the 39% that did not prefer working in teams, we found very little desire among Gen Yers to "go it alone." Most of their responses centered on quality control, productivity, and results as the reasons for not liking working in teams. The respondents realized that not every task requires a team for solutions. Sample comments were:

- "I would prefer to work in a team if I can guarantee that the people I'm working with are competent. If not, it's solo."
- "I can hold myself accountable for my results."
- "I would prefer either alone or on a team, depending on the project and deadlines."

All of these traits do not add up to self-centered and selfish individuals, but to people who actually care about others and who have the capacity to care about you and your organization. Again, it is up to you to make them care, give them ownership of their job, communicate frequently with them, and help them buy into what your company is all about.

Myth 5 — Gen Y Is Pampered and Spoiled

In some ways middle class (and up) members of Gen Y really were pampered. They have Baby Boomer parents who indulged them and catered to their every want and need, from fixing traffic tickets to completing college applications for them. According to EmploymentReview.com, Gen Y's parents have spent more time with them, their fathers were more involved with rearing them, and their parents have been more hands-on with them than any prior generation. Naturally, some of them are spoiled. However, the majority of them are not. They simply have different priorities and see the world differently. They grew up knowing they were valued. They have high self-esteem and they have no need to do what you want *just because you want it.* They are used to being treated as if they mattered and being given reasons for taking a particular course of action.

All individuals want to be recognized for their accomplishments. Celebrating success by going out to lunch or dinner, and being recognized by key business leaders, goes a long way toward making young workers feel valued. Experienced employees may have gotten used to not being acknowledged. Gen Y hasn't and won't!

> ## KEY POINT
> **Gen Y cares about balance in their lives.**

According to the Families and Work Institute, Gen Y sometimes has a reputation for being pampered because they tend to put more emphasis on nonwork areas of their lives like family and leisure. However, they work just as many hours — and in some cases more — than the Baby Boomers and Gen Xers did when they were a similar age. Gen Y is also perceived as spoiled because these individuals are not reluctant to live at home or take money from their parents. This is addressed specifically in Chapter 4, but suffice it to say that Gen Y simply views accepting help from their families as the logical use of available resources and a way to save money. To them it's not being pampered, it's being prudent and practical.

As already noted, research shows that Gen Y cares about family and friends, social causes, and volunteerism. Give them challenging, meaningful work and they will care about your company, too. However, they are not purely altruistic. They must be able to see some benefit to themselves. If you provide structure, clear rules, and benefits, most Gen Yers — even the spoiled ones — will embrace your culture when they see the benefits.

Case Study

Lott Marketing
Ron Lott

I was amazed at the way you challenged us business leaders about our prejudices toward Gen Y. It helped change my understanding about why they do what they do. Recently, I had the following experiences that support the need for leaders to look differently at the situation.

An intern we have, a college student, has been working with us for a few months and has not been particularly impressive. He had been assigned a fairly menial task in our test kitchen and his performance was lackluster.

Our CFO asked if he could use him on an important project. We warned him about the young man's questionable work ethic and commitment. After a brief discussion we reluctantly agreed, and our CFO took on the leadership of this intern.

Needless to say, we were amazed at the turnaround. The new assignment was a very difficult task and required a great deal of commitment. He is doing a fabulous job. He just needed a meaningful challenge…and leadership from our CFO to tap into his talent.

As a leader, I have thought a great deal about how we must adapt as we move forward. There is an analogy that works for me. A talented Gen Y candidate is like an untested, finely tuned motor in a sports car. This motor wasn't designed to perform at its peak in a school zone at 25 miles an hour. Nor was the engine designed to sit in a garage and have its performance measured by simply revving it up every once in a while.

Like a fine automobile, you must put it in gear...fully engage it in order to really understand its performance capability. With Gen Y, we, as leaders, must be prepared to engage our new, highly tuned talent. Only then can we truly judge their performance and contribution.

On a very personal note, my son, a Gen Yer, used a week's vacation to take a course to obtain certification to deal with children at risk. And one of our employees is taking all of his vacation and two weeks without pay to do missionary work in South America.

How You Must Deal With These Myths

Gen Y has been unfairly stereotyped. It is crucial that these stereotypes do not exist in your organization or in the hearts and minds of your employees. All of us will live up — or down — to expectations about us. If we are treated as responsible people, we will act more responsibly. If we are treated as slackers, we will tend to act like slackers.

If your organization has a negative attitude about Gen Y, all the books, seminars, and guides in the world — including this one — will not help your staff accept and work with Gen Y. And, make no mistake about it, if anyone in your organization is prejudiced toward Gen Y, Gen Yers will pick up on it. You need to set a clear policy from the top or you can forget about attracting and keeping this new generation of employees.

KEY POINT

You need to confront bias about Gen Y.

Whether you are a Boomer or Gen X yourself, it is incumbent upon you as a leader to check your pulse and your organization's pulse on this issue. How do your current employees feel about Gen Y? Have they bought into the stereotypes and misconceptions about Gen Y? What are their expectations for these future employees? Are they dreading working with them, or looking forward to it? Do they understand why Gen Y is the way they are and what makes them tick? Do they understand the fresh skills Gen Y brings to the company? And, most important, can they accept Gen Y's differences and work with them?

You Need to Be a Role Model

You cannot eliminate prejudices and stereotypes about Gen Y that are latent in your organization until you confront them first in yourself. What do you honestly think about Gen Y? Do you consider this new generation of workers a problem to be solved, or a vital asset to be developed? Do you still believe the negative stereotypes? Are you

> **"We know from our previous winners that individual bosses really can change the working lives of the people in their team..."**
> —Sarah Jackson, chief executive of Working Families, about their best boss contest in Britain

resentful that you have to adapt to this new type of worker? Do you wish they would change instead of your having to?

Now is the time to shed those prejudices and negative feelings. These are the people whom you will be leading for the next few decades. They are the twenty-somethings already working for you now. They are your future and, because of the coming labor shortage, ultimately you will need them more than they need you.

It is imperative that you set the tone unequivocally and welcome Gen Y with open arms. Your employees are watching and so are your current and future Gen Y workers.

Do Not Lower Your Standards

Putting aside unfounded prejudices with respect to Gen Y does not mean leaving behind your good judgment, common sense, or standards. It does not mean you will no longer recruit or retain qualified employees. Put another way, you do not recruit and retain unqualified employees simply because they are Gen Y.

Not every Gen Yer is a potentially great employee and not every Gen Yer already on board should automatically be retained. Nor are we suggesting that you pamper or coddle Gen Y employees who lack the skills, the integrity, or the other intangibles that you require. Like any other generation, they have their weak links. The mark of excellent leadership is to be able to look beyond stereotypes to see the talent and potential within Gen Y, yet still hold them to the standards you have set for all employees.

There are Gen Yers who truly are self-absorbed, lazy, and spoiled and live down to the negative stereotypes. You do not want these people as employees. However, Gen Y as a whole has a good work ethic, wants to contribute and be productive, and can become an important asset to your company. It is important that you do not mistake Gen Y's legitimate desire to progress, their need for communication, or their insistence on meaningful work as self-centeredness, "slacking," or disloyalty. As a leader, it is your job to expose and eliminate any prejudice toward Gen Y that exists in yourself and your organization. You must be able to look beyond the superficial preconceptions you may have about Gen Y to harness and nurture the talent and potential that lies within. At the same time, you must still demand that Gen Y meets the standards you set for all employees.

Coach's Corner

Don't Settle

When I was an assistant coach at the University of Kentucky, the recruiting coordinator for the football program was Coach Tommy Limbaugh and he took a lot of time with Billy Donovan and me to share with us his philosophies on recruiting. He had spent a career studying recruiting and was a master at it. He told Billy and me that there were two kinds of mistakes that you can make in recruiting. One is okay; the other is not.

The first one is that you go after a talented person — someone who could really help your organization, your team,

someone who could really help you win the championship —
but in the end you don't get him. That's okay. On that same
day, over 330 other basketball programs in the country didn't
get him either. That mistake's fine. You're going after people
who can help you win the championship.

If you make the second kind of mistake too often, you're
going to be out of business. The second mistake is when
you go after somebody and you get them and they're really
not the answer. They're not good enough to help advance
your organization, your team. They're not good enough to
help you win the championship. If you make that mistake too
often, you're in big trouble.

Conclusion

People born between 1977 and 1995 now make up the
largest generation in history, Generation Y. There are a lot
of negative myths and stereotypes about Gen Y: They're
lazy, job hoppers, and so forth. These are only true when
they're in jobs they don't like and with poor managers.
When Gen Y is led properly, Gen Y is a major resource that
you can use to revitalize your organization. Why not take
advantage of this resource?

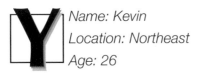

Name: Kevin
Location: Northeast
Age: 26

Kevin's background:

- graduated from a small college with a degree in business management

- currently works as a sales account manager for a company that sells construction materials worldwide

Kevin has big dreams, and he is going to do what it takes to achieve them. He wants to own his own business by age 30, and in the meantime build up capital and move up in his current company. He says this drive to achieve big dreams sets Generation Y apart from older workers, along with being open-minded and willing to think outside the box.

He believes in working efficiently. He wants to work hard, but do it smarter and harder than everyone else. He is not willing to waste time. Because of this, he greatly appreciates that his company allows him to work as many or as few hours as it takes to reach his sales numbers. He says that one week he might work 70 hours and the next week 20, and there's never any question if he wants to take a few days off. He stays organized personally and professionally so that he doesn't get either burnt-out or fired.

The opportunity to take risks and be responsible for his decisions keeps his mind stimulated, which staves off the boredom and lack of challenge that caused him to quit his previous job. When Kevin wants to try something different, his manager asks him if he thinks it makes good business sense, and even if the manager doesn't necessarily agree, he's willing to let him try it. This strategy has proven to be successful because Kevin's recent $1,000 risk earned the company over $40,000, and the company is starting to use his idea with other clients.

Kevin feels that his company is concerned about its employees, instead of viewing them as disposable. He feels like a part of the family, and he truly believes his product is the best in the market. The company provided him with six weeks of paid training before he started selling, and he will receive another four weeks of training in a couple of months. His company tells him that the sky's the limit, and they believe in him.

Chapter 4

Understanding Gen Y's 6 Key Skills

Shakira, age 23, held a liberal arts degree and had created a website design business that she ran in college. She'd also traveled a lot, doing one year of study abroad. She was hired by a company but wasn't sure if she'd like the job. However, she figured she could always quit if it didn't work out. Fortunately, her manager gave her a complete orientation and asked where she thought she could contribute. Then he let her take on projects as she went through the regular newcomer training.

Shakira immediately improved the company website, making it easy for anyone to revise using any word processing program to cut and paste. Then she got out the "monthly" newsletter that hadn't been issued for a year. In doing that, she developed relationships with a lot of different people on the phone as she collected information. In addition to her regular training she created a workgroup of young Gen Y employees that video-conferenced and brainstormed ideas for her division. Within six months, she was a rising star.

We now know that Gen Y is an indispensable labor pool for the replacement of our retiring workforce. We also know they are not spoiled, selfish, demanding, or lazy as some think they are. The truth is, Gen Y has much to offer our organizations.

Gen Y Comes with Real Skills

In prior generations, new employees did not bring advanced skills to the job. Much time and money had to be spent training them to do some very basic job-related tasks. New employees did not know more than their future employers nor did they come equipped with instantly applicable expertise.

None of that is true with Generation Y. For the first time in history, a generation is entering the workforce with skills in certain areas — particularly technology — superior to their bosses and current coworkers. We believe one of the major challenges many leaders will face is accepting this reality. Since there is no precedent from which to work, many organizations will be too slow to adjust. By adapting quickly, you can profit from Gen Y's skills and enthusiasm to create a stronger organization.

While we are saying Gen Y brings certain superior skills to the job, we are *not* saying they are also bringing all of the wisdom and life experience necessary to apply these skills productively. Here is where leadership kicks in.

> **"Leadership has a harder job to do than just choose sides. It must bring the sides together."**
> —JESSE JACKSON

Leaders need to grasp the implications of this new paradigm and provide support for both the new and current employees. For the new employees, leaders must mentor and guide them using the wisdom gained throughout the years. For current employees, leaders must make certain the new Gen Y talent is not dismissed, overlooked, and eventually squashed. And they must find ways for Gen Y skills to spread to experienced employees.

Gen Y's 6 Superior Skills

Key Skill #1:
Gen Y is Tech Savvy

Gen Y is highly educated and many will bring advanced degrees with them to the workplace. Gen Y is extremely tech savvy and, for the most part, will be far ahead of your existing employees when it comes to the latest technology. They are perfectly comfortable with computers, iPODs®, iPhones®, and so forth. They already know how to use Excel® and PowerPoint®, do mail merges, scans, and attachments. If you need something from the web, chances are excellent that your Gen Yer can find it more quickly and efficiently than your current staff.

Managers around the world generally recognize Gen Y's tech skills. For instance, one Australian survey found that 94% of employers are happy with the technology skills that Generation Y employees bring to the workplace. Recognition of the talent is not the issue. The issue is damning it with faint praise. Managers too often dismiss Gen Y's technological skills as a given, thereby diminishing the accomplishment. Worse yet, managers then tend to call on Gen Y to fix some minor issue on their computers, often multiple times for the same thing.

> ### KEY POINT
> **Don't take Gen Y's tech skills for granted.**

Dismissing the skill set and then trivializing it sets the exact wrong leadership tone. First it shows a lack of appreciation for Gen Y's tech skills. Second, it communicates, however unintentionally, the organization's willingness to accept outdated skill sets in experienced managers. Finally, and again unintentionally, it sends a message that this company is not a learning organization.

When it comes to technology, Gen Y has knowledge and proficiency. Gen Yers should be used — not taken advantage of — as a resource. They will not mind sharing their knowledge, as long as it is not dismissed or taken for granted. They will expect their coworkers to at least *attempt* to learn the new skill information. One 22 year old repeatedly showed older coworkers how to do minor tasks on the computer, patiently taking them step by step through the process and encouraging them to write the steps down. After showing them how to do the same tasks dozens of times over a year, she quit.

Case Study

Naumann/Hobbs Material Handling
Bob Hobbs, Sr.

Employ Technology

Bob Hobbs started his business career in 1963 after graduating with distinction from Arizona State University. In 1965 Bob joined Naumann Lift Trucks as a customer services salesman, and by 1976 was the president and general manager. In 1979 Bob purchased the company, which is now known as Naumann/ Hobbs Material Handling (NHMH).

"I realized several years ago that in order to prepare the next generation of leaders, I needed to lead by example. Like most folks my age, I did not grow up with technology. There was nothing natural or intuitive about it for me or most of our managers. For us to succeed, I needed to step out of my comfort zone and embrace the new technologies. The reality is, you *must* overcome your anxiety with technology or you will not succeed. Also, and maybe more important, you *must* lead by example.

"I also think it is important for leaders to demonstrate that they are always open to learning new things. Being successful in business is about leading people *and* change. When you lose your willingness to change, you lose your ability to learn.

"My advice to leaders would be:

- Stay abreast of current technology. Both your ex-perienced staff and your new hires will be watching.

- Technology can help you manage your succession plan. If an executive leaves today, it can be business as usual for those who have prepared.

- Use technology to help you track and measure your progress toward your goals.

- If you haven't embraced technology and you want to build a business or lead a team, there is no chance you will succeed.

- Surround yourself with people who are comfortable with whatever technology you're going to embrace because you are not going to know it all.

- Do not insult your newest talent by constantly treating them like a 'help desk.' If you need help more than twice on the same issue, the problem is you.

"We have really concentrated on overcoming our initial hesitancy with technology. Now, all of our Baby Boomer managers are extremely savvy and I think this is impressive to our new folks. We are able to attract great talent in many ways because we are seen, rightly so, as a growing and progressive organization.

"My goal has always been to see NHMH continue to grow and prosper long after I retire. We have always been committed to our team; that is why it made such great sense to form an employee stock ownership program. Now, everyone on the team is an owner."

Key Skill #2:
Gen Y is Diverse

According to the US Census Bureau, Generation Y is the most ethnically diverse generation in history, with only 61% of its members identifying themselves as Caucasian. This generation's social circles are also the most diverse with respect to religion and race. Only 7% of this generation says that all of their friends are of the same race or religion. Diversity has been demonstrated to be a desirable and healthy workplace component.

In contrast, other generations of employees needed "diversity training." Many came from extremely homogenous backgrounds and were not exposed to different races, cultures, or creeds until they arrived in the workplace. It was a serious challenge to teach these insulated workers how to co-exist and work with people different than themselves. Millions of dollars and hours had to be spent on diversity training to accomplish this goal.

Gen Y is open-minded and accepting of those different from themselves. Working and interacting with people outside of their own ethnic group is the norm. For instance, after a stint in the Peace Corp, one Caucasian Gen Yer got a job with a nonprofit organization running educational programs in Muslim countries. He was happy to play host to the teachers and students when they visited the US. And when his boss went on maternity leave he had no problem taking over many of her interactions with managers in different countries. Not only is Gen Y comfortable with the increasingly diverse workforce (and client base), they can make others feel comfortable. This is a benefit to you and your organization and links very closely with the next skill.

Key Skill #3:
Gen Y Understands the Global Marketplace

From the moment Gen Y could interact with a computer they learned about the *World Wide* Web. At no point in their lives have they ever been without access to information from around the world. At a very young age this generation connected with peers abroad. This connection has continued throughout their entire lives. While Gen Y may have grown up in neighborhoods segregated in various ways, their worlds are surprisingly integrated and in many ways they cannot comprehend an environment that is not global.

This generation has never known the Berlin Wall, the USSR, or the Cold War. They have never lived without an international space program. For their entire lives they have used and purchased goods manufactured outside the United States.

Gen Y Thinks Globally

Once their high school education began, the global economy was only further reinforced. Many high schools participate in foreign exchange student programs and Gen Y have either participated themselves, known a classmate who has, or attended class with someone from another country and culture.

In American colleges and universities it would be nearly impossible for a Gen Y student not to interact with someone from another country, religion, race, or culture. Classmates, professors, and alumni are a constant reminder to nearly every college student in American that we are living in a global community. For example, at Arizona State University, 15,441 ethnic minority students enrolled in the fall of 2007. In 2006, 22% of the ASU faculty were minorities, and in 2007, 29% of ASU's freshman class reported a minority status. Undergraduate students comprised 34% of the total international student population, and freshman international students represented 24% of the undergraduate class for fall 2007.

KEY POINT

Gen Y is comfortable with other cultures.

Helping to further this awareness is the availability of study abroad programs. According to the Institute of International Education Open Doors Survey, in one year there were 205,983 American students studying abroad through credit programs. And it works both ways. According to the Open Doors survey, in the 2005–2006 academic year, new foreign student enrollments at American colleges and universities were about 143,000 students. This means that over four years there are over half a million foreign students in US colleges. In other words, US college students have a tremendous amount of exposure to other cultures.

Gen Y's attitudes toward diversity and international contact are a bit like their feel for technology. They take it for granted and are comfortable being on the cutting edge. They don't need to be "trained" to appreciate cultures. They'll seek out opportunities to expand their knowledge and contacts. For instance, they love to travel to foreign countries.

Key Skill #4:
Gen Yers Have Good Self-Esteem and Are Independent

This generation has very strong self-esteem because they have enjoyed parental support and involvement like no other generation. Gen Y often grew up as the center of their parents' lives with a sense that they were special and could do anything.

The positive result of Gen Yers sense of specialness for your company is that they are eager to take on responsibility and believe they can accomplish anything. Because their parents have treated them as "winners," they believe they also can win at work. They have a positive, can-do attitude that can be a huge plus for your organization.

Gen Y is also very independent. They grew up in nontraditional settings that taught them to be autonomous. They spent time in daycare or time at home alone as latchkey children. One of four comes from a single-parent household; three of four have working mothers. This background makes Gen Y comfortable and confident when taking on independent projects and assuming individual responsibility. *Inc* magazine called them confident, independent, and enthusiastic. Many have what it takes to be entrepreneurs. And they can harness their independence and entrepreneurial potential to your company goals as well.

Key Skill #5:
Gen Y Has a Sense of Security and Is Ambitious

Because of the support they have enjoyed from their parents, Gen Yers know they are loved and cared for. They have a deep-down sense of security that is healthy. This safe feeling makes the members of Gen Y believe in themselves and feel optimistic about the future. They are less afraid than other generations to ask questions and try new things. They have figured out that it is better and less time consuming to ask questions than to waste time trying to figure things out. They also like to learn and are willing to do things differently.

Gen Y is ambitious but ambitious in a good sense. They can envision a good quality of life and it is something they aspire to. This makes Gen Y hard driving and motivated when they accept and believe in a goal. They look forward to challenges. According to research by NAS Recruitment Communications, they are looking for opportunities to show off their skills. After a lifetime of involvement with sports and other activities, they are naturally more competitive than prior generations and want to do things faster and better. All of these traits make for a more motivated and confident worker.

Key Skill #6:
Gen Y Has Life Experience in the Marketplace

One of Gen Y's more subtle attributes is their experience as lifelong customers. They have been making buying decisions since they were toddlers, choosing between Burger King and McDonalds, Barbie and American Girl, Nike and Reebok. Their parents have allowed them to make purchasing decisions to a greater degree than any prior generation.

Gen Y teens have an average of $100 per week of disposable income, more than any earlier generation and they have made countless choices throughout their young lives about how to spend it. Some have debit cards in elementary school, many have credit cards in high school, and all have some form of credit purchasing power in college. They pay attention to and understand marketing and advertising. As lifelong customers in the business world they understand how it works. This real-world experience as a customer can be valuable to a company.

Gen Y Understands the Customer Perspective

Because Gen Yers have been lifelong consumers, they have developed an expectation and understanding regarding customer service. They understand how someone should be treated as a customer. If one does not receive the kind of service one desires, they are free to shop elsewhere.

For years, businesses have talked about customer service for external *and* internal customers. Previous generations have come to accept a certain lack of customer service from fellow employees. Companies have invested millions of dollars to enhance this internal customer experience in order to improve organizational efficiency. This point is extremely relevant to you as a leader.

Your new employee will not simply *hope* to be treated like a customer. As a worker, Gen Y *expects* to be treated like a customer. You have to sell the company, its procedures, and yourself to them before they will "buy" you. As we will address later, today's leaders must understand this and make sure the organization's support systems are in sync.

> **"The key to great customer service is a satisfied employee."**
> —ROGER DOW,
> MARRIOTT HOTELS

Max Depree, author of *Leadership is an Art*, states, "Treat your employees like volunteers." The point is, employees have options. Just like customers, if they're not treated well Gen Yers *will* take their business (skills) elsewhere.

Conclusion

Gen Y presents a unique and exciting leadership challenge. Gen Yers are indisputably bright and talented, yet they think differently, have very different needs, and will require a very different style of management. At first, Gen Yers may seem to be "high maintenance" to a Boomer or Xer. You will have to do many things in new and different ways to attract and retain them. However, the effort will pay off in better leadership for all your employees.

Coach's Corner

Leadership Is Key

Jeff Van Gundy played Division III college basketball at Nazareth College. He joined our coaching staff at Providence College, and we immediately recognized his brilliant mind and passion for the game.

Eventually Jeff became one of the most respected coaches in the NBA as Head Coach for the New York Knicks and later for the Houston Rockets. Great players like Patrick Ewing and Mark Jackson were quick to praise him.

It did not matter that Jeff himself played small college basketball. It didn't matter that these NBA players knew that Jeff wasn't nearly as gifted or skilled at basketball as they were. Instead, they looked to Jeff with respect because of his leadership, vast knowledge of the game, and passion. In short, they knew that because of his work ethic and expertise, he could help them improve as players, and win. Jeff's ability as a coach could help them achieve their goals.

Gen Y will force you to take your leadership skills to a new level. You will have a lot less room for error. You will have to do things better and quicker. Why? This group has more freedom and job options than any other group in history. If they see things they don't like in you, your employees, or your organization, they are going to leave. They do not think they have to "tough it out" or "pay their dues" the way other generations did.

They are also more sensitive to seemingly little things, less willing to put up with management mistakes, and less likely to give you and your organization the benefit of the doubt. They will not wait long for you to change or fix something. If they are receiving mixed messages, or leadership is not "walking the talk," they will leave.

Name: Andy
Location: West Coast
Age: 28

Andy's background:

- attended a very selective liberal arts college in the Northeast and majored in computer science and physics

- worked at a campus job after he graduated

- at a friend's suggestion, he moved to Silicon Valley and started working as a software engineer for an innovative and successful personal electronics company

Andy enjoys what he does because he likes working on cool stuff and receives a good balance of pay and vacation. He's doing something he believes in, and it's exciting. For each project, the objectives are clearly laid out and given a timeline, and he's allowed to go about specifics as he sees fit. His hours are really flexible — he doesn't have to be in the office except for meetings. He thinks that a company can achieve really interesting results if people are given freedom to work when and where is best for them.

His workplace is a very social environment — his coworkers are his friends. He likes working with people who are highly competent and friendly. He turns to coworkers, who are in their mid-30s for career advice because they're experienced in software engineering. He would leave this job if his friends left the company, if he was given a bunch of bad assignments in a row, if his girlfriend got a job back east, or if they got sick of the "ridiculous California housing prices."

Every job he's ever had has been handed to him. He's

convinced that it's totally about networking. For one of his jobs, a friend said, "Come work with me," so he did.

In Silicon Valley, Andy says, they like to think of themselves as more progressive, like the fact that he can work at 3 am if he wants to. At a job in Vermont, Andy had a Baby Boomer boss who had what Andy has since come to identify as an "East Coast mentality." There was a rigid structure, and he was more focused on tradition than looking at issues and problems analytically. Among other issues, the boss told him that he had to work normal business hours just because "that's how we've always done it." In contrast, his current supervisor is good to work for because he works *for* Andy and his team. His current supervisor takes care of most of the organizational side (like attending meetings, scheduling, and knowing what the team is all working on) so the team can be efficient and get things done.

Andy's definition of a good job:

- working with highly competent and friendly people
- being good at the job
- interesting work that's exciting for him
- doing something he believes in
- flexibility

Chapter 5

New Realities for Leaders

*Christine, now 28, had gotten a good job out of col-
lege. She liked it, but she wanted to acquire a wide
range of experiences. So when things got slow at work,
she quit. Over seven years, she had five jobs and a
couple of brief "retirement" periods. She enjoyed most
of the jobs and felt that she learned a lot because of
the variety. When there was a delay between jobs, she
sometimes moved home, where her mother, stepsis-
ter, and brother were glad to have her around. Meanwhile, Christine made a wide variety of friends and
sometimes she'd travel with them. Christine figures
that you're only young once and she plans to experience life before she settles down — if she ever does.*

We've already discussed how Generation Y is different. In this chapter we cover eight more general
characteristics of Gen Y and how these characteristics can
impact your leadership strategies.

As a leader or manager you'll have a tendency to fall
back on your normal leadership style. Yet you know that

every individual is different. In the case of Gen Y, you can use your knowledge of their attitudes and behaviors to adapt your leadership style for greater effectiveness. Gen Y represent a new reality.

> "Leaders are made, not born...You become proficient in your job or skill, and then you become proficient at understanding the motivations and behaviors of [your] people."
> — Brian Tracy, author and speaker

8 New Realities About Gen Y

1. Gen Y is delaying marriage and parenthood.
2. There is no stigma attached to moving back home.
3. When Gen Y quits, the problem is you!
4. Gen Y "leases" a job, not "buys."
5. Multiple jobs are a badge of honor.
6. Your leadership is constantly being evaluated.
7. Their circle of influence is also watching.
8. The extended family is coming back for Gen Y.

You Need to Enforce the New Realities

As a leader, it is hard enough to get followers to act when a *written* rule has changed, let alone when there are new *unwritten* rules. Tremendous time, energy, and money are wasted in organizations because after a new procedure is announced and documented, a significant percentage of the employees still try to do it "the old way."

Awareness of these differences in Gen Y is important. These differences have implications for everyone in your organization. However, what those implications are will not always be clear. As a leader, you need to be in the forefront of handling these implications. Where they impact people directly, you need to make sure that others are changing to meet the new reality — for instance in accepting Gen Y without bias.

> "Approximately 20% of the workforce will fight change. If resisters are left within the team or workplace, they can become the proverbial 'rotten apple that spoils the barrel.' However, many resistors can be changed."
> —CHARLES MILOFSKY & CARL HUFFMAN, IN *THRIVING ON CHANGE IN ORGANIZATIONS*

There is a natural tendency for people to fight change. When people resist rule changes, written or unwritten, it is because they think they can. Deep down people have a belief or desire that they can continue to do it the old way, without any consequences or repercussions.

> "Leadership is the art of getting someone else to do something you want done because he wants to do it."
> —DWIGHT EISENHOWER

As leaders we need to fully understand the unwritten rule changes and not allow wasted energy fighting change. The best example we can think of is a tax change by the IRS. We may not like the new rule; it may not be favorable to our situation, but we cannot pretend it does not exist. The IRS will make sure there are consequences associated with ignoring the new rules. As a leader, your role is like that of the IRS! You need to communicate the new rules and make sure they are understood. You need to make sure that failure to work with the new reality has consequences in your organization.

Reality Change #1:
Gen Y Is Delaying Marriage and Parenthood

Many of their differences are a direct result of Gen Y's lack of familial responsibilities. Gen Y is delaying marriage. According to the US Census Bureau, the age at which men and women are getting married is steadily creeping up from year to year. In the 1960s, when some of the oldest Baby Boomers were reaching their twenties, the average age for men to marry was 22 years and the average age for women was 20. By the 1980s, the age had increased to 24 years for men and 22 years for women. In the 90s, it was 26 years for men, 23 years for women. By 2005, the average age for men to get married was 27 years and women 25 years.

For both sexes, there is now an extra five years (that Baby Boomers did not typically have) to explore the job market, change jobs, move to different cities, and even return home to live with parents. Without the financial obligation to support another person or the limitation of a spouse's separate career plans, needs, or commitments, Gen Y has much more freedom to take risks and make changes.

Similarly, Gen Y is also delaying parenthood. According to the National Center for Health Statistics, the average age for women to have their first baby in the 1970s was

21 years. By 2000, it was at a record high of 25 years. Similarly, according to the 2002 National Survey of Family Growth, men are delaying fatherhood. In the 1970s, half of men who became fathers for the first time did so within the five-year interval of ages 22 to 27. In the 1990s, half of men became fathers between the ages of 23 and 32, with many first-time fathers in their thirties.

KEY POINT

Without the responsibilities of supporting a family, Gen Y has the freedom to explore alternatives or leave unsatisfactory jobs.

Reality Change #2:
There Is No Stigma Associated with Moving Back Home

In the past, when a young Baby Boomer or Xer couldn't find a job or a job didn't work out, there was disappointment and embarrassment. These generations were not happy about moving back home with their parents. This is not the case at all with Gen Y. For the most part, Gen Yers have close relationships with their parents and feel extremely comfortable returning home and letting their parents help them — and their parents are often happy to do it. Gen Yers believe that living at home is a smart and logical way to limit their expenses. They certainly do not see moving back home as a failure.

In a 2004 monstertrack.com survey, 57% of the college graduates surveyed were planning on moving back home with their parents. Gen Y is also willing to accept money and other kinds of help from their parents when they have a problem. They see taking help as the efficient use of available resources. This provides a tremendous financial safety net for Gen Y that other generations never had and contributes dramatically to their sense of freedom and willingness to risk change.

Reality Change #3:
When Gen Y Leaves, the Problem Is You!

In the past, when an employee left a company the assumption was that the individual was somehow flawed, found wanting, or not satisfactory to the organization. Perhaps he or she did not have the necessary skills for the job or the right temperament. Future employers would question frequent short job stints. Why couldn't this person hold a job for any length of time? What was wrong with him or her?

Today, when a young worker leaves, the finger is pointed at the employer — the stigma is on the organization. Why couldn't you retain this young person? What did you do to alienate him or her? Why couldn't you provide challenging work? Why didn't you give the necessary feedback? And the word will spread to other Gen Yers. A company can very easily get the reputation of being hostile to Gen Y employees.

Of course, some turnover is healthy. You don't want to keep the people who don't fit in and contribute. However, you can no longer afford to hire people and wait to see if they "stick." You need to have a system for "onboarding" and assimilating newcomers. You need a system for training them. You need a system for mentoring them. Only then will you get the right people performing the way you need them to.

> A recent survey suggests today's employers are most worried about hanging on to good employees and bringing in new ones, even in the current economy. When asked about their greatest staffing concern, 39 percent of senior executives interviewed cited employee retention, while 22 percent said recruitment.
> —ROBERT HALF SURVEY OF TOP EXECUTIVES, OCTOBER 2008

Reality Change #4: Gen Y "Leases" a Job

Because of their increased freedom and lack of familial responsibilities, Gen Y has a different mindset about commitment to an organization. They do not sign on for life. They have a much shorter horizon. In contrast, when previous generations took their first job they were looking for a greater degree of job security; they could envision working with that company for 10 or more years, and possibly even assumed they would retire from that same company.

Gen Y would be happy with a one- or two-year work experience. They are not worried about a long-term commitment. The Opinion Research Corp. found that only 21% of Gen Y felt that "having a secure, steady job" was important to them in choosing a career. They are leasing the job, not buying it. They are more or less taking a long test drive. They plan to check out the job before they make a serious commitment to it.

Our research found that 74% of respondents do not plan on staying in their jobs for more than 3 years. Think about buying versus leasing a vehicle. Buying is a completely different commitment than a three-year lease. A lease is a limited transaction. You pay X dollars per month for a defined usage and period of time. You are merely paying for what you use, not developing any long-term equity.

This is the exact mindset of Gen Y. A company pays them X dollars a month and for that payment the organization gets a defined amount of time and energy (work) from the Gen Y employee. Like a car lease, more miles can be used per month, but ultimately if you exceed your limit, there is an additional charge. Once the lease is up, the consumer is free to move on to another vehicle.

> "I'm convinced that we can write and live our own scripts more than most people will acknowledge."
> —Stephen R. Covey, author

If Gen Y doesn't like the job, they're comfortable quitting and looking for another one. They will accept work at a less demanding job, perhaps one that is not even in their field (for example, waitressing or bartending) and bide their time until the right job comes along. They are also comfortable going back to school for graduate degrees or even doing volunteer work for organizations like the Peace Corps, Teach America, or Americorps instead of working.

Gen Y is able to live quite inexpensively. If a Gen Yer does not move back home, he or she can find a reasonably priced room in almost any city in the country just by going online and checking the ads on CraigsList.org. Gen Y would rather get by on a shoestring budget than make "big bucks" at a job he or she doesn't really enjoy or care about.

> "Today's students have to look forward to the excitement of probably having three or four careers."
> —GORDON MOORE, INTEL CORP CO-FOUNDER

Reality Change #5: Multiple Jobs Are a Badge of Honor

Gen Y seldom signs on with the expectation of being around for a long time. They want to learn something from a job or have an experience. Once that is done — or not available — they expect to move on. In fact, it is almost considered an aberration if Gen Y has been with only one company in the course of five years. A Gen Yer who leaves a job is viewed by his peers as making a smart move to get out of a bad situation or into a better one. There is also a sort of adventurous, exploratory approach to employment. Why wouldn't you want to try different jobs? If you don't have a spouse or family to support, if you are free to move anywhere in the country, if your parents will help with your expenses, why not try something new? Maybe there is a better job out there just waiting to be discovered.

This is where your relationship with your current Gen Y employees becomes key. If you are retaining them effectively, if they are satisfied, they will be a big reason for new Gen Y employees to come on board. They will be the living proof that there are good jobs within your company that are worth staying for.

Reality Change #6:
Your Leadership Is Constantly
Being Evaluated

Since past generations of workers stayed at their jobs for years, maybe even decades, their view of leadership also had a long horizon. Traditional leadership thinking was to focus on the long haul and implement strategies with a five- to ten-year time line. In this paradigm, leaders were viewed from a distance, and developing a personal leadership style versus an organizational leadership style was rarely considered. Since employees tended to stay for longer periods, leadership flaws were often overlooked, ignored, or simply accepted as commonplace.

Generation Y has shattered this paradigm. The new rule is that leaders need to be there, out front, present, and accessible. Leadership is about *now,* not what can happen in five or ten years. Today's leaders need to be aware that they are constantly "on" and there is nowhere to hide. Generation Y is constantly critiquing their leaders, closely watching words and actions, accessibility, how they (and others) are being treated, and comparing their leaders to other possible options.

> **"Being a leader is like being a lady; if you have to go around telling people you are one, you aren't."**
> —Margaret Thatcher

Coach's Corner

Evaluating Leadership

One striking difference I have noticed over the past few years is that players are constantly evaluating your leadership. Back in the day, if a coach yelled at a player, that was it. That player didn't say, "When so and so did the exact same thing, nothing was said."

I think now players evaluate leadership, and part of that evaluation includes comparing how they're treated relative to others. I truly believe Gen Y is extremely fair, but also sensitive to how you interact with others. If you treat others poorly, they'll hold you accountable for that just as if you had treated them poorly. If you treat someone better than you treat them, they'll hold you accountable for that, too. They might even hold you accountable if you treat them better than you treat someone else, and they'll wonder why you didn't treat that other person as well as you treated them. They evaluate your leadership and they want to make sure you're giving everybody equal time. And the right amount. Not just equal…but the right amount. A major difference in today's players is they evaluate and compare leadership.

Not only is personal leadership being constantly monitored, so is strategic leadership. In the traditional model, strategy development and execution were the domain of the executive team and for the benefit of the shareholders. It was rare to see an organization truly link corporate strategy to day-to-day activities.

Gen Y now demands otherwise. In fact, Generation Y can chose an employer based upon overall corporate strategy *and* their own ability to contribute to its execution. Gen Y will research a company's strategy and commitment to their customers, employees, and the environment. Strategies that discuss this "triple bottom line" will intrigue and attract Gen Y talent.

The Triple Bottom Line

In addition to the traditional profit bottom line, the triple bottom line adds social and environmental concerns. These include effects on all stakeholders such as customers and communities, as well as environmental impacts.

"There is no doubt Gen Y is different when it comes to evaluating leadership," says Bob McNeice, an expert on sustainable business practices. "Gen Y is not only constantly evaluating the personal leadership they witness, they are also looking at an organization's strategic plans and how a company exerts its leadership in the environment at large."

"There is no doubt Gen Y is attracted to firms that embrace sustainable business practices," says McNeice. "All of the research I have done shows that more and more of this generation say they want to use their business degrees to contribute to society. Over and over we hear that talent wants to make social responsibility a priority. Having the reputation for sustainable business practices and being socially responsible are important factors for becoming an employer of choice. Nearly three quarters of all graduates are looking for organizations that have strong social responsibility reputations.

"It is important that business leaders understand the difference between sustainable business practices and 'being green,'" McNeice adds. "I believe Gen Y has become jaded towards the term 'green' and believes it has been grossly misused. Since Gen Y is particularly savvy as consumers, they do realize many green products have overstated their actual performance."

Not only are Gen Yers evaluating individual leaders, but they are also looking to see if the organization is "walking the talk."

Case Study

Fairmount Minerals

Chuck Fowler, president of Fairmount Minerals, does not see "going green" as a passing fad. In fact, for many years, Fairmount Minerals has focused its strategic plan on building a sustainable business. "We believe the definition of success is when everybody associated with the Fairmount family thinks about people, planet, and prosperity when making each decision."

Every stakeholder at Fairmount Minerals has a chance to contribute not only ideas but also to be an active part of the solution. Goals are set, teams are formed, and *real* action is taken. Everybody in the Fairmount family understands the ultimate goal…"Do good, do well."

Does it work? At Fairmount Minerals, success is measured by how well they achieve the triple bottom line of people, planet, and profit. As for the economic impact of this strategy, over the last 30 years Fairmount measures its growth not in 8 or 10% increments, but in hundreds of percentage points.

How has your sustainability strategy resonated with your new Gen Y employees?

Over the years I have seen a significant shift with new employees. Ten or fifteen years ago employees needed to understand the concept of sustainability. Today's applicants instantly understand the idea of sustainability. I also find Gen Y really gets the triple bottom line approach. I think Gen Y understands that sustainability is not just about "being green." It is also about performing their jobs more efficiently.

Does any part of the strategy stand out more for Gen Y?

One thing I have noticed about Gen Y is their openness to community service. It seems as if community service is an extension of what they already do and is a very natural commitment. We have been committed to this process for quite a while now. All of our stakeholders know we are sincere about sustainability, and Gen Y appreciates those efforts. They jump in with both feet.

Any other observations about Gen Y you would like to make?

As an example, let's take one of our newer locations and the employees we have hired there. I find this group *wants* to be there. This is not just something to pay the bills. These folks want to contribute.

I am also finding that sustainability is extremely motivating to our new employees. Their efforts have real meaning beyond just a job task. These folks are wonderful employees, and we are finding them to be very hard workers.

Reality Change #7:
The Circle of Influence Is Also Watching

When Baby Boomers and most Gen Xers started working, part of their experience was learning how to navigate the business world *on their own*. Rarely, if ever, did Boomers and Xers look to their parents as a sounding board when things were not going well. If they did, chances are they would have received input supporting the *employer, not them*. Many Boomers and Xers have heard, "I'm sure there is a reason why such and such is happening. What are you doing to cause it or fix it?" Boomers and Xers learned early that their parents would not automatically take their side. Only in the most egregious situations would parents disregard an outside authority like a coach or teacher, and side with their offspring. It was the responsibility of the Boomers and Xers to "figure it out."

The new rule is *completely* different. In most cases, important circles of influence — friends, family, and other Gen Yers — are also evaluating your leadership and how you handle particular situations as they relate to their person of interest. No longer does the authority figure get the benefit of the doubt. Circles of influence almost instantly side with the Gen Yer first, and sort out the facts later.

Circles of influence are putting increasingly greater focus on their persons of interest and are less likely to see (or care about) the bigger picture. In fact, circles of influence may even *dig* for negative issues. Once such issues are uncovered, the circles of influence can then feel involved and supportive as they comfort their persons of interest.

It is critical that today's leaders recognize this new rule and develop strategies to be proactive. Including the circles of influence in company communications such as newsletters and press releases may help balance their perspective.

Reality Change #8: The Extended Family Is Coming Back for Gen Y

Extended families are back in new ways for Gen Y that make their circles of influence even larger. Long ago, for Boomers' parents or before, extended families meant grandparents living in the same house (or on the same farm) with children and grandchildren. Or it meant grandparents moving in for the last years of their lives.

Today Gen Y is exposed to extended family in two ways. First, they often create their own psuedo-families. Between friends, siblings, and half-siblings, Gen Y often creates an extended family unit that offers them social, emotional, and even financial support. This is a new reason why Gen Y balances work and "family" differently than Boomers.

Second, Gen Y is more likely to be exposed to elderly grandparents when they themselves are adults. Their grandparents are living longer than past generations, so are often active and around beyond Gen Y's childhood. Gen Y would have a natural bond with their grandparents. As the old joke goes, the two get along because they have a mutual enemy! Grandparents are often more accepting than parents as well as being a source of resources and advice.

Gen Yers, in turn, act as occasional caregivers. This gives them additional experience and furthers the contact with an extended family. It's also a reason for Gen Y to value flexibility. For instance, one 23-year-old quit working at a boring job to look into starting her own business. In the meantime, she takes one day a week to visit her two grandmothers separately, take them to appointments, and so on.

Career Planning for Gen Y

Be open to the possibility of a Gen Yer having multiple jobs within your company in the course of a few years. Sidewise moves are very acceptable to this group. Gen Y may begin in one department and move to others because they offer more responsibility, experience, or ownership. Get comfortable with the notion that Gen Y needs to feel they are making progress and it is a good thing if that progression takes place *within* your company instead of elsewhere. Gen Y will eventually find the right fit if *you* are flexible and open.

To recruit well, you must retain well. Word will spread that Gen Yers can enhance their resumes and experience at your company.

KEY POINT
Gen Y will challenge your leadership skills in new ways.

Coach's Corner

Everyone Is a Leader

It all starts during the recruiting process. I tell players and their circles of influence that we want to help develop each and every one of them as leaders. Each and every one of our players wants to be a leader. There isn't a prospect who wants to come into our program and allow the leadership to be from the other guys. Although leadership may take different forms, we want everybody to be aware of the unique opportunities to use their personalities and their gifts to be leaders. A freshman, a newcomer, may have a different leadership role than a senior co-captain, but nonetheless, through the course of our season, through the course of the year, there will be opportunities where he has a personality or a gift or the insight where he can offer leadership. Leadership is constantly growing and evolving. You can't wait until there's an opening to then allow someone to start becoming a leader; it's an ongoing continuum.

We still have a senior member or someone with tenure and experience be the captain of our team, but that doesn't displace the need for everyone else to be aware of opportunities to lend their own leadership. At any one time, everyone is a leader, and everyone else is a follower or listener. Different situations call for different team leaders depending on what gifts and talents may be needed and the opportunities that may present themselves. To the extent that you see yourself as a leader, I believe, the more likely you are to take ownership. If you see yourself simply as a follower, then you're far less likely to take ownership at a deep and meaningful level. Your mindset is more likely to be, "well, when it's my turn to be captain, here's what I'll do."

In a traditional top-down leadership paradigm where the cables only run north-south, those cables are easily severed. The leadership chain can easily be broken. When it's more circular, more matrix-like and the cables run in every direction, it's very difficult to break the leadership chain.

Conclusion

Gen Y brings many good things to the workplace — advanced degrees, technical skills, diversity, experience as a consumer, and an appreciation of the world market. Gen Y also has innate characteristics like ambition, high self-esteem, and competitiveness that can make them highly motivated, independent, and optimistic workers.

Your challenge as a leader is to craft jobs or frame the situations for Gen Y that tap into these natural talents. Gen Y's natural ambitiousness will turn into motivation only if Gen Y believes in the goal. Gen Y's competitiveness will turn into efficiency only if Gen Y feels the work is meaningful. Gen Y's ability to learn, ask questions, and try new things will turn into productivity only if the work is challenging. Gen Y's independence will turn into new ideas for your organization only if Gen Y feels a sense of responsibility.

Does this mean you make your entry-level Gen Y employee project manager of your biggest contract? No. But Gen Y's work must be linked to a bigger project, or a component of it must be something Gen Y cares about, or there must be some challenging aspect to it, or Gen Y must be able to see something with increased responsibility in the near future.

Your challenge is to recognize and maximize Gen Y's special talents and positive attributes. Expect the most out of them and then help them achieve it.

Y Name: Albert
Location: Southwest
Age: 26

Albert's background:

- spent the last two years of high school in an accelerated math and science program run by a large state university

- graduated from a prestigious private college with a B.S. in business, where he earned a 3.5 GPA and held offices in many extracurricular organizations, such as student government and a musical theater group

- interned at a *Fortune* 20 company during college

- hired at the *Fortune* 20 company as an analyst; stayed there for two years

- worked as a freelance marketing designer

- now works as a market researcher for a local promotional organization

- currently volunteers on the county's Drug and Alcohol Planning Council

Albert has had more than his fair share of bad bosses in his few years of work experience. Some of the bad qualities of these supervisors included being controlling, subversive, abusive, and having a strange personality. One was stuck in the mentality that since he'd done something a certain way in the past and it worked, that was the way Albert must do it again, even if the previous results weren't as good as Albert's way could produce. One of his bosses was in his forties, and Albert claims that he just didn't know how to run a business. Another bad quality was insecurity. Confidence is not something that supervisors should lack when dealing with Generation Y, who grew up on the mantras of self-esteem and leadership.

With the different personalities and organizations that Albert has had to adjust to, he has become a self-proclaimed chameleon. He sees leadership, communication, negotiation, and political savvy as the keys to success. He also values working efficiently, and some of the industrial age practices that his past jobs continue to use have driven him crazy. In his head there is a picture of how the ideal organization should operate. He knows he has made political mistakes out of his naivete and inexperience, and understands that he and his peers need to recognize their limitations.

According to Albert, Generation Y wants to truly accomplish something important. The challenge for Baby Boomer supervisors is to direct that energy and get what they can out of this motivated, driven, and confident generation.

Albert's characteristics of a good job:

- self-directed project work

- diversity of work

- opportunity to make an impact rather than just being a cog in the wheel

- possibility of upward mobility

Chapter 6

Increasing Awareness of Your Personal Brand

When Akeem, age 22, received a new task from his supervisor, he started on it as ordered. But then a number of issues came up which caused him to think about their ramifications. However, when he asked his supervisor if the new issues had been considered and if he could make a few changes, his boss jumped down his throat! The boss essentially told him to do it the way they'd always done it because he said so! As you would expect, Akeem was hurt and didn't volunteer any further suggestions. Akeem's supervisor took an authoritarian approach to management that few people would appreciate. Yet it's a common management "strategy."

The next major building block for a winning recruiting and retention culture is awareness. Once a leader fully understands the situation, it is critical to take this information to a much deeper level. A leader must take a step back in order to *really* assess the situation.

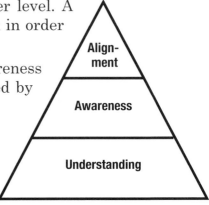

There are three key awareness levels that must be addressed by the leader:

1. awareness of the fundamentals
2. awareness of personal leadership tendencies and their impact
3. awareness of cultural and organizational tendencies and their impact

Brand name (n., bran(d)•nam)
having a well-known and usually highly regarded or marketable name *(Merriam-Webster's Online Dictionary)*

It is rare when leaders actually take the time to analyze their own personal leadership brands. In fact, it is rare when leaders even realize they *have* a leadership brand. We all are aware of product brands and the tremendous investments that are made to create household names. Yet few leaders are aware of the investment they should be making into branding *their* leadership. A leader who takes the time to become branded as a desirable leader will attract and retain the best of Gen Y.

What Is Your Leadership Brand?

Your leadership brand is the style or manner in which you provide direction, implement plans, and motivate or inspire people. There are generally three main styles of leadership: *authoritative, collaborative,* and *delegative.*

Authoritative leaders do not seek outside input or advice, generally make all decisions independently, and give very specific direction in expectation of a standard response.

Collaborative leaders take more of a team approach, seek input from employees whose skills and expertise they value, and give more open-ended direction, allowing for individual adaptation and modification.

Delegative leaders, although ultimately responsible for the decisions made, give others virtually complete power to make decisions, place the highest trust and confidence in them, and defer to their superior knowledge.

Research shows that there are particular circumstances where each of these styles is most effective. For instance, when time is short and the leader is the expert, an authoritative style often works best. Great leaders normally use a combination of these styles, tailoring their use to the particular circumstances and individuals.

> ### KEY POINT
> **Being aware of your own leadership brand is the first step to better results.**

Coach's Corner

Know Your Leadership Brand

In my first year of coaching at North Carolina State, we were playing at home against the University of North Carolina, coached by the legendary Dean Smith. Our stadium, Bayne Reynolds Coliseum, was approximately 50 years old.

It had been a warm day and, typical of the coliseum, there wasn't a lot of air flow; in fact, it was downright uncomfortable, hot, and sticky. As the players competed, their fingers would turn prune-like, similar to when you stay in the water too long. As the game progressed, our fans were in the faces of the Tar Heels players. Our fans were on their feet screaming non-stop. It was an unbelievable environment, almost threatening for the opponents. Dean Smith had a team, as was typical for North Carolina, filled with tremendously talented players — great players. We were clearly outmanned in terms of talent, yet our fans were doing everything they could to help us.

I noticed that, as the game progressed, as hot and uncomfortable as it was, Dean Smith never took his coat off, never loosened his tie. I think what he was trying to convey to his team was that they were the more talented team, that even under these threatening conditions, this hostile environment, all we have to do is perform with poise and composure. So he didn't sweat, he didn't flinch, he didn't loosen his tie, he didn't take his sport coat off. He portrayed to his team that he was going to be unaffected by the environment. That they were going to do what they do; they were the better team, and if they did that, they would be successful.

Dean Smith knew his leadership brand.

John Chaney at Temple University, another legendary coach, also knew his brand. At Temple Coach Chaney took a lot of kids who in many ways were underdogs. So when he coached, even before the jump ball occurred, his tie was off and loosened, sometimes all the way down to his sternum. His shirtsleeves were rolled up above his elbows. He didn't wear a sport coat. It seemed to me he was subtly conveying to his team that as underdogs, I'm in this fight with you and I'm ready to scratch and claw, bite and kick, do whatever it takes to help us be successful. He didn't have the same kind of team that Dean Smith had; he had a different brand — he was more of an underdog — whereas Coach Smith had great talent year in and year out. Both coached masterfully knowing their different brands.

It is important that you identify your leadership brand because it will determine how you communicate with your Gen Y employees, and the type of work you are willing to entrust to them. Gen Y wants and needs to communicate with you. They have grown up with much feedback and positive reinforcement from their parents. They have enjoyed the ability to communicate with their

> **"Create customized career paths: This will create a sense of control that Gen Y desires and will give them a measure of their progress in the organization... If you want them to do something, tell them why."**
>
> — NAS RECRUITMENT COMMUNICATIONS

peers via cell phones, text messaging, instant messaging, and so forth. They need feedback about what they have already done and they want input into what they will do. Gen Y also wants very much to be a participant in decision making, to have responsibility, and to have at least some control over the work they are doing.

If your leadership brand is too authoritarian, you will repel Gen Y. Authoritarian leaders are the antithesis of the boss they are looking for. These leaders will have to modify their style to become more Gen Y compatible. On the other hand, if your leadership brand is naturally collaborative or delegative, you should be able to work well with Gen Y.

Consultant's Corner

Leadership of People Is the Point

In nearly every organization in which we have ever worked, we have encountered managers who were promoted because of their proficiency at the task at hand. Whether it is accounting managers, IT managers, shop floor supervisors, or any other kind of manager, they were promoted because they were good accountants, programmers, or machinists. More rare are the managers who were promoted because they had superior *people* skills and reasonable knowledge of the task at hand. In other words, people who were promoted because of their *leadership* skills.

In today's environment, technical skills are the price of admission. But overreliance on them may be counterproductive. We've all known cases where the best salesperson was promoted and was a lousy sales manager.

Simply being the best at a function is not a reason to be promoted. It is critical for everyone who supervises *people* to understand *people*. As good managers know, the job is to get things done *through* others. Their own skills at the work they supervise become irrelevant except for training and evaluation.

Take the time and make the investment to develop your team's people skills. Learning finance, programming, or the way a machine operates may be difficult, but many people master these skills. A good manager who wants to become a leader works just as hard, if not harder, at the people skills as he or she ever did at mastering technical skills.

Communication Fundamentals

As in any sport, or most activities for that matter, there are a series of fundamentals that must be mastered before someone can move on to more advanced levels. Even if a performer is an all-star, their coaches usually take time to revisit every fundamental. Legendary football coach Vince Lombardi used to start his preseason camps by saying, "Gentlemen, this is a football." Even the great Green Bay Packers teams needed to refocus themselves on fundamentals and be *aware* not to overlook the obvious.

There are three key fundamentals we need to revisit before moving to the next level. While these may seem obvious at first, please do not overlook their importance. In many ways, nothing else can be successfully implemented unless the leader is *aware* of these distinctions between how the generations see the world.

Then and Now	
Gen X/Boomer	**Gen Y**
Conditioning	Wellness
"Tree hugger"	Green/sustainable
Job jumping	Leveraging opportunities
Telephone	Cell phone
Walkman	iPod
Encyclopedia	Google
Mid-life crisis	Quarter-life crisis
Rejection letter	Follow-up letter

Choose Your Words

You must choose your words with care when you communicate with Gen Y. Words that mean one thing to a Baby Boomer or Gen Xer may mean something completely different to Gen Y. Also, Gen Y is much less formal than prior generations. The way they communicate with you may be very different.

Even the words we use to describe your leadership role vis-à-vis Gen Y mean something. You aren't going to "deal with," "handle," or "train" Gen Yers as if they were a problem or an animal you were working with. You are going to collaborate with, communicate with, and lead Gen Yers. That's what today's leadership is.

Consultant's Corner

Words Matter

During a recent corporate function, we were brought in to address all of the employees about the need to create personal strategic plans. Our client wanted a high-energy, fun presentation that would drive home the point.

To illustrate how to develop solid plans that may have many moving parts, we used juggling as an analogy. To the casual observer, juggling looks very complicated with many things going on at once.

The truth of the matter is, basic juggling is simply one key movement, repeated over and over. To teach people to juggle, we have them create a framework and develop targets or goals. We then have them practice by trying *not* to catch the balls so that the balls drop to the floor in the targeted area. This teaches folks where to place their hands when they are actually catching the balls.

To illustrate our point, we told the audience to picture two "Jethro Bodine" cereal bowls on the floor by their feet. Their task was to drop the juggling balls into the imaginary bowls.

Interestingly enough, the Gen Xers and Baby Boomers in the audience immediately began to practice. Our reference to the old television show, "The Beverly Hillbillies," and Jethro Bodine made perfect sense. The Gen Y participants hesitated and then asked, "What is a 'Jethro Bodine' bowl?" They had no idea and had never seen the Beverly Hillbillies.

While this added to the fun of the presentation, it did drive home a valuable point — English is a living language. Words change meaning, references become outdated, and popular culture invents new references all the time.

As leaders, we must choose our words and our references wisely. Our goal is to be understood. A misused word or phrase may at best not be understood and, at worst, may offend.

Nonverbal Communication Counts

How do you walk around the office? What is your posture like when you meet and greet employees? Where do you stand or sit when you talk to someone individually? Facial expressions, posture, and body positioning all matter. Also be conscious of the physical environment at your organization. How is your office decorated? What does it say about you? How is your lobby area decorated? What does it say about your organization? Gen Y is very observant and will respond to nonverbal cues, even subtle ones.

Coach's Corner

Listening to Gen Y

On January 15, 2002, our North Carolina State team was playing at Clemson. With 48 seconds to go, a time out was called with our team trailing by one point. We had the ball.

As our team ran off the floor to the bench, I already had in mind a play that we could run and I felt very confident that it would work in this situation. However, as the team approached the bench, Archie Miller, our senior point guard, grabbed me and suggested that we run what we called a bump action.

Based on his intuition and feel for the game, without hesitating I immediately deferred and opted to go with his suggestion, discounting the play I had in mind when the time-out was first called. We then executed the plan to perfection as Anthony Grundy scored a lay-up and tied the score, 77–77, but was also fouled on the play. He made the free throw to put us ahead 78–77. Clemson then scored on the next possession to re-take the lead by one point, 79–78. But we scored the final basket of the game when Josh Powell tipped in a missed shot with two seconds to go, giving us an 80–79 win.

Even if the play I wanted to call had worked, we would only have tied the game. Since we were open to ideas, and our players knew it, we were able to accept the input, avoid overtime, and post a great win.

In this case, as in most cases, listening equals winning.

Communication Involves Listening

As with most fundamentals, this is an obvious communication principle but one that cannot be overstated with Gen Y. They want to be heard. They want to talk to you. They want to give you their perspective. You need to listen to them!

KEY POINT

Gen Y may be especially anxious to give you input when they are first hired. They are seeing things from a fresh perspective and have new ideas. This is a very important time to listen. If you squelch Gen Y now, you may *never* get their enthusiastic input for your organization.

It takes multiple positive reinforcements to equal the impact of one negative comment, so you need to be very positive with Gen Yers early. If you show Gen Y that you can listen, are interested in their ideas, and actually will consider implementing what they suggest, you will earn their respect and attention. You will also profit from their increased interest and commitment to your mission. If you tell Gen Y to hold their ideas until they understand "how things are done around here," you may lose them. At all costs, avoid the ubiquitous "We thought about that, but…" response.

As a leader your body language must align to your message. Often we are not conscious of times when our words and our appearance are misaligned, and we send the exact opposite message we intended to send.

The first step in aligning your spoken and body language is to really be *aware* of your prejudices toward Gen Y. If you are harboring too many negative feelings, it is bound to be a distraction to your spoken words.

Make yourself *aware* of your physical presence. Conduct a self-audit of how you (and your physical space) may be communicating without your even knowing it.

Conclusion

Most leaders and managers are less aware of their personal styles than you might expect. Most of us have done what we do so long that we often operate automatically without much self-analysis. Because Gen Yers respond best to different styles, they can help you become more aware of your own leadership brand. As many mentors of Gen Y say, they learn as much as their mentees because of the fresh view they bring. Gen Y will be particularly useful to you as they come onboard. Gen Y (and any newcomer) sees things with fresh eyes. As you listen to them you'll gain, and their loyalty to the job will increase.

Name: Vivien
City: Southeast
Age: 24

Vivien's background:

- graduated college from a large university ranked in the top 30 with a double major in philosophy and public policy

- immediately pursued a masters in public policy and management at a top 25 university

- while working on her masters, she interned at a community grant-making fund

- after graduation, she continued working at the fund where she interned

- currently is their Director of Sector Leadership

Vivien wants to change the world. She started working at her current job, a grant-making fund, as an intern while she was pursuing her Masters degree. She knew she wanted to continue working there after she graduated because she was invested in the organization and in her clients. She wanted to accomplish her goals and evolve in her position. She wanted to keep building on the knowledge she is continually gaining and improve on future projects.

Vivian believes Generation Y stands out because of their desire for and ability to take input and feedback. She sees herself as open-minded and willing to understand her flaws. Her boss supports her by validating her work through the recognition of her accomplishments and by welcoming new ideas. Vivien sees the difference between genuine appreciation and unintentional, demeaning pats on the back. The latter feels different because a superior just brushes off your ideas or accomplishments and has no invested interest in them.

Vivian says that "Generation Y is different because we do not want to waste time waiting to move up within an organization. If we're dissatisfied with the upward mobility, we'll be entrepreneurial and start something of our own. The same goes if we have a passion in an industry that doesn't conventionally make much money." Thanks to the success of the Baby Boomers, Gen Y often has resources to burn and take risks. Along with this, Vivien says she's willing to mix her personal and professional lives as long as she's having fun and is passionate about her work.

Despite the many options available to Vivien after she completed her masters, she decided to stay at the organization where she interned. To Vivien, the reasons to stay at any organization include:

- invested in the organization
- invested in the projects she is currently working on
- building her knowledge
- finishing the work on projects
- evolving her position so it is even more to her liking
- improving on previous projects

- the organization's good reputation
- liking coworkers and organization's leadership
- day-to-day work is exciting and allows her to connect with people
- her boss allows her to choose her projects
- her boss creates buy-in to projects and ideas
- understands the organization's working and purpose as a whole
- her boss recognizes her strengths and puts them into play
- is recognized for her work
- is given the freedom to pursue her wants and likes, and opportunities for learning within the organization

Chapter 7

World-Class Performers

Karla, age 25, really cared about her first job in a school district. She had a personal vision to use business management methods in education. She wanted to develop and apply new, world-class methods to the educational setting. After working for the school district, she was accepted to an MBA program that could further her goal to be a top performer bringing new skills to improve the educational process.

During the past few years, we have spent countless hours researching world-class performers. We have interviewed dozens of people who perform at the world-class level, including athletes, actors, musicians, politicians, and business executives. We found that they possess a common set of behaviors and skills. These same behaviors and skills can be learned and adapted for business leaders in any industry or market.

World-class performers and leaders:

1. Use performance feedback or "game film."
2. Turn unconscious, negative tendencies into conscious, positive choices.
3. Practice energy management.
4. Realize that what is required for improvement may be counterintuitive.
5. Develop a tactical and measurable action plan.
6. Have vision.

Skill #1
World-Class Performers and Leaders Use Performance Feedback or "Game Film"

In every profession, people who desire to improve their performance know they must reflect on what they have done in the past in order to do it better in the future. Athletes review game film, actors study film clips, and musicians listen to recordings of themselves. Teachers are observed and evaluated by their supervisors; doctors have peer reviews; lawyers read transcripts of depositions and trials. Every world-class performer has a tool that enables him or her to examine and evaluate his behavior, to see what is being done well or poorly, and to pinpoint areas for improvement or growth. World-class performers then make the conscious decision to correct their weaknesses.

While you may not have actual game film to analyze, there are tools that can help you identify your strengths

and weaknesses. These tools are personality profiles, 360°
evaluations, and employee surveys. These types of tools
can provide you with the "game film" you need to become a
better leader.

One of the best tools we know of to increase your
awareness is personality profiles. Personality profiles
identify behavioral tendencies, personality traits, and
types. These tools help in two ways. First, they help you
understand *yourself*, and, second, they help you recognize
behavior patterns in other people so that you can understand
them better. As a leader or manager, you need to work with
a variety of people, on a variety of levels. It will help you do
your job better if you can identify how different employees
think, react, and want to be treated as you supervise and
reward each one. This is especially true of Gen Y employees
who are particularly sensitive to how you interact with them
(and others!), the words you use, and your management
style. Gen Y thrives on feedback and communication. The
better you understand your own behavioral tendencies and
those of Gen Y, the better you can communicate.

Perhaps you unknowingly dominate conversations,
ask questions without listening to the answers, or have
little patience. Perhaps you are too critical, uncomfortable

"The communication style of leaders helps us distinguish
great leaders from the wannabes. When facing a problem the
great leader says, 'Let's find out,' while the wannabe says
that 'nobody knows'... Great leaders have the capacity to
listen while wannabes can't wait for their turn to talk."

—Reed Markham, PhD

with change, or overly concerned about details. Everyone has blind spots — areas where they need to improve. But these blind spots can be particularly detrimental when interacting with Gen Y.

KEY POINT
Your challenge is to *adapt* your behavior to communicate and act in the most effective way.

Chapter 8 has an exhaustive discussion of DISC, the most widely used personality-profiling program. DISC will give you the "game film" you need to uncover the behavioral tendencies that you need to work on in yourself.

Skill #2
World-Class Performers and Leaders Turn Unconscious, Negative Tendencies into Conscious, Positive Choices

Studies show that 90% of what we do is rote. We have routines, habits, and familiar practices that are more or less automatic. But great leadership is not a passive, un-thinking activity. It is the opposite of routine and rote. It is thoughtful, dynamic, and proactive.

As discussed above, some of our unconscious habits, routines, and tendencies are negative. The little things we don't even realize we're doing can have a disproportionately large impact, especially with respect to Gen Y.

For example, one of the more common tendencies we see is multitasking. In today's busy world everyone tries to accomplish multiple things at once. If this becomes an unconscious habit when you are interacting with others, then you are in a danger zone. Every employee, particularly Gen Y employees, will begin to believe their input is not valued if you are not fully attentive.

World-class performers seek to uncover these unconscious tendencies and develop conscious triggers that control or direct them. Particularly when dealing with Gen Y, we need to be sensitive to the way we communicate and interact. The DISC profile discussed in Chapter 8 will help you understand and identify your tendencies and turn them into conscious, positive actions.

Skill #3
World-Class Performers and Leaders
Practice Energy Management

Every world-class performer we have ever met practices some sort of energy management in addition to time management. At some point during our careers we all are exposed to a time management course. We learn there are only so many hours in the day and to prioritize our tasks accordingly. Time, we learn, is a finite resource.

World-class performers further learn that energy is also a finite resource. How to spend that energy is a critical decision, and it is not taken lightly. Maximum energy is invested in areas that can improve performance and little or no energy is wasted on events or situations beyond their control. As a leader, it is critical not to waste energy on events beyond your control. It is equally important not to continually rehash the same old issue or try to wish a challenge away. Wishing is not a strategy!

There are three consistent energy wasters we see business leaders repeat in regards to Gen Y.

Energy Waster #1
Why Can't They Be Like We Were?

Every older generation has probably sung that same sad song. Why isn't today's generation like we were, perfect in every way? It's time to accept and adapt to reality: "What is, is." Don't waste energy wishing that Gen Y was like prior generations of employees. They're not and, as discussed earlier, they're not playing by the same set of rules that prior generations did either. They certainly have different interests and needs. They are looking for very different things in the workplace and they are going to require you do some very different things to attract and retain them. As discussed in earlier chapters, they're different, not wrong. They even may be better. Don't stew over who they are, embrace it. Work with it.

Energy Waster #2
Why Do We Have to Change...Why Can't They Change?

Many of us had to "pay our dues" working for a lousy boss at a mediocre job for many years. We "toughed it out," why can't Gen Yers do the same? The fact is that Gen Y has figured out that they don't have to tough it out when work conditions are poor. They realize that they have the option of leaving and finding fulfilling employment elsewhere. They are keenly aware that a whole generation of Baby Boomers will be retiring and Gen Y is very much in demand. They have delayed marriage and parenting and are free of familial responsibilities. They also have a financial security net in the form of their parents.

Other generations, Baby Boomers and Gen X, did not have the freedom or the mind-set to quit. We had to "grin and bear it." We had families to support, mortgages to pay, and we could not count on our parents to foot the bill. Fortunately, for most of us, the wait paid off. We survived the poor bosses, the menial tasks, the lack of feedback, and so forth. Gen Y is not so patient and is keenly aware of many alternatives. The sooner we accept this new reality the better.

Three Types of Folks in Your Organization

The Gen Y difference can be useful to you in changing what we believe is a weakness in most management cultures.

Our observation over the years leads us to believe most organizations are broken down into three types of folks: Teamers (20%), Fence-sitters (60%) and Lottery Ticket Winners (20%).

"Teamers" are the folks who are loyal and dedicated employees who always give their best. They tend to be positive folks who trust their leaders and always strive to do their part. Unfortunately, since these folks require little "maintenance," managers and leaders tend to ignore them and do not give them much time or energy.

The second group, "Fence-Sitters," usually make up the majority of an organization's employees. These folks tend to be the silent majority. They are not overtly negative *or* positive.

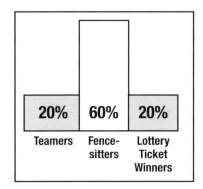

Their attitude is "wait and see what develops." Again, since Fence-Sitters are usually "silent," managers do not spend much time with them either.

The final group, the "Lottery Ticket Winners," are the "squeaky wheels." To them, nothing is ever right. They are, so they think (and say), smarter, more qualified, and more talented than their boss (or anyone else for that matter). Seldom do they offer any proactive ideas, but they *always* are the first to point out the negatives.

Since this group is most vocal and demanding of attention, managers tend to spend the overwhelming majority of their time and energy with this group. Teamers tend to just shrug the lack of attention off while the fence sitters quickly learn that in order to be noticed, you need to be negative.

Managers convince themselves that if they could just win over these negative folks everyone else will follow. Therefore, managers *waste* countless hours and enormous amounts of energy trying to motivate employees who are frequently a lost cause.

Don't Coddle the Negative People

When we are working with leaders, we tell them a story to help identify an organization's lost causes. We call it the "Lottery Ticket" story.

A husband and wife wake up one Sunday morning, check the newspaper and discover they have just won the lottery, a $45 million dollar jackpot! The paper says there are two other winners, so their take will be $15 million.

The couple is immediately overwhelmed. They have a wonderful life now. Happy, healthy, and they do not want for anything. Both of them are afraid this windfall will change everything, and not for the better. In fact, they believe their lives couldn't get much better. They have read countless stories about how lives were ruined after just such a windfall.

After hours of discussion and soul searching, the couple decides they do not want the money. They flip a coin and the husband wins the toss. What he wins is that on Monday, as he walks into work, he is to hand the ticket to the first person he sees.

On Monday morning our generous husband sees Joe, the office naysayer. True to his promise, he approaches Joe, explains the situation, and hands him one of the three winning $45 million lottery tickets.

Joe takes the ticket, puts it in his pocket and says, "Oh sure, you give me the ticket I have to split," and walks away.

That is a "Lottery Ticket Winner."

Our story elicits uncomfortable laughter from the audience when we tell it. Everyone knows the point we are making. For some folks, even being *given* a winning a lottery ticket is not enough. Yet it is just this type of person who demands our time and energy. The regrettable mistake is, we give it to them.

The result of our misplaced efforts is that we are not leading. We are ignoring the Teamers and teaching the Fence-Sitters that inappropriate attitudes are rewarded with time and attention.

Our *very* strong advice is if you have folks who would respond negatively to a winning lottery ticket, **stop giving them your time and attention**. Start giving your time to the Teamers. They deserve it, and you will be teaching the Fence-Sitters the correct leadership lesson.

Your goal for the Lottery Ticket Winners is simple. They can either:

• start pretending to be positive,

• start being positive,

• shut up altogether,

• or leave.

If you have lottery ticket winners who will undermine your change management efforts toward Gen Y, address it now…and head on. Gen Y doesn't like naysayers either. When you've enlisted Gen Y, they'll help you focus on change and improvement rather than the complainers.

Energy Waster #3
Defensiveness

World-class performers do not waste their energy on being defensive about situations. If a coach, director, conductor, or mentor offers challenging advice, world-class performers stop and listen.

Likewise, when faced with new members on the team, members who ultimately want to contribute and maybe even take their jobs, world-class performers waste no energy being insecure or defensive. They know it is a drain on precious resources.

As a leader, it is important to manage your (and your team's) insecurity and defensiveness. As discussed earlier, Gen Y is very educated and tech savvy. They generally bring superior skills to the job in one area or another. They will know more than you about some things. You may have to ask them about something or have them explain something to you or your other employees. Don't be defensive about this. It doesn't mean you cannot lead or manage this bright generation. You have other superior skills and knowledge and your experience is irreplaceable. Be happy Gen Y has skills to add to your organization and never lose faith in yourself as a leader.

Skill #4
World-Class Performers and Leaders Realize that What Is Required for Improvement May Be Counterintuitive

World-class performers are able to think outside the box and, specifically, force themselves to re-think and change their game plans in order to improve. The saying "you can't teach an old dog new tricks" does not apply to successful leaders because that is exactly what they do — they "learn new tricks."

Some research shows that leaders and managers tend to learn one style when they are younger and continue to apply it throughout their careers. When situations change, they often fail when facing new challenges. Gen Y can help save you from this. Particularly when dealing with Gen Y employees, doing what you always did, or what comes naturally, or what is comfortable, may actually be the opposite of what you should be doing. This generation sees and interprets things differently. They have much different expectations and needs. What you did instinctively for Baby Boomers and Gen Xers may not work for Gen Yers.

For example, it used to be that getting called into the boss's office was akin to being sent to the principal's office when you were a kid. In the past, the boss was fairly isolated and unapproachable. He or she didn't really rub shoulders with the average employee and rarely talked casually to new, young employees. Being called in meant you had made a mistake or were in trouble and the boss was going to confront you with the mess you made. It was usually embarrassing and uncomfortable to see the boss. In fact, the boss only seemed to be interested in you when you were in trouble.

Gen Y Wants Feedback

Today, Gen Y wants and expects to be called in by the boss. Gen Y wants to talk to the boss to share ideas, get face-to-face feedback, and ask questions. In fact, Gen Y will be upset if they do not get to talk with the boss.

You may be operating under the old system and think intuitively that communication is only for correction. You may think intuitively that it is not "normal" to talk to new, young employees and it could somehow diminish your position. Yet in order to be a world-class leader you must now do what is counterintuitive. Gen Y's need for communication is actually a good thing because it will give you an opportunity to constantly reinforce your mutual vision and keep your finger on Gen Y's pulse.

The way you communicate is only one example of the counterintuitive behavior you must now adopt. The reality is, you will have to do things in almost every area of recruiting, interviewing, onboarding, and interacting with Gen Y that are different and not "what you always did." Be prepared to stretch your comfort zone and adapt.

Skill #5
World-Class Performers and Leaders Develop a Tactical and Measurable Action Plan

World-class performers not only set goals, they break each goal into measurable, bite-size chunks that are committed to a plan.

A good leader will not just say "I wish we could hire outstanding Gen Y employees;" he or she will outline the many steps that must be taken to accomplish this. The next chapters contain the nuts-and-bolts strategies and processes to help you create and implement your action plan for recruiting and retaining talented Gen Y employees.

Skill #6
World-Class Performers and Leaders Have Vision

Perhaps the most important attribute of world-class leaders is their vision. In terms of Gen Y, this will also be the major challenge for leaders. Countless books and articles have been written about vision and we will not attempt to re-invent the wheel here. You know what vision is and how critical it is to your success as a leader and to the success of your organization. But in this era of Gen Y hiring, the role of vision is more complex and multifaceted. It is a sort of "vision PLUS."

Identify Gen Y's Personal Vision

Obviously, you need to have a clear corporate vision and communicate it effectively to Gen Y. There's nothing new about that. What is absolutely critical here, and so different from the past, is that *you must go farther and determine what the Gen Yer's vision is for him- or herself.*

> **"Effective leaders help others to forge their aspirations into a personal vision."**
> John Kotter, author,
> Harvard Professor

Determining a Gen Yer's personal vision can occur during the initial job interview, in a training exercise, during a one-on-one review, during a scheduled feedback session, or in the break room over coffee. But it has to happen. You must identify and understand Gen Y's personal goals and interests.

In the past, job candidates may have been asked a question something like: "Where do you see yourself in ten years?" The smart applicant (who was usually desperate to get the job) would enthusiastically spout something along these lines: "Why, doing a good job working here, of course!" Older generations of employees would generally say what they thought the interviewer wanted to hear. Gen Y will say what they really mean.

Interviewers need to be ready to hear very different answers to that same question. A Gen Y candidate may well say something like, "In 10 years I hope to have started my own business," or "My goal is to learn as much as I can in my first few for-profit jobs, get my Masters of Social Work, and pursue my dream of working in the nonprofit sector."

Today's interviewer, who is not trained and ready for these types of answers, may be caught off guard. Many extremely talented candidates will be excluded. In reality, a good interviewer today should be looking for these answers. A nontraditional answer should be explored rather than being a reason to exclude the Gen Y candidate.

KEY POINT

When you find out what the individual Gen Yer's vision is, you will find out what he or she cares about and is really willing to work for.

Develop a Shared Vision

Once you have identified a Gen Yer's vision, you must take the final step and link your vision for the organization with the Gen Yer's personal vision. Show the Gen Yer that his or her vision and goals dovetail with yours, that, in fact, not only do they coincide, they can be achieved together. To be a world-class leader, you must be able to convince a Gen Yer that he or she can achieve his or her personal goals by *staying with your organization and working together with you.* You do not want Gen Y to consider his or her time at your organization just a stepping stone toward the job they really want or the goal they really have.

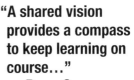

"A shared vision provides a compass to keep learning on course..."
—Peter Senge, author, The Fifth Discipline, The Art and Practice of the Learning Organization

Gen Y Sees the Work World Differently

Gen Y has a shorter job horizon than experienced employees. They are looking at a point one year in the distance or perhaps two. As discussed earlier, Gen Y has a different mindset about commitment to an organization because of their increased freedom and lack of family responsibilities. They do not sign on with a company for life. When most of us Boomers or Xers took our first jobs we were interested in job security. We envisioned the possibility of working with that company for many years. Gen Y is only looking for a one or two year work experience. They are not thinking about long-term commitment. They are "leasing" the job, not "buying" it, and they may or may not renew their lease!

All humans have a tendency to avoid what is uncomfortable or painful — the "fight or flight" reflex. Gen Y's reflex time is shorter. Because they have so many options and a financial safety net, it is easier and more tempting for Gen Y to leave when things get tough. They may overreact to situations or problems that are temporary or correctable. They may focus too much on the present and not enough on the future.

Because Gen Y may not have faced significant challenges before — at least not without the direct support of their circles of influence — they may have a lower tolerance for uncomfortable situations. And because they have many options in life, they are often less willing to put up with discomfort on the job.

Gen Y may be made uncomfortable by things you take for granted. Perhaps it is coworkers who don't extend a welcome. Or a boss who doesn't say hello. Or company values that focus only on profit. Or even the lack of public transit to your offices. You'll need to probe for these subtle issues since Gen Y will assume that you are aware of them.

With instant access to opportunities via the Internet, Gen Y can choose "flight" more easily than dealing with an uncomfortable environment. "Generation Y has a significant advantage over any other generation; they have information instantly at their fingertips," says David Campeas, CEO of PrincetonOne, a staffing agency. "At any time, in seconds, they can use the Internet to see what is available. If a boss does not "walk the talk" or does not respect their input, instead of stewing over it, they can immediately look for alternatives," says Campeas. "Gen Yers are loyal, but not automatically to a company. Loyalty must be earned by consistent leadership practices."

Your challenge is to stretch Gen Y's horizon. Help them identify and commit to a goal that is bigger than a one- or two-year commitment. Enlist them in lengthier projects. Is there something you have wanted to accomplish but have not had the time or resources to complete? Assign these tasks to your Gen Yers and be sure Gen Y understands their strategic importance.

Help them understand that temporary obstacles, which can be resolved by good leadership, do not trump the bigger, more valuable goal. Help them see that despite present challenges or difficulties, they are still on track to achieve their long-term vision.

Sell Your Vision Constantly

You know Gen Yers are "extreme communicators." You will have as many opportunities to talk to them as you can make the time for. This is a good thing because it will help you reinforce your mutual vision, something you absolutely must do. Make it a point to include a discussion of vision in every conversation with Gen Y. Any time you have the opportunity to talk, re-sell the vision. Ask them if they are on track. Ask them if their vision has changed. Ask them if they feel they are making progress toward their goals. Ask them what you can do to help.

Conclusion

We've outlined the results of our research on what makes world-class performers. Other research suggests that most leaders and managers develop their own personal styles (or brands) of leadership early in their careers and then stick with that style. Thus, they can fail because they don't adjust when the situation changes. Generation Y is a major change in the workplace and provides you with the opportunity to adapt your style for the better. If you'll accept the challenge, you'll come out ahead because world-class approaches not only work with Gen Y, they work with all your staff.

 Name: Julie
Location: Midwest
Age: 26

Julie's background:

- graduated with majors in journalism and communication from a college ranked in the nation's top 90 universities

- found her first job in New York City on idealist.org

- found her second job through a friend who was leaving the position she wanted

- found her third job through a friend who is an influential woman in the community, and who

passed around Julie's resume to potential
employers

- currently works as the communications manager
at a grant-making foundation

At the age of 26, Julie has already had three jobs, the
longest of which lasted 15 months. She describes this
as par for the course these days. She wants a job that is
challenging, offers diverse opportunities for projects, and
is flexible enough to allow her to work outside her normal
area, hours, and location. She would also like to understand
peoples' jobs in different departments and collaborate with
them. Even though she hasn't stayed at one organization for
very long, she's not one to immediately throw in the towel.
She says that it's not fair to the employer to leave without
asking for what she wants. She has let her former
bosses know that she was unhappy and given them the
opportunity to fix the problems. If her complaints are ignored,
then she has to consider how much she really wants to work
there.

Working at a nonprifit organization fulfills part of Julie's
desire to change the world and advance the greater good.
She is motivated to succeed professionally because it affects
her overall personal happiness — her professional life is
intermingled with her personal life. She generally works
normal hours, but if she wanted to give her all to a certain
job or project, that would become part of her personal life.
However, she would like for her organization to be more
innovative, including keeping up with changes in styles and
technology for the nonprofit sector and funding atypical,
unique ideas.

To retain top talent, Julie says that it is imperative to
value high morale as a part of the culture. If it's an unhappy
work environment, it's difficult to succeed. While money is

important, it's not the most important factor. Julie would rather be happy with less money than miserable and making a six-figure salary, because she wouldn't have time to spend it.

The generational challenges Julie has encountered are that older people:

- are more set in their ways

- are not open to change, even if it's better and more efficient

- have a hard time respecting young colleagues as peers instead of assistants

- had a different work environment during their professional development, so they don't really understand what it's like to be starting out now

- are more prone to be loyal to one organization

Julie says she spends more time with her boss than with her boyfriend, so the qualities she's looking for in a good boss include someone who:

- challenges her

- doesn't look at her age or experience, but looks at how she works for them

- continually gives her better projects

- listens

- manages their own time well

- is flexible and understanding

Chapter 8

Personality Types Matter (Self-Awareness)

Betsy, 24, is happy with her new job but somewhat worried that her boss, Tim, doesn't like her. He has never said that her work is poor nor has he ever criticized anything, but neither has he ever complimented her on her work. This makes her very nervous. More importantly, one morning she saw him in the elevator and he barely acknowledged her, only grunting a terse "hello." He generally strides through the office with a stern, preoccupied look on his face.

Tim always keeps his door closed and has never stopped by Betsy's office to talk. Furthermore, when she approached him to ask a few questions about a project, he seemed annoyed with her for worrying so much about the details. He kept cutting her off and twice changed the topic. Betsy wishes Tim would just tell her what she is doing wrong and why he doesn't like her. She doesn't know how much more of this tension she can take.

What went wrong? The sad thing about our case study is that Tim actually does like Betsy. He just doesn't show his approval or acceptance in a way that Betsy understands. Tim is a Baby Boomer who believes in minimal communication. He will let Betsy know when something is wrong. If he doesn't say anything, she is doing well. He would "call her on the carpet" when something is unacceptable and he assumes Betsy knows this. He never talks to his older employees and they are fine with that.

Tim will only go to someone's office if there is an urgent problem. He doesn't believe in making small talk with subordinates, and particularly not with new hires. He would have been alarmed and uncomfortable if his boss had talked to him when he was first starting out. Tim is not really a "morning person." He doesn't say more than a few words even to his wife in the morning. There is no way he could be chatty with employees early in the day.

Tim is a "bottom line" guy. As we will discuss shortly in relation to the DISC profile, he is a "High D." He is not really concerned about the details or socializing with employees. He is happy to let employees manage the little stuff and just present him with the final facts. He gets impatient with endless, detailed questions or discussions when the simple idea is so clear to him. If he cuts people off, it's just because he's gotten all the information he needs and he doesn't want to waste time — his or theirs. It certainly doesn't mean the work is not good or he doesn't like the employee.

A Lack of Self-Awareness

The above case study is a classic example of poor communication between people with different expectations, communication styles, and personality profiles. Betsy is interpreting Tim's actions to mean something that they don't. Tim is insensitive to what he is doing and the message he is projecting to this Gen Y employee. He is not tuned into her need for feedback, her sensitivity to unconscious behavioral tendencies, or his need to adapt. Tim would be stunned to learn that Betsy thinks he doesn't like her. He is oblivious to the subtle signals he is sending her.

Coach's Corner

Awareness

I have always been impressed with the teachings of a priest named Father Anthony de Mello. He talked about the road to enlightenment, and one of his most repeated and emphasized tenets was awareness.

In fact he would repeat the word three times when he spoke...awareness, awareness, awareness. You don't schedule awareness; it's a state of being. Just like it would be a necessary state on the road to enlightenment to a mystic, it's a necessity for the business leader who wants to be enlightened. Sometimes the best teacher is failure. If you're not aware and something happens as a consequence, it heightens your awareness. You learn to be aware the next time around. Leaders should allow it to occur naturally through their ordinary workday. You can't schedule it; you can't always plan for it; it's a state of being.

Leaders should develop the discipline of listening. Some of the best input you get as a leader may come from a different source every day. It could be someone who works in the cafeteria who gives you information. It could be a custodian; it could be an email, a conversation. It's very fluid. Be aware…aware…aware.

It's hard to be aware if you are not available and approachable.

Tim is not alone. Many people are not meeting the communication needs of Gen Y — or their other employees for that matter. As we have said throughout this book, Gen Yers are extreme communicators. They have grown up their whole lives with instant and almost constant communication from email and Instant Messenger® to cell phones and texting. They are in touch with each other and the world. Gen Yers also have had a tremendous amount of feedback from their parents who are very involved in their lives. Gen Y is so tuned in to communication and feedback that *when you don't communicate with them it is a negative communication.*

It's All Communication

As we learned in our case study, a closed door is interpreted by Gen Yers as meaning you don't want to talk to them. The failure to engage in casual conversation means you don't like them. A failure to compliment them on a job means you didn't think it was well done.

You must be able to communicate effectively with Gen Y at every point of your employment interaction: recruiting, interviewing, orienting, training, and managing. Your ability to communicate will directly affect your ability to retain Gen Y. You must also be able to recognize the subtle, unconscious things you are saying or doing that might alienate Gen Y at any stage of your interaction with them.

Fortunately, there is an excellent tool, the personality profile, which will help you do this. We discussed the use of "game film" by world-class leaders in Chapter 7. Now we will explore it in detail.

People Are Different!

This chapter has three main points that are obvious in general but important in the details of their application.

- First, people are different.
- Second, it's useful for leaders to know about those differences and how to relate to them.
- Third, you can use knowledge of individual differences to improve performance.

Despite the fact that everyone knows *intellectually* that we are all different, at a primitive level we judge others by ourselves. We expect others to be like us. We manage others the way we want to be managed. When someone doesn't respond the way we would, we are uncomfortable.

The Golden Rule vs. The Platinum Rule

From the positive side, treating others as we'd like to be treated is a version of the golden rule. Not too much wrong with that. However, there is a newer Platinum Rule,™ to treat others *as they want to be treated!* This small distinction makes all the difference with people who differ from you.

Gen Y is definitely different. As we have discussed in all the prior chapters, they have different wants and needs, care about different things, are motivated in different ways, and — most important — have very different communication needs. Gen Y is also the most diverse group in history. They are very different — from their managers, from other employees, and from each other. Thus, it is even more important to treat them as individuals. The easiest way to do this is to become aware of their personal styles and give them a little undivided attention.

Coach's Corner

Don't Peek!

What I will sometimes do during practice is go over and talk to a player on the sidelines and give him my undivided attention, even though practice continues to take place on the floor. I will purposely turn my back on the rest of practice so I am only focused on a single player. This sends a strong message to the player that he is, at this moment, the most important person and has my undivided attention.

The key, for me, is not to peek at what else is going on around me. I am confident the other coaches have the rest of practice handled. If my focus strays from this individual player, it would send the exact opposite message I intend.

Business leaders need to find opportunities to turn their backs on some day-to-day minutiae and give their Gen Y "players" some undivided attention. Put the phone on "do not disturb," ignore the email for a few moments, and show your players that, in this moment, whomever you are speaking to is the most important person in the organization. No matter what the temptation, *don't peek.*

Using Individual Differences

As a leader, you need to work with a variety of people on a variety of levels. It will help you do your job if you can identify how different employees think, react, and want to be treated as you supervise and reward each one. The better you understand and communicate with each individual, the better the results you'll produce. This is particularly true for Gen Y.

HOW Do People Differ?

There are a lot of ways to describe how people differ. We can talk about their values, goals, motivations, thinking styles, and so on. Such differences make each of us unique. Differences are easy to see but can be hard to interpret. When we observe others behaving differently, we may not understand them or we may wonder why they would behave that way. Managers sometimes feel it is their job to change people, when all they really need to do is help them perform. Trying to change workers is an uphill job and is often unnecessary.

In the heady days of Silicon Valley around the year 2000, many companies provided free cola and pizza for their computer programmers. These workers stayed all night and worked for days at a time when they were "hot." They didn't fit into the regular schedule that traditional management might have preferred. But the computer firms adapted. They encouraged employees to sleep at the office. They just wanted to get their software on the Internet in a hurry.

This is an extreme example. It may not work for your organization, but the point is, people work differently and have varying needs. Your job as a leader is to inspire employees, set the vision, and motivate. Your job as a manager is to get the most out of them, to facilitate their efforts, and get the work done. To be the best leader you can be, you need to adapt your style to the situation at hand. *Rather than trying to make everyone adapt to your style, it is more effective for you to understand theirs.*

Personality Theory

The classic way to categorize profiles and understand different people has been through the use of personality theories. Personality is the study of individual differences. You can also consider personality to be a collection of habit patterns or personal styles. It is how you differ from others. Some of your personality depends on your experiences in life. Different people learn different things and are exposed to different events. However, much of your basic personality comes from your genes. Studies from the University of Minnesota show that identical twins raised apart will usually end up with very similar personalities.

A personality profiling system you trust will help you read people and communicate better with them. By gaining an understanding of personality styles, you'll be better at accepting and appreciating others. As a bonus, when you study personality, you will also understand yourself better.

The DISC Personality Profile Program

There are many well-established and valid personality profiles. We recommend and use DISC, the oldest, most recognized, and most-widely used commercial personality profiling program. It was developed more than 75 years ago by Dr. William Moulton Marston.

DISC stands for Dominance, Influence, Steadiness, and Conscientiousness, the key personality traits. We will describe the four primary styles, but most people have a blend of two or even three behavioral styles.

Primary DISC Types

The first DISC type is *Dominant*.

People who score high in this area are Direct, Drivers, Demanding, Determined, Decisive, and Doers. They are goal oriented rather than people oriented. They're not shy about telling others what to do. They tend to move fast, talk fast, and think fast.

High "D" Behavioral Tendencies:

- Action is critical.
- Demand results.
- Know what needs to be done, not necessarily how to do it.
- May miss emotional cues from others.

The second DISC type is _Influential_.

People who score high in this area are Inspiring, Impressive, Interacting, and Interesting. They are people oriented rather than task oriented. They are socially skilled, persuasive, and friendly. They make people comfortable and are imaginative, optimistic, and easily distracted.

High "I" Behavioral Tendencies:

- People interaction is critical.
- Want to be around others.
- Social recognition is important.
- May prioritize socializing over task completion.

The third DISC type is _Steady_.

People who score high in this area are Stable, Supportive, Steady, and Structured. They are people oriented, but tend to have a few close friends rather than being outgoing. They are accommodating and peace seeking. They like stability and supporting others.

High "S" Behavioral Tendencies:

- Task completion and process is critical.
- Want to be a part of a team.
- Change is to be feared.
- Work step by step.

The fourth DISC type is *Conscientious*.

People who score high in this area are Cautious, Compliant, Calculating, Careful, and Contemplative. They are task oriented. They tend to be careful thinkers and perfectionists. They are logical, organized, and follow rules.

High "C" Behavioral Tendencies:

• Details are critical.

• Want to have all the facts and data.

• Motivated by being "right."

• May not handle criticism well.

Remember, this is just a summary overview of the four primary DISC types. Most people are a combination of types and their behavioral tendencies are more complex. However, most readers will be able to identify themselves as predominantly one of these four types.

In our case study at the beginning of the chapter, Tim was a High D. His style was to be direct, concise, and to the point. It is common for a High D to cut people off and grow weary of details. High D styles are not particularly chatty or warm. Betsy, on the other hand, had many I and S tendencies. She was looking for warmth and conversation. She talks freely with co-workers and would love to talk to Tim as well. To her, Tim's one-word greeting was negative. It meant Tim didn't like her. Betsy also had some "C" characteristics in that she was very interested in details. If Tim had reviewed DISC profiles of himself and Betsy he could have handled everything much better.

Adapt, Adapt, Adapt!

Tim needs to adapt and so do most leaders. Knowledge about yourself and others through DISC is only meaningful if you adapt your behavior in response to it. Once you recognize the personality styles and behavior patterns of yourself and others, you must take the next step. You must *adapt* your behavior. *Knowing someone's personality type is useful only to the extent that you tailor your behavior to communicate with people based on their individual profiles!*

Using DISC for Communication

If you still treat everyone the same, the value of DISC is lost. However, if you change your communication approach to match the needs of different people based on DISC, you are more likely to get the responses you want from each one.

Adapting your communication strategies to the audience is obviously a good idea for all of your interactions. It is especially *critical* for retaining Gen Y. Gen Y *must* know you are listening, care about them, and respect their ideas.

Let's look at how the DISC profile can be a guide for basic communication. You will need to pay attention to whom you are talking and adapt your approach to them.

If the person you are communicating with is **Dominant (High D):**

· Avoid small talk. Get to the point quickly.

· Don't react to their impatience.

- Don't give details unless asked. State what you want or need.
- Present facts, list benefits.
- Be decisive.
- Don't tell them what to do; ask their opinion.

If the person you are communicating with is **Influential (High I):**

- Be friendly and interested in them.
- Take time to socialize.
- Avoid details of the task; follow up in writing.
- Build the relationship.
- Ask for their input.
- Use emotional appeals.
- Suggest courses of action.

If the person you are communicating with is **Steady (High S):**

- Be patient with them.
- Listen to them.
- Take time to explain things.
- Show an interest in them.
- Give details.
- Project calm, including in your body language.
- Don't hard sell an idea.
- Listen more than you talk.

If the person you are communicating with is **Conscientious (High C):**

- Provide details.
- Don't be loud or overly expressive.
- Show that risk is low.
- Don't open with new or unusual ideas.
- Answer questions clearly and directly.
- Don't criticize.
- Don't be blunt.

Consultant's Corner

Interviewing Tendencies

Here are some interviewing tendencies of the DISC types.

High "D"

- controls the conversation and direction of the interview
- will be challenging in questioning
- asks questions that are "to the point"
- may not tolerate long-winded answers

High "I"

- Holds a casual, conversational interview
- May talk more than listen
- Uses a gut-feel approach to candidate selection
- Is impressed by solid references

High "S"

- Prepares a list of questions and agenda
- Looks for consistent performance concerning education and experience
- Listens thoughtfully during the interview
- May not challenge vague answers

High "C"

- Is impressed by a detailed resume
- Will hold the interviewee to a high standard
- May not build trust and rapport
- May allow the interviewee to control the conversation

Using DISC Styles

Your challenge is to use each style's strengths and get them to adapt to your needs. The High D interviewer must be careful not to dominate the conversation or interrupt what he or she perceives to be overly-long answers. The High I must resist the urge to base decisions about the candidate on gut feelings and must be careful not to talk more than listen. The High C might be too demanding since they hold themselves to very high standards and may do so for others. The High S interviewer might not challenge vague answers or inconsistencies.

The point is, all the personality types can do a good job of interviewing *if they understand what their tendencies are and adapt them.* DISC gives them the "game film" to do so.

The Accuracy of DISC Profiles

There is a lot of research to support the reliability and validity of the DISC system. Reliability means that scores are consistent over time or within the test instrument. Validity means that the test predicts something accurately. Test scores within the dimensions and over a six-month period are very stable (r = .90) for DISC. It also corresponds significantly to a number of similar personality scales such as the Big 5. DISC scores can differentiate good performance from poor performance in studies of sales performance and managerial ability. They can predict turnover rates, job injuries, management selection, and other outcomes. For example, in one study, top salespeople differed from other professional workers on all four dimensions.

In our experience, DISC results are extremely valid overall. However, they certainly can be wrong in some areas. One good way to test the validity of your own DISC profile is to ask someone close to you if it seems to reflect your personality. Ask someone you trust if your DISC results seem to be "you."

Using Your Scores

It is interesting to note that some people react negatively to their DISC profiles or dispute the findings. They don't want to believe they are "High this" or "High that." Remember, there are no right or wrong personality types with DISC. Being a hard charging D has both advantages and disadvantages. The same with the sociable I profile as well as the S and C profiles.

Since the purpose of DISC is to help you understand your behavior, you must be willing to use your DISC profile results as feedback (one of the rules of world-class performers). When people receive scores and interpretations that they don't like, they react in three ways:

1) deny,

2) acknowledge and work to improve, or

3) acknowledge and not care enough to change.

If you — or your employees — deny the results, one of two cases will pertain. Either the problem is there and you are not seeing it, or the profile is wrong. Your best response is to check yourself for denial, and focus on the parts of the results that can help you. In other words, spend your time focused on information that you can put to use.

World-class leaders do not waste time being defensive. We talked about accepting the fact that Gen Y might have skills superior to yours. DISC is another opportunity to let go of defensiveness. If your profile is showing you something that you don't like, don't be in denial about it. Address it! If the profile shows some negative behavioral tendencies, don't waste your time wishing your profile were different. You are going to be asking your employees to adapt based on their profiles; you must set the example for them by adapting based on yours.

In earlier chapters we asked you to acknowledge possible Gen Y prejudice in yourself before you confronted your employees. Similarly, you must address any developmental areas revealed through DISC and then challenge your employees to do the same.

Using Individual Differences for Better Performance

Understanding your personality and the personalities of those around you can help you lead and manage in numerous ways.

Self-Assessment

Logically speaking, you'll want to understand yourself before you apply a system to others. Of course you know yourself well, but thinking about yourself with a particular framework like the DISC can give you a different perspective. For example, High Ds pride themselves on getting things done. However, they can come to realize that in dealing with others a greater reliance on social skills may be important in getting the tasks done. Focusing on the goal is not always as important as knowing how to get other people to share your goal. Your own self-assessment will not only help you be more flexible, it will help you understand others.

Hiring

Hiring the next generation of workers means utilizing new recruitment methods. Eric Chester, author of *Getting Them to Give a Damn: How to Get Your Front Line to Care about Your Bottom Line*, suggests that employers should not focus on hiring the "best" people, but the "right" people. In professional football some coaches draft "the best talent

> **"Hiring people is an art, not a science, and resumes can't tell you whether someone will fit into a company's culture."**
> —HOWARD SCHULTZ, STARBUCKS CEO

on the board" others "the best fit for our needs." Sometimes it's best to bring in a person who is strongest in a particular position or who fits well with your team, not the best general athlete.

A job may be more suited for a particular personality type. For instance, an impatient person shouldn't be put in a position to deal with slow, repetitive work. People who are more social and outgoing relate better to customers, and so on. Capacity to do the job is not enough for a good fit in an organization. A new hire also has to fit the corporate culture and want to do the job. DISC will not precisely determine job fit, job fitness, or success. It describes a person's work behavior patterns, style, traits, and "type." You're looking for the behavioral patterns that fit your job and organization. Your goal is to find a good fit by matching personality inclinations to your specific situation.

Career Planning

You can also use profiles for the career development of existing employees. Helping people analyze their styles and skills can be valuable for them and the organization. Using DISC and other tools, you can develop employees, as well as help them determine their best positions. When you are coaching an employee, a profile can serve as "game film" to be reviewed.

Team Building

When creating work teams you need a variety of skills and personalities. If everyone in a team likes to be in charge — or if everyone is a follower — your team won't function well. If everyone on the team has the same style, you may get conformity of thought from the lack of diverse opinions or approaches.

Depending on the task, you may need big idea thinkers, detail-oriented workers, devil's advocates, and so on. For instance, a typical team needs both a task leader and a social leader. Superior teams require a certain chemistry. Understanding personality can help you create a chemistry that leads to great teams. With an awareness of different personality styles you can also teach employees how to understand, communicate, and interact more effectively with one other.

Flexible Leadership Style

The "best" leadership style depends on the situation and the people you lead. You'll need to adapt your style to the situation and people involved. Different personalities respond differently in the same situation. For instance, people handle stress differently. As a leader or manager it is your job to get the most out of your employees. That's why this book has emphasized how Generation Y is different from previous generations. Depending on their personalities, you can adapt your behavior as you reward and interact with your employees. For example, social types (I and S) like to have more contact and discussion during a job while task types (D and C) want to focus on the job. The former types tend to like peer recognition, the latter monetary rewards.

Preventing or Resolving Conflicts

When you understand people, you are more tolerant and less likely to get upset. You can communicate about problems better and avoid or resolve them. When conflict arises, you are better able to deal with the issues without being distracted by personality and style differences. You don't assume that the other person is wrong because they are different than you.

Game Film

Having a DISC profile of *yourself* will help you to better attract and retain Gen Y employees. In every profession, people who desire to improve know they must reflect on what they have done in the past in order to do it better in the future. As we've mentioned, every world-class performer has a tool that enables him or her to examine and evaluate his behavior, to see what is being done well or poorly, and to pinpoint areas for improvement or growth. World-class performers then make the conscious decision to correct their own weaknesses.

KEY POINT
Understanding your own and others' DISC profiles is a valuable tool.

Manage Your Film Clips

We tell leaders that their actions and decisions are like a full-length movie. Ultimately, their success depends upon directing a quality production.

We then challenge leaders to always be aware that they are constantly being judged on the *film clips,* not the full production. Most leaders tend to focus on the full movie and do not manage their film clips. Leaders may rationalize away an action, decision, or inaccessibility on their part because they are focused on, and judge themselves by, the entire movie.

Generation Y is judging leaders on what they can see and experience, not what is happening behind closed doors. When a leader is "out there," he or she must be aware that the audience does not know what may have happened before this scene or what is happening afterwards. The audience only sees this short clip. Today's leader *must* be aware of this new rule and constantly manage their film clips.

Game film is particularly helpful because it allows the viewer to slow things down, study execution, and become aware of mistakes, omitted opportunities, and what was done well. While you do not have actual game film in the world of business, the personality profile you get from DISC can serve as such.

DISC allows you to take a snapshot of your behavioral tendencies, unconscious actions, and traits. Your profile can help you see your strengths and weaknesses as well as your style of communicating. This will help you at every point as you interact with Gen Y and other employees.

Your DISC profile will alert you to your tendency to unknowingly dominate conversations, to ask questions without listening to the answers, or to cut people off. Perhaps you are too critical, uncomfortable with change, or overly concerned about details. Maybe you are too analytical or antisocial. These unconscious characteristics could alienate Gen Y. DISC helps you see them so you can control or eliminate them.

On the flip side, DISC will show you what your strong suits are in dealing with Gen Y and you can focus on consciously utilizing your positive traits.

Coach's Corner

Overlooking the Fundamentals

In my experience, when our team isn't playing well or we're struggling, we have a great need to return to the basics, to review the fundamentals.

There's not a practice that should go by without a real emphasis and review of the fundamentals. That's what we focus on. Any time we get away from those, that's when we tend to struggle. It's not the elaborate plays or the tricky schemes that make the difference; it's always basic fundamentals.

Sometimes leaders tend to get ahead of themselves. There is a tendency to think, "I am beyond that now," and look for a fancy play to succeed while overlooking the simple things. If they stopped to review the fundamentals, they could spot when they weren't listening, saying thank you, or being available, to name a few.

Developing Yourself as a Leader

As a leader, you need to work with a variety of people, on a variety of levels. It will help you do your job if you can identify how different employees think, react, and want to be led. This is especially true of Gen Y employees who are quite sensitive to how you interact with them, the words you use, and your management style. Gen Y thrives on feedback and communication. The better you understand your own unconscious behavioral tendencies and those of Gen Y, the better you can communicate with them and work with them.

Once the behavioral traits and tendencies of employees are understood, a great leader adapts his or her behavior accordingly and leads each employee differently. A leader has to respond to the current situation by adapting the communication to the audience. When you're aware of both the need for communication and your own style, you are in a strong position to relate better to your workers.

Think about the successful, world-class people you know personally. Are they successful with just technical skills, or do they succeed with a combination of technical skills and social intelligence? Think of how you feel when you interact with these people and think about their bottom-line performance. The combination of technical skills and self-awareness works!

Conclusion

Personality-profile programs identify behavioral tendencies, personality traits, and types. These tools help in two ways. First, they help you understand *yourself* and, second, they help you recognize behavior patterns in other people so that you can understand *them* better. DISC is the most recognized and most widely used personality-profiling program. You need to interact differently with people depending on their behavioral styles and personality types. Using the DISC to adapt your approach to them will help you be a world-class leader.

 Name: Rashan
Location: Northeast
Age: 28

Rashan's background:

- graduated from a selective liberal arts college in the Northeast, where he majored in literary studies and Mandarin Chinese

- after college, he was hired by a book publishing company, where he has remained for five years as he continues to move up the ranks

- currently fulfills the role of publicity manager

Reading good books and telling people about them is something that Rashan would do even if he wasn't getting paid for it, so publishing is a perfect fit for him. He loves his job because his passion for good literature makes his everyday work meaningful. He chose to dedicate his professional life to literature because it's a part of his personal life as well. He thinks this integration is the key to succeeding and being happy in his career.

Advancement through the company's titles, and increases in pay, keep him at the company. He actively explores his options at other companies, and every time he receives an offer with higher pay or a better title, he returns to his current company and asks them to match it.

One day, Rashan would like to run his own publishing business. He wants his tastes in literature to define which contemporary books people will consider classics in 100 years. He is motivated to be the best, and he is willing to make the necessary choices. According to Rashan, potential is meaningless unless you live up to it.

Rashan was raised to respect his elders; therefore, he prefers not to butt heads with members of the older generations. However, such a driven man cannot help but wish for them to make way for his young ideas and energy. He respects wisdom and experience, but he wants older coworkers to move out of the way so he can advance.

Rashan would leave a job if:

- his work didn't feel meaningful
- he was continually forced to do things he didn't like
- the quality of his assignments was poor
- he got a better job offer that he could leverage with his current company
- It wasn't a good balance of pay and quality of life

In Rashan's mind, someone is successful if they are:

- financially independent
- making their own way in the world
- happy on a daily basis

Chapter 9

Emotional Intelligence

Christine was shocked when her best Gen Y employee walked into her office and gave her his two-week notice. Matt, age 26, had been there almost two years and Christine had no idea he was unhappy. He had never complained to her about anything. In fact, she was going to compliment him on the quality of his work at his annual review. Further, he was getting a very competitive salary and was also due to get a small percentage bonus on his two-year anniversary. Matt played on the firm hockey team so Christine assumed that he felt like part of the organization. Maybe his decision to leave was the result of some family problem. Christine wasn't really sure what his family situation was. Now she is really stuck; there is no one in line who can step in to take Matt's place. Replacing him will be a big distraction from her regular work, and will put a lot of pressure on her department. Then there will be the costs of training and onboarding the new employee. Christine is now very worried about her other Gen Y employees. Will they leave soon?

What **went wrong?** Christine is the poster-child for poor leadership in the area of Gen Y retention. Clearly she is completely out of touch with Matt. Instead of seeking him out on a regular basis to learn more about what he is doing and how he likes it, she meets with him only once a year for an annual review. Because he hasn't complained, she assumes he is content. Matt hasn't been getting bonuses periodically that are linked to his actual job performance, only a small annual bonus tied solely to his job tenure.

Although she considers him one of her best Gen Y employees, Christine is saving praise for Matt, to deliver it in a one-time review, instead of periodically complimenting him for jobs well done. She assumes his competitive salary is enough to keep him onboard. Christine does not realize that money alone is not giving Matt job satisfaction. Even the extras like being on the hockey team aren't making Matt care about his job. Christine didn't take the time to learn about Matt's family life so that if, indeed, Matt's job departure was related to family needs, she could work with him to provide more flexible hours or other accommodations. Christine's lack of communication with Matt has cost her organization a great employee, and if she is treating her other Gen Y employees the same way, she *should* worry, because they'll be leaving next.

One newer area of individual difference that has received a lot of attention is Emotional Intelligence or EQ. Christine had a low EQ; high EQ is a valuable characteristic to look for in both your leaders and your new recruits.

What Is Emotional Intelligence?

EQ can be defined roughly as emotional awareness and control that translates into strong people skills. "Understanding emotion in oneself and others is at the root of good people skills," observes Dr. Vanessa Urch Druskat, Associate Professor of Organizational Behavior and Management at the Whittemore School of Business & Economics at the University of New Hampshire. "EQ helps you to recognize how your own emotions impact the people with whom you interact." While aspects of EQ had been studied sporadically for years, it was Daniel Goleman's 1995 book, *Emotional Intelligence,* and a *Time* magazine article on the book, that popularized the concept.

KEY POINT

You want to look for employees who have "people smarts" and emotional control.

Dr. Druskat, whose award-winning research has examined how teams and leaders effectively manage complex interpersonal challenges, believes "emotion is present in *every* interaction with another human being. Stopping the emergence of emotion in an interaction is harder than stopping a sneeze. Emotionally intelligent people recognize this emotion and treat it as information that allows them to manage the conversation so that it is effective."

Why the Interest in EQ?

We think that the reason emotional intelligence attracted so much attention was that people believed it explained why some individuals were very successful who didn't have the traditional "smarts" indicated by IQ tests. When everyone in a company is fairly intelligent, IQ may not be predictive of success. In that case Emotional Intelligence — particularly as it pertains to people skills — may be a much better predictor of success.

Some people have all the MBA smarts you'd want, but don't work well with others or make good leaders. On the other side are the people who aren't brilliant but they work well with others and inspire their teams. They make good leaders. You probably know of many cases like this yourself — on both sides. If those with low social-emotional skills have strong technical skills they can do well in "back-office" jobs. On the other side are the people who aren't the most technically proficient but they work well with others and they inspire their teams.

> "Interpersonal communication and other so-called soft skills are what corporate recruiters crave most but find most elusive in MBA graduates..."
> —*Wall Street Journal*

In Dr. Druskat's view:

Emotionally intelligent leaders know how to ignite the kinds of emotions that make our work meaningful. Inspiration involves stirring positive emotions. A strangely little known fact is that motivation requires emotion....Without emotion, motivation does not exist! It is emotion that gets you out of bed in the morning. One can get out of bed because of fear or because of "inspired excitement."

The concept of emotional intelligence (EQ) caught on in a big way without actually being precisely defined. Organizations have always been interested in how to measure talent. You want to hire the best and invest your training dollars in those who will benefit the most. The EQ concept said that people could be successful, independent of traditional intelligence.

Until EQ came along, most non-job-specific measurement looked at IQ and achievement tests that focus on verbal and mathematical skills as general intelligence indicators. However, it's been known for a hundred years that people had *different kinds* of intelligence. Howard Gardner and others have discussed up to nine types of intelligence and there are probably more. For instance, mechanical intelligence is seldom listed — that hands-on ability some people have where they can fix any piece of machinery. (Some of the other noted types of intelligence include musical, spatial, and kinesthetic.)

Three Ways to Define EQ

The first big problem with defining EQ is that there is theoretical disagreement about what it is. How you define EQ makes a difference in things like whether it can be taught. Different researchers think it is a kind of intelligence, a personality trait, or a learned skill. For instance, Wikipedia defines EQ as "an ability, capacity, or skill to perceive, assess, and manage the emotions of one's self, of others, and of groups."

Depending on whether EQ is a kind of intelligence, a personality trait, or a skill, you would measure it differently. These three approaches are related to how each of the three noted research groups in this area have approached EQ.

Peter Salovey and John D. Mayer, in a 1990 journal publication, originally defined EQ as "the ability to monitor one's own and others' feelings and emotions, to discriminate among them and to use this information to guide one's thinking and actions." They later changed their definition to "The ability to perceive emotion, integrate emotion to facilitate thought, understand emotions, and to regulate emotions to promote personal growth." They intended this to be a kind of intelligence, but focused on emotional skills. Their model focuses on four related types of emotional abilities:

1. Recognizing emotions — your own and others — represents the basis for emotional intelligence.

2. Emotionally intelligent people can use their own emotions to help the task at hand.

3. The most complicated ability is to understand the

subtle cues of the emotion language of others and to project emotional messages to others.

4. The end point is the ability to effect emotions in both ourselves and in others. You can manage your own emotions and other people's.

Daniel Goleman's model of EQ also discusses four emotional competencies:

1. Self-awareness about your own emotions and the ability to use gut feelings in decision making.

2. The ability to control your own emotions and to deal with change.

3. The ability to understand other's emotions and emotional relationships.

4. The ability to emotionally inspire and influence others.

The third research approach comes from Reuven Bar-On who also developed one of the first measures of EQ that used the term "Emotion Quotient." However, his definition of EQ could also describe maturity or competence. He defines emotional intelligence as understanding oneself and others, relating well to people, and adapting to and coping with your environment.

For our purposes, what seems clear is that the ability to understand and manage our own emotions, and working to understand others' emotions, is at the core of relating successfully to other people. Dr. Druskat believes that "managing our own emotions is one of the most critical elements of EQ. It doesn't do us much good to understand our emotions if we can't use that understanding to behave effectively in a given situation."

Gen Y and EQ

Research by Travis Bradberry and Jean Greaves on over 500,000 people (*The Emotional Intelligence Quick Book*) showed that EQ tends to increase with age. Gen Ys would have less self-awareness and practice managing their emotions than older workers. On the other hand, the well adjusted Gen Yers who you want to hire are very group oriented. This suggests that they may have higher social skills than others.

A Good Manager Needs to Have High EQ Social Skills

One area of EQ-related research shows that first impressions strongly influence judgments. As we've mentioned earlier, to deal with Gen Y, you need to set aside any prejudices against the young and project positive emotions yourself. Your "natural" first inclination is possibly to be cool to Gen Y, especially people with piercings, tattoos, or other visible differences. You need to suspend any negative impressions you form and make an effort to project a warm first impression to your young workers.

> "...for jobs of all kinds, emotional competencies were twice as [important] as were technical skills and purely cognitive abilities combined. In general the higher a position in an organization, the more [EQ] mattered; for individuals in leadership positions, 85 percent of their competencies were in the [EQ] domain."
>
> —Daniel Goleman

Gen Yers Are Group Oriented

Goleman's research and the research of many educators in the area of emotions and emotional intelligence have had a large impact in school systems. Thus, Gen Yers who came through their school systems in the 1990s were likely exposed to EQ training. Also, colleges and universities have been pressured by companies who hire their undergraduates to do much more team learning and teamwork in their classrooms so that graduates are more ready to work in teams than previous generations. However, experience matters, and translating EQ skills, like conflict management, as it develops from school into work organizations, is not a simple matter. Thus, the greatest application for EQ in the Gen Y work situation is the necessity for managers and leaders of Gen Y employees to demonstrate EQ in their interactions with these employees.

Because Gen Y employees are likely to be very different from the managers themselves, all aspects of EQ are relevant to managing Gen Y. A good example is the Gen Y employee who unrealistically expects to be quickly promoted. Recognizing and managing such expectations is the first step. The second step is working to understand more about this expectation and what it means (for example, what kind of experience is the person looking or hoping for). Finally, it is necessary to manage this person's emotions by behaving in a way that doesn't snuff out the person's motivation, but channels it into more accurate expectations and, if the person can handle it, more challenging work.

Self-Awareness

This is the cornerstone of EQ. Leaders need to recognize their own unique personalities, skills, values, and tendencies. They need to do so to understand how they are different from others, and to aid them in understanding the various dimensions on which people differ (see the earlier chapter on DISC). It naturally follows that in addition to increasing their self-awareness, it is the leader's job to get to know and understand the unique traits, skills, and tendencies of individual employees. This helps you understand the tasks that will most interest and suit each employee, and also the way an employee needs to be treated in order to bring the best out of that individual.

"Analyzing" Yourself

To communicate effectively with today's workforce, *you* must have emotional intelligence about yourself.

Tomorrow take 15 minutes to review the following tips to practice your people skills.

1. **Reflect on your personal style:** What are your tendencies, both conscious and unconscious? Think about ways you need to adapt to successfully communicate today.

2. **Who will you see today?** What are their tendencies...what type of interaction will they prefer to maximize communication?

3. **Put your antenna up!** If you expect to enter into new relationships today, be conscious of your

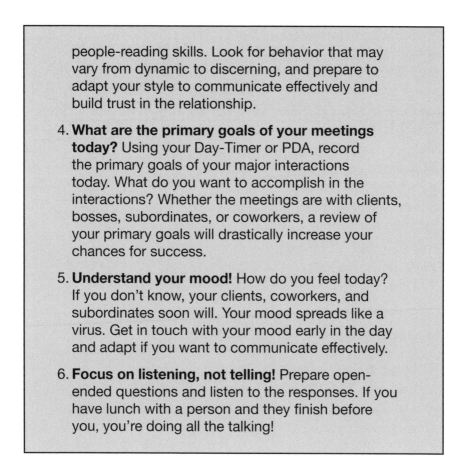

people-reading skills. Look for behavior that may vary from dynamic to discerning, and prepare to adapt your style to communicate effectively and build trust in the relationship.

4. **What are the primary goals of your meetings today?** Using your Day-Timer or PDA, record the primary goals of your major interactions today. What do you want to accomplish in the interactions? Whether the meetings are with clients, bosses, subordinates, or coworkers, a review of your primary goals will drastically increase your chances for success.

5. **Understand your mood!** How do you feel today? If you don't know, your clients, coworkers, and subordinates soon will. Your mood spreads like a virus. Get in touch with your mood early in the day and adapt if you want to communicate effectively.

6. **Focus on listening, not telling!** Prepare open-ended questions and listen to the responses. If you have lunch with a person and they finish before you, you're doing all the talking!

Self-Management

Managing oneself is a critical skill for successful interactions and for effectively influencing others. Some employees may be best influenced using a directive command; others may need a more empathic influence style. Managing one's own tendencies so that one is optimally effective in different situations and with different employees is a skill demonstrated by those with high EQ. It is a skill that can be learned.

Other Awareness

Once a leader understands his or her own unique tendencies (including emotions), values, and skills, it is easier to know what to look for when seeking to more fully understand the tendencies, values, and skills of others.

> **"A growing number of organizations are now convinced that people's ability to understand and to manage their emotions improves their performance, their collaboration with colleagues, and their interaction with customers."**
> —*Fast Company*

Managing Others' Emotions

Leaders who become practiced and skilled at interpreting the emotions of others will find it fairly easy to become practiced and skilled at reading or interpreting the emotions of people in audiences or groups. The next step is managing those emotions. For example, one can calm a nervous group by providing information in a confident, calm, and clear way. You can increase tension in a group that is too relaxed and calm by demonstrating tension. Increasing the motivation of a group usually involves communicating a message in an inspirational way. Many of the most admired leaders of our times studied inspiration so that they would know what it looked and felt like to audiences. This isn't always intuitive — it requires knowing, understanding, and empathizing with your audience and authentically aiming them in a direction in which they will be inspired.

Emotional intelligence is seen in organizations or groups with cultures or climates that support EQ. Your goal should be to create an emotionally intelligent climate so that even nonemotionally intelligent people have an increasing chance of behaving in an emotionally intelligent way. Some of the dimensions which can create this climate, as identified by Dr. Druskat, include:

1. interpersonal understanding
2. confronting members who break norms
3. caring behavior
4. team self-evaluation
5. creating resources for working with emotion
6. creating an optimistic environment (oriented toward a hopeful future)
7. proactive problem solving
8. organizational awareness (i.e., how our work links to the work of others in the organization)
9. building external relationships (for example, with relevant others outside the team)

KEY POINT

Emotional intelligence can be developed in yourself and Gen Y.

Conclusion

Emotional intelligence is a concept that calls your attention to a fact you already knew — that raw technical ability does not always translate well to a job. The ability to manage your own and others' emotions is valuable in managers and leaders, as well as Gen Y hires. For most jobs, you're looking for people who can work well with others and who have good emotional maturity. Being aware of EQ should help you be a better leader, choose more capable managers and interviewers, and select new employees who fit best in your company.

 Name: Pat
Location: Northeast
Age: 28

Pat's background:

- BS degree in biology

- master's degree in education

- moved to major metro area to teach science in elementary school

- currently teaching high school forensic science

Pat grew up and attended college in his hometown city in the Midwest. After graduating, he decided to decline several teaching offers to seek a "change of scenery." Pat knew he wanted to teach in an environment in which the parents were involved, and he found the right opportunity in a major Northeastern city.

After two years of teaching eighth grade science, Pat is now in his second year of creating and teaching high school forensic science. The program is his to develop, and he has set out to create a challenging and rigorous curriculum. Pat stated, "I feel the work load is overwhelming at times, but that is not an issue. I enjoy hard work. Every day is a new challenge. Just when you think you have mastered everything, something new comes your way."

Pat is motivated by challenges and readily accepted the opportunity to start a program from scratch. "I'm all about challenging situations." Pat also said, "It is exciting to tackle something new. If a goal is realistic and attainable, I am all in."

Many of Pat's friends are also teaching, and he thinks they sincerely enjoy teaching. Through conversations with his peers, he realizes they are all there to make a connection with the students. Pat said, "We all really strive to do excellent work. My friends and I often discuss how we think about negative teachers from our past in order to motivate ourselves and not repeat the same mistakes."

To Pat, the characteristics of a good boss are:

- someone who is supportive

- someone to assist you and help you to learn from their experience

- no micro management

- someone who allows you the opportunity to take ownership of an assignment

- someone who trusts you once you have proven yourself

Chapter 10

Change Management

Charlese, age 22, was told when she was hired that she was part of a "new wave" in the organization. Charlese wanted to help make a difference in the world. The huge nonprofit organization she joined had run things the same way for more than fifty years. Charlese had skills in data segmentation, customer relationship management, list selection, and multivariate analysis. Used right, these skills could help the organization find new donors, build closer relationships with individual donors, and build partnerships with larger corporate donors. Unfortunately, when Charlese laid out new methods to test, there was always an excuse why it couldn't be done then. And when she organized an internal working group to discuss how to make changes in procedures, it turned out that everyone else hoped to keep things the same. When she realized that the organization wasn't committed to the change they'd talked about when they hired her, she bided her time until a job with a more progressive nonprofit group came along.

What went wrong? Change is hard to design and harder to implement. Most large organizations have *lots* of inertia and internal resistance. The job description that attracted Charlese was not championed by top executives who were willing to push improvements throughout the organization. And commitment at lower levels had

"No company can escape the need to reskill its people..."
—Gary Hamel & C.K. Prahalad, Competing for the Future

never been recruited. The organization *said* they wanted to change but hadn't made the alterations to systems that would be required to implement and sustain the larger change.

This chapter gives you a general outline of how to both implement change *and* keep change going. Of course this topic has been the source of many books on its own. Here we give you a brief overview within the context of dealing with Gen Y. Many change programs are started, but few are successful over the long term without strong leadership. Gen Y can be both a source of change for you and a powerful tool to accomplish it. When you use Gen Y effectively, you'll be able to implement changes more easily.

What Is Change Management?

Change management is a systematic approach to dealing with change, both from the perspective of an organization and on the individual level. For an organization, change management means defining and implementing procedures and technologies to deal with changes in the business environment and to profit from changing opportunities (*Webster's Dictionary*).

Any major adaptation within an organization requires a great deal of effort to be successful and that includes changing the culture of your organization. Change is one of the hardest things to accomplish in any company. Many efforts under various names like reengineering, total quality management (TQM), or Six Sigma, have failed as often as they've succeeded.

Implementing Change

There are many change management methodologies out there, but in the end they all contain the four essential components of any good change plan:

- vision and strategy
- organizational alignment
- workforce enablement
- sustainability

Vision and Strategy

Just as with everything else in life and leadership, it all starts with a vision. Your first job is choosing your vision and staying aware of it. Whether you're a coach, parent, or CEO, your vision of the future is what guides you and those you influence and lead. A coach motivates his or her team with the vision of a winning season and the accolades and sense of accomplishment that winning brings. A parent instills values in their children because of a vision of who those children can be when they are grown. A good CEO paints a vision of where the company is headed so that employees have a clear line of sight to the future and the part they play in it.

> **"If you don't know where you're going, then any road will do."**
> —The Cheshire Cat to Alice, in *Alice in Wonderland*

As a leader in your organization, having a vision is critical to your organization's long-term success. Without it, employees don't understand where the company is headed or how they fit into the organization. The challenge is that over time this vision will change. Market conditions, new products, emerging technologies, and a changing workforce (Gen Y) will have an impact on the direction in which your organization heads.

So how do you keep a multigenerational organization engaged and committed to an ever-changing business landscape? You develop the company's internal capacity for change. Just as a coach conditions his athletes so they can better compete, so too can you condition your employees to embrace change. And it all starts with a clear vision and open, honest communication.

Your senior leadership must be committed to bringing the vision to realization and must actively play a role in supporting it. This is critical to employees buying into any proposed change. Without leadership support, employees will label your new vision as just the "flavor of the month" that will fade away as other things take priority.

To increase the change capacity of your organization, you must utilize a consistent methodology. By managing change with a consistent approach, you allow your employees to anticipate what is coming next and, as a result, they will be less resistant.

For example, if you consistently used the following framework, employees would know what to expect when a major change is announced.

A. Change kick-off presentation (senior leadership) with Q&A session

B. Employee survey (How do they feel about the change? What are their concerns?)

C. Communication of change details (multiple media formats)

    1. Roundtable discussions with executives

    2. Interdepartmental meetings to identify new processes

    3. Newsletter

    4. Intranet webpage

D. Training

    1. Business processes

    2. Systems/tools

E. Re-survey (where are the gaps?)

F. Develop post-change support system

G. Implement the change

H. Monitor, sustain, and improve

Consistently following a methodology similar to the one above will enable your employees to know in advance that they will be going through a well-defined process that will allow them to understand, buy in, and commit to the proposed new process.

A consistent framework also addresses a critical need, not just for your Gen Yers, but for all generations within your company. It allows them to be actively involved in shaping the change that will occur. This is absolutely critical to your success and brings us to the second component of a change plan: organizational alignment.

Organizational Alignment

Having a clear, compelling vision of the future, while critical, cannot be successful without the buy-in and commitment of the whole organization. In order for employees to be engaged and committed to any change effort, leaders must develop a comprehensive communication plan that provides the answers to the following "Big Six" questions:

1. Where are we heading?
2. Why are we doing this?
3. How will I be impacted?
4. How do you know this will work?
5. What is expected of me?
6. What training and support will be put in place so I can be successful?

Addressing these questions throughout the change effort in a thorough, honest manner — with an emphasis on *honesty* — will go a long way toward gaining trust and support. Having grown up in the digital age, Gen Yers are bombarded with marketing and sales messages every day in a variety of formats. As a result, they are particularly adept at identifying communication that is less than truthful. Bottom line: If you try to "spin" information to cover up or downplay something that is less than desirable, they'll be able to tell.

This candid communication needs to occur across multiple formats, town hall meetings, newsletters, Intranet pages, FAQs, roundtable discussions, and staff meetings. In marketing, there's a "Rule of 7" that also applies to any change program. The Rule of 7 is a fairly well known marketing concept that says an individual needs to see, hear, or be exposed to a message at least seven times before responding in some way. In other words, if you don't have a communication plan that reaches your employees at least seven times in a variety of formats, you significantly reduce your odds of success. It simply doesn't sink in, or is not taken seriously, or is misinterpreted

A missing piece in many communication plans is an involvement strategy. How can you get your employees involved in the change? Their voices need to be heard. By allowing them to participate in crafting the solution and assisting in implementing the change, the level of employee engagement will rise and the amount of resistance you face will decline. If done correctly, this will also help to bridge the different generations in your organization while building trust.

> ### KEY POINT
> **To be effective, communication must be in both directions.**

Workforce Enablement

For many people a major reason for resistance to change is a perceived loss of control. In their current jobs, they have some level of comfort. They can do their jobs fairly well, know where and to whom they can turn for help, and have built up some level of expertise. Their work has, to some degree, become routine. Introducing a culture change may cause this routine to be disrupted, and this possibility of disruption can lead to uncertainty and fear.

As mentioned above, one of the critical questions employees need to have answered in any new process is, "What training and support will I have?" The answer to this question, regardless of the program being undertaken, should have two parts: training on what has changed in the business processes, and systems training. Many companies focus solely on the systems or "how" training. Enter "xyz" into field #1, select option C in your pull-down menu, et cetera. While "how training" is a necessary component to any change, it fails to answer the question, "Why?" That's where the business process training comes in; it provides the larger context that the systems are a part of. Understanding the "why" in your culture change effort is critical to its long-term sustainability.

How you deliver training across generations is also important to maintaining employee engagement. Whether or not you agree with the list on the following page, there are differences between Gen Y and other generations in what styles of training they prefer. Gen Yers are often called "digital natives." They've grown up with PCs, video games, text messaging, and the Web, and are particularly skilled at picking up information quickly through electronic

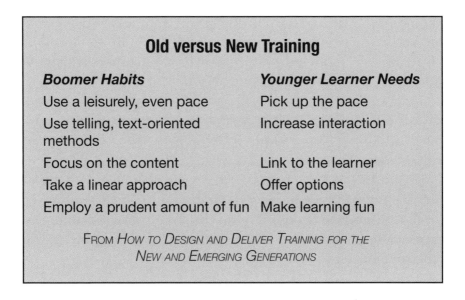

Old versus New Training

Boomer Habits	Younger Learner Needs
Use a leisurely, even pace	Pick up the pace
Use telling, text-oriented methods	Increase interaction
Focus on the content	Link to the learner
Take a linear approach	Offer options
Employ a prudent amount of fun	Make learning fun

FROM *HOW TO DESIGN AND DELIVER TRAINING FOR THE NEW AND EMERGING GENERATIONS*

media. Technology is at the center of their personal and professional lives. The rest of us are sometimes referred to as "digital immigrants" — those who have learned to use technology as we've progressed through our careers, but that technology is not part of us. This is a critical difference that needs to be addressed when delivering training. Offering multiple training options, at least one electronic and one instructor led, provides the greatest chance for broad engagement across all the generations within your company.

Sustainability

Sustainability is the final but most overlooked component to successful change. Why? Because it is by far the most difficult to achieve. Many companies that initially alter their cultures find that things have regressed within six months. The key here is discipline. In today's fast-paced business environment, once a change is implemented it is off to the "next big thing" and it is assumed that new programs will automatically carry forward.

Before that can occur, however, the change has to be embedded into the organization and be perceived as the natural way of doing things. This takes time and focused effort *after* the implemented action. Repeated coaching of individuals, consistently recognizing and rewarding desired behaviors, and providing support tools (posters, reference guides, email reminders, and the like) well beyond the implementation phase are all critical to maintaining the change long term.

Coach's Corner

Making Change Stick

 In the middle of December of my first year at Arizona State, it became increasingly apparent that we would continue to have a very difficult time defending any of our opponents man to man. The problem was that up to that point in my coaching career I had never coached anything other than man-to-man. We played zone here and there, either under an assistant's direction or simply for a quick change of pace, but it wasn't our deal. To win, we had to change. By the end of the season it was allowing us to be much more competitive. We continued to play it even into the next season where we had the single greatest improvement in college basketball from one season to the next.

The change didn't come easy. When you change horses

you often get worse before you get better. The leadership team's conviction is critical. If we had vacillated, it would have been more difficult for the team to believe in what we were doing. It was important once we made the decision to change that we committed to making it work. It wasn't the kind of situation where we had the luxury of experimenting, dangling one foot in the water to see if it was warm enough, so to speak. It was one of those kinds of decisions that once you made it, you did not have the luxury of turning around if you were going to have a chance at success with it.

My four points for change success are:

1. Make sure you and your leadership team show a united front.

2. No second guessing the decision (not even in "private" conversations).

3. Show your commitment to success; burn the boats — there's no turning back.

4. Manage the leader's communication, both verbal and nonverbal.

Make sure that your management team demonstrates the conviction and commitment to what you're doing. If you want others to believe in it, you can't waffle yourself. No one must ever see a lack of commitment on your part.

Conclusion

Implementing change is one of the most difficult things to do in an organization. Improving attitudes toward Generation Y in your company is a good place to start. This is an important issue, yet it is confined to a narrow topic.

And what you'll learn from such a limited change effort can eventually be leveraged to make broader changes. We've given you a brief model of how to approach change. Most important, commit wholeheartedly and focus on the sustainability of any new program.

Name: Bridget
Location: Southeast
Age: 30

Bridget's background:

- attended a public university in the northeast receiving a degree in radio and television communication

- during college worked as a television news reporter

- interned with a major national advertising agency and fell in love with marketing

- currently works as a marketing director for a national food retailer

Bridget is now in her fourth job and feels this one is "the right fit." She believes it is important to do something you love and something about which you can be passionate. Having worked as a news reporter in the past, she enjoys the opportunity to represent her company in frequent radio and television interviews. While she loves the work, it was not the job that attracted her to this company.

Her current organization is known for its commitment to

"giving back" and this core value resonated with Bridget. She was particularly impressed with a micro-loan program that provides seed money to women in third-world countries to start a business. She sees how these loans help people in a very real and meaningful way. Seeing her employer "walk the talk" with these core values is what attracted her to the company.

Bridget feels many employers still believe money is the biggest motivator and paying folks more will increase retention. She believes that for her and her peers money is not a major driver. While money is important, she feels believing in the core values, your product, and your direct leadership will trump money every time.

Bridget believes many organizations do not understand Gen Y's motives and values. She feels managers are imposing an outdated belief system on newer workers. Her advice is to not expect Gen Y to chase the old American dream. Her feeling is the old American dream is to live to work, delay life experiences, and even to put important relationships on the back burner. Gen Y wants to work hard *and* play hard.

Bridget believes she and her peers were raised with strong ethics and values. These ethics and values *include* a strong work ethic *and* a strong family ethic. Family is one area where she will not steal time to give to work. She will work just as hard as anyone, but not at the expense of the rest of her life.

To Bridget, a good leader is someone who:

- is highly self-motivated

- shows respect for others

- is tough but fair

- walks the line between friend and boss
- is a team player
- works hard

Chapter 11

Increasing Organizational Awareness for Change

Elena, age 28, was becoming increasingly frustrated with her job. Over the past year or so, her department head had become much more of a micro-manager and seemed to constantly take credit for his team's successes. In addition to his "hands-on approach," as he called it, Elena felt he was not communicating about what was going on in the organization and how her work contributed to the overall goals.

Elena also found herself losing respect for her teammates. When opportunities arose to address these issues with the boss, no one spoke up. She often felt like a lone voice in the wilderness when it came to these conversations. She began to feel that her teammates were being hypocritical because during meetings they would not say a word, but afterwards they could not stop complaining about the situation.

When Elena approached her boss about finding some way to improve communications, she was shot down. He told her she must be the only one with an issue, because no one else had even mentioned it. To prove his point, he referred to the corporate values of open communication and his own personal open-door policy. Since no one seemed to take him up on his "openness" but Elena, he reasoned the problem was with her.

In the past 12 months two key team members resigned and Elena knew of at least three more who were actually looking for other jobs. While she loves the work and the overall corporate values, Elena feels she will also need to leave if she doesn't see more alignment between words and actions.

What went wrong? Elena was hit by several things in her situation. Her boss micro-managed, took credit for the team, and didn't share information. He demotivated Elena and the team. When confronted, he showed no awareness of the true situation and denied the existence of a problem. The corporation had values Elena liked, but allowed a bad boss to spoil one group. The recent resignations should have been a red flag for his superiors. They should have had periodic, anonymous employee surveys to uncover the situation. Her teammates refused to confront the boss or work to change the situation. The good ones simply left. Elena will be following them soon.

Analyzing and Improving
Your Organization

In addition to having an understanding of themselves and the new rules of business, leaders must have their fingers on the pulses of their organizations and be aware of problems within them. As Colin Powell said:

> *Leadership is solving problems. The day soldiers stop bringing you their problems is the day you have stopped leading them. They have either lost confidence that you can help or concluded you do not care. Either case is a failure of leadership.*

There will be many problems as you try to lead your organization into the new Gen Y era. Make it your business to know what they are.

Just as world-class performers study game film of themselves to uncover tendencies, leaders must study game film of their organizations to find team tendencies. Once tendencies are uncovered, a game plan must be put in place to address these issues.

Every coach knows that it is not enough to simply develop a solid game plan. A great game plan, poorly executed, will result in a loss. Execution is critical. We believe there are three key steps every leader or manager must take in order to uncover team tendencies, prepare their team for success, and coach effectively for change:

1. Conduct an organizational/team assessment.

2. Develop an effective change management strategy.

3. Sustain the change.

Your Organizational Assessment

Business leaders worth their salt know it is important to understand how engaged and satisfied their employees are. Surveying tools, used mainly by HR (employee surveys) and marketing (customer surveys) have provided invaluable data to drive an organization's strategy. Based upon the feedback, new employee programs are developed to increase morale and new products and programs are implemented to secure customer loyalty.

For years businesses have conducted employee and customer satisfaction surveys to understand the current environment. Completed surveys are *game film*. Data can then be reviewed to uncover strengths, weaknesses, opportunities, threats and *tendencies*. Surveys do not need to be limited to simply employee and customer satisfaction instruments. Over forty aspects of organizational "climate" have been measured in the last 50 years, from attitudes toward coworkers to attitudes toward advancement.

Before you can prepare the team to implement your game plan, you first must know your starting point. Surveys can be used to gather a wide range of feedback. There is no reason these successful tools should be limited to HR and marketing. As a leader, you can develop your own surveys that allow you to gain insights into your organization. Once your game plan to attract and retain Gen Y is in place, surveys can provide you with just-in-time data to make the adjustments necessary for increased success.

We strongly recommend that leaders conduct some sort of "attitudes toward Gen Y" audit or survey in order to get a pulse on the current management team, from top to bottom. Conversely, we also urge organizations to survey their current Gen Y population (if the population is large enough to create an anonymous and statistically valid survey).

KEY POINT

Measure the organizational climate in your workplace.

Developing a Survey

There are nine tips we would offer in developing your survey:

- As the leader, create a clear and compelling introductory message. Your "call to action" will affect how people respond to the survey.
- Make sure everyone knows the responses will be anonymous.
- Keep the survey focused, do not be tempted to add other issues into the mix.
- Shorter surveys are better than long ones — no more than 25 questions.
- Use straightforward wording.
- Group your questions in a logical flow.
- Find out both the rating of an item and its importance. You want to be able to prioritize the results.
- Ask several open-ended questions.
- Thank people in advance for their cooperation.

Gathering this game film will provide tremendous insight into your team's attitudes, hiring, and management practices. Once you have received the data, it is critical for you to take the time to:

- Thank everyone again.
- Analyze the data quickly.
- Communicate the results.
- Link every positive change to the team input.

This final point is critical. As we discussed earlier, everyone has a different communication style. If we were to see one consistent mistake made by leaders, it is the failure to *constantly* link improvements to team feedback. You can never tell the team enough times, "We are doing ABC because you said it was important." That creates ownership and buy-in.

Prepare the Organization for Success — Your Change Management Strategy

Gen Y presents a unique and exciting leadership challenge. They are indisputably bright and talented, yet they think differently, have very different needs, and will require a very different style of leadership. In comparison to previous generations, Gen Y may seem to be high maintenance. You will have to do many things in a new and different way to attract and retain them.

Most important, Gen Y will force you to take your leadership skills to a new level. You will have a lot less room for error. You will have to do things better and quicker.

Why? As already mentioned, this group has more freedom and job options than any other group in history. If they see things they don't like in you, your employees, or your organization, they are going to leave. They do not think they have to tough it out or pay their dues the way other generations did. They have a shorter horizon.

They are also more sensitive to the little things, less willing to put up with management mistakes, and less likely to give you and your organization the benefit of the doubt. They will not wait long for you to change or fix something.

Most of your team will find these challenges disturbing. Many of your managers will feel no change is necessary. They believe that eventually Gen Y will conform to the current way of doing things. In talking with leaders around the country, many feel they can "fix" Gen Y.

Your Change Efforts

Gen Y is not a problem to be fixed. They are not broken. As the leader, it is your job to take your organization to the next level. You must lead a change management effort.

Your Gen X and Baby Boomer managers and supervisors who have come up through the ranks, have learned a set of employment rules that no longer exist. This old reality has been deeply ingrained over the years. They are very comfortable with how they currently manage new employees. In fact, there is an extraordinarily strong support system in place (other like-

> "If I had six hours to chop down a tree, I would spend the first four sharpening the axe."
> —ABRAHAM LINCOLN

minded managers) that reinforces their beliefs. However, this must change.

As you begin to transition your culture, you must understand and accept the anxiety and natural pushback that occurs as you move to your desired future situation. People respond differently to change, and it is important to understand how the various styles respond to this challenge.

KEY POINT
Sustaining change is harder than implementing it.

Change Tools

Communicating a clear vision of the future is, once again, critical. You need to help your team *visualize* the desired outcome and understand why it is in their best interests to adapt. The vision should be communicated often, to the entire team as a group, and to each team member individually. You may need to do a great deal of coaching during this stage.

A great tool to utilize in these discussions is "modeling." Pick an individual or group you feel "gets it." When interacting with your team, link the desired behaviors with the model. All world-class performers look for someone who has mastered a skill and also seek models on which to base certain parts or elements of their performances.

Here is also where the surveys will be important. During this time of transition, people do not know *how* to do something, which causes them stress. If they also do not know *why* something needs to be done, there is very little chance the new behaviors will be exhibited.

Having conducted surveys allows you to better explain the "why" of the plan. You will have the data you need to relate your actions to the input you received from the team. As a leader, you are not pushing this change down, you are responding to the needs of the team. You can only make this link if you have asked for input and then really listened.

It is during this time of transition that your leadership will be most tested. It will be critical for you to be committed to the future results, communicate early and often, and maintain your belief in a positive outcome.

The third step of a change management process is maintaining and adjusting the new situation. Another way of saying this is sustaining the change. How do you keep your team or organization from reverting back to old habits?

Four Steps to Sustaining Change

Measure, Measure, Measure

There is an old saying that "People respect what you inspect." It is also true that people respect what you count. In your organization, what are the key metrics or performance indicators that will show you are improving? Determine what to count, then count it! Also, post it where your team can see it and track their performance. A scoreboard tells everyone who's winning and is often enough alone to motivate increased performance.

Consultant's Corner

Scoreboards

We have used a variety of metrics over the years for our clients. The key is to pick *meaningful* targets and to review them often. One such scoreboard is modeled after a sign I used to see as a child outside the entrance gate at the steel mill. Posted for all to see was a sign telling the world how long the plant has operated since a "lost time injury."

Several of our clients have taken this idea and used it at their management meetings. A sign that says, "We have gone ___ days without an unplanned turnover" is posted for all to see (an unplanned turnover is a resignation versus a termination).

Another scoreboard is modeled after the deficit clock. Some of our clients keep track of the *cost to replace* lost talent. These numbers are posted at the management meetings as a way to track the financial impact of turnover.

Link the Front Line

Here is another opportunity to communicate to your front-line managers and supervisors. These are the folks who will be *critical* to your recruiting and retention efforts. Link every positive improvement to their initial input and their ongoing efforts.

Make sure your managers and supervisors are trained to

support your efforts. If you have revamped one of your hiring and management systems, make sure everyone knows how to use the system. We are constantly amazed at how often this step is overlooked. Nearly every company makes sure training occurs when a mechanical or technological change occurs. Management wants to ensure they receive the desired ROI for their investment. However, when a *human system* is changed, training is slow to follow.

Rewards and Recognition

Who in your organization is demonstrating the best practices? Has the best numbers? Who is, in other words, winning? Showcase their success. Reward their behavior and thank them for their accomplishments.

> **"What get rewarded gets repeated."**
> —KEN BLANCHARD,
> *THE ONE-MINUTE MANAGER*

These folks should also be rewarded with *time*. Spend time with these winners. Find out how and why they have been successful. Ask these folks to help craft and analyze your next survey. Like attracts like — these folks are what you need to be a winner.

Performance Management

The final step to sustaining your plan is to incorporate the desired behaviors and outcomes into your performance management system. If you are monitoring the results in your annual, quarterly, and monthly reviews, you will see positive results.

Work with Human Resources to make these behaviors a requirement for the position. Have the desired behaviors written into the job description. One thing for sure is, your next group of managers and supervisors will know how important it is to recruit and retain talent.

The Need for Alignment

As discussed earlier, your first problem might be the stereotypes and prejudice toward Gen Y that exist in your company. It might be your own misgivings about Gen Y. Other problems with respect to attracting and retaining Gen Y will be revealed through environmental scans. These surveys will reveal the gaps in your organization, the areas where you need to change, and your blind spots.

You need consistency with respect to Gen Y. If any step of the recruiting, interview, hiring, training, onboarding, or managing process is out of sync, Gen Y will notice and be put off. This is where operational leadership is critical. You must oversee a consistent, unswerving, in-step, organization-wide effort to be Gen Y friendly and Gen Y compatible.

Once you have determined what specific areas need to be improved or corrected, you must be sure that action is taken at every level, by every employee, at all times. Your decisions and policies must be in alignment with your goals three hundred and sixty five days a year. Likewise, your employees must be consistently on board with your game plan and strategies.

Conclusion

Be constantly aware that improving requires a proactive effort on your part. You need to assess the situation in your organization and create the change you want. Conduct a survey, then use the results to align your organization with your true values. Sustaining change is harder than creating it. Measure and record what you want to happen and it *will* happen. When your organization is walking the talk, the climate will be improved for Gen Y and everyone else.

 Name: Kim
Location: Midwest
Age: 29

Kim's background:

- first in her family to attend college

- graduated from a small college in her home state

- earned a masters in social work from a top 15 university whose social work college is ranked in the top five

- worked for years in the nonprofit sector before recently making the switch to for-profit

- currently works to create incentives for *Fortune* 500 companies

Growing up at the front end of Generation Y, Kim took advantage of the many opportunities that were available for the first time. Women and people without resources or connections were attending college in full force, so Kim was able to get her Masters degree. Despite this supposed equality, she still struggles with being taken seriously at work. Older, male coworkers don't treat her as a peer, and she winces every time she is called "sweetie pie" or "kid." She knows that the hurt she feels is unintentional, but she wonders if there are hidden implications.

As a single woman, Kim wants to succeed because she wants to be able to take care of herself today and in the future. She doesn't want to have to depend on others. She strives to prove herself in the business world, and she thinks that neither age nor gender should determine her pay. If and when her results are better quality than her 40-year old coworkers, she wants to be paid more. She is frustrated because her managers never think she has enough experience and they don't put enough value on her Masters.

Kim is determined not to adopt her parents' mentality of "work as hard as I can so the company doesn't let me go." She has seen her parents get laid off from restructuring, and because of this she has no loyalty to any particular company. Instead, her loyalty is to herself and her career, making sure she continually builds her skill set and has options. That's not to say she doesn't strive for excellence in everything she does; just the opposite, in fact. She throws her entire self into projects and has just recently realized that she was doing a great job at the expense of her life. She was losing parts of herself to develop professionally, but now wants to work more on priorities, under the mindset that the world won't end if she doesn't do something.

Kim's definition of a good leader:

- sets clear objectives for my job

- helps me measure my success

- develops the skill set that I want to learn

- asks me what experience I would like to get out of my job

- provides for my training and growth in the organization

- realizes the potential in everyone

- will help me with my problems

- is confident and goal-driven

- listens

- works to understand each employee

- helps me solve problems by getting other parties involved who may be out of my realm of control

Chapter 12

Alignment in Recruiting

Jim is in charge of the recruitment of Gen Y for his company. He contacted the job placement offices at the three colleges from which most of the company's new hires had come because his firm had a good track record with them. He focused on marketing majors because that is what his firm specializes in. Jim had a gut feeling about the kind of person he was looking for, but not a specific list of traits or competencies. He has done this for years and was pretty sure a marketing major from one of the three colleges would fit the bill.

Jim did not think the job description needed to be updated because the responsibilities and duties had not really changed over the past five years. He decided to skip the job recruiting fairs because they were so labor-intensive. He thought that posting the jobs online would be a much better use of his time. It was easier and quicker, and he could reach a lot more Gen Yers using the Internet. So far, Jim has received only a few responses from marketing majors and the resumes emailed to him are not impressive.

What went wrong? Jim is not adapting to the new kind of recruiting required by Gen Y. He is doing things the way he used to. Jim is limiting his prospects drastically by restricting his search to the same schools and single college major he used in the past. He does not realize that hires from different schools with different majors can work equally well at his firm. Jim's focus on a single specific major is too narrow. He also needs a specific candidate profile, not just a "gut feeling" about who will fit well at his company. The job description he has used for the past five years must be updated to specifically include new requirements and new job components. Although the Internet is a quick and easy way to post jobs, it is no substitute for the personal contacts made at recruiting fairs or through networking. Jim was wise to use the Internet but also must put in the personal time of face-to-face recruiting to attract the best Gen Y candidates.

How to Approach Recruiting

In recruiting, there is never a one-size-fits-all solution. Every strategy, every game plan needs to be adapted for the current situation and talent on hand. There are, however, several basics that must be in place in order to build a successful strategy or game plan.

The four "must have" fundamentals for any successful recruitment and retention strategy are:

- recruiting plan
- interviewing process
- onboarding process
- retention strategy

In the next chapters we will address each of these points in detail. As a leader in your organization, we suggest you handle this information the same way a coach builds a winning team. First, stress the fundamentals and choose plays that your team can execute *flawlessly*. Less is more to start, and consistent execution of a few plays is better than spotty execution of many. As your "team" develops, you can add additional plays (tactics) for your game plan.

The Basics

Recruit for Your Brand

To know the kinds of people you want to recruit, you need to make explicit what your own organizational personality, culture, or brand is. A company that sees technology as its advantage should hire different types of people than a company that sees customer service as its advantage.

A good example of this is Enterprise car rental. For many years, Hertz, Avis, and National *were* the car rental market. They all pretty much did things the same way with offices at airports. Enterprise quietly became the number one car rental firm by doing a number of things differently, such as putting small offices at car repair places. However, the most significant thing they did was change their recruiting and hiring game plan.

In general, car rental offices were not staffed by college graduates. Enterprise not only hired college grads, but they hired a certain type of grad. As *Forbes* magazine put it some years ago, Enterprise hired from the graduating half that made the top half possible! This gave them an edge with a group of students who were not in great demand. But Enterprise was interested in more than just grades. They looked for people who had demonstrated *social* skills. They had been social directors of their fraternities or sororities, and the like. They were *people* people and this showed in customer service and office management. These new hires made Enterprise extremely successful.

Most companies have very similar candidate profiles, except for their academic majors. Not enough companies have thought about what sets them apart and makes their brand different. When you understand your brand, it will help you hire people who will fit you *and* your customers better.

With the help of your management team, take time to develop your value proposition *as an employer*. Most organizations understand their value proposition *as a business*, yet rarely have we seen leadership teams take the time to develop a list of attributes that set them apart as an employer.

KEY POINT

Decide on your special brand as an employer and project it.

As you develop this list, make sure you do not just list adjectives and attributes. Have your team describe each point, why it is important, and how it sets you apart from the *hiring* competition. Once this list is developed, make sure your recruiters can link each item back to the recruit's goals and vision.

Consultant's Corner

Your Hiring Value Proposition

One very successful company we work with was having difficulty linking their value proposition to the recruiting process. They had developed a great list of items that set them apart from the hiring competition, yet they were unable to drive these advantages home during the recruiting process.

Their list included things like:

- family atmosphere
- ability to contribute immediately
- opportunities based on performance, not tenure

We offered our client a technique often used in benefits selling. This technique links the benefit to the recruit.

Because of…

You can…

Which means…

Which really means…

For example,

Because of	the fact we reward performance,
You can	set yourself apart almost immediately.
Which means	even though you have only been here a short time, you could assume significant responsibilities.

Which really means	you will be in control of your destiny and can fast-forward your career by years, and work on some very exciting strategic projects.

Develop Specific Candidate Profiles

The first major recruitment tool that you need is a Candidate Profile. Unfortunately, most profiles — when they exist at all — are boringly generic. They contain standard criteria not particularly tailored to your real job needs. You must think carefully about the kind of person you really want and what competencies you are looking for. Be specific, not generic. Relying on gut feelings, as did Jim, the recruiter in our opening profile, just doesn't make it. Gut feelings depend on our emotions on any given day, not legitimate criteria. Create as precise a profile as you can, considering not only job skills but also intangible characteristics. (See Appendix A for a list of 45 key competencies that you might need in a candidate.)

Developing a precise job profile can be a learning experience, particularly if you involve current job holders in the effort. Some companies need a specific profile of technical skills. Then their focus is the skills needed for the job and, accordingly, they must have a current and accurate job description. (Developing the job description is discussed below.) Other companies may focus on intangibles like motivation or personality in their candidate profiles.

Develop Accurate Job Descriptions for the Job NOW

The third key tool you need to successfully recruit Gen Y is a relevant and accurate job description. There obviously has to be a fit between candidates and job descriptions, so you must be sure your job descriptions are precise and current. In our example, Jim mistakenly thought that a five-year-old job description was current enough. If only as a result of changes in technology, most jobs change in the course of five years. Gen Y will be reading your job description carefully, and may call you on discrepancies between it and reality if they get your job.

Many organizations don't provide enough real details about the job to applicants. Gen Y wants to know the real nitty gritty of day-to-day work. You and your recruiters need to provide a full picture of what the work is actually like. Done right, this can protect you from the danger of high expectations on the part of Gen Y.

The best way to develop an accurate job description is to enlist the aid of employees who hold that job or a similar one. What are the day-to-day components of the job? What are the skills they need? Capture their valuable input and craft a job description that reflects this reality. Do not count on older, possibly dated job descriptions. Capture a job description for what is required *now*.

Another tool to use is 360-degree feedback. This type of analysis is typically used to examine job *performance*. It gives managers comprehensive feedback from everyone

who comes in contact with them — bosses, subordinates, peers, customers, and suppliers. It gives a more complete picture of performance than only top-down ratings by managers.

This 360-degree technique can be used to design a job *description* based on input from multiple people who interact with the position to be filled. It can provide a more complete and objective picture of what the position requires. It can also be used as the basis for training new hires. For instance, Gen Y will be likely to pay more attention to job descriptions based on the representations of the people with whom they will be working rather than more generic descriptions of the jobs.

Set Your Standards High and Seek the Best

Sometimes people will hire others who are not quite as good as they are so that they can maintain the upper hand. You may have heard this expressed as "A" people tend to hire "B" people, "B" people tend to hire "C" people," and so forth.

In today's competitive world where many resources are available to everyone, having great employees might be your *only* competitive advantage. If your company is to grow and become more successful, the people you hire must be able to eventually replace you. Instead of hiring *adequate* candidates, always seek to hire *great* ones. You will have a better chance of becoming — or remaining — a great company.

David Ogilvy, who built a major advertising agency from scratch, expressed both the upward and downward potential of this habit when he said:

> *If each of us hires people who are smaller than we are, we shall become a company of dwarfs, but if each of us hires people who are better than we are, we shall become a company of giants.*

Do not fall into the trap of thinking your new hires should be just like your best old hires. Some companies are almost superstitious about this. If their last great hire came from Carnegie Mellon University, they look for more people from Carnegie Mellon University. If their last great hire had a major in English, they look for more English majors. This is the formula Jim mistakenly used in our opening example. It is *not* the way to find the best new people.

Include Your Dress Code

Although it might seem like a very minor issue, when it comes to successfully attracting and hiring Gen Y, addressing your organization's dress code from the start is a huge benefit. Explaining your dress code up front in the job description can help you avoid conflict down the road.

A frequent complaint that companies have about Gen Y is their inappropriate dress. Their dress can be sloppy, too sexy, or extremely casual. They have tattoos and piercings. They just don't fit the corporate image. Like any group, Gen Y is trying to establish its identity through dress, mannerisms, and jargon.

Gen Yers will usually conform to a dress code if it makes any sense and is made clear to them. Explain to Gen Yers that your customers have certain expectations of the people with whom they interact, and that you also have certain expectations concerning the decorum of employees during office hours in your workplace. By including the dress code in your job description, it gives them clear notice of your expectations *before* hiring takes place. If they ultimately accept the job, it will be with the understanding that they will comply with your policies with respect to dress, tattoos, piercings, and so forth.

If your Gen Y recruit happens to be inappropriately dressed on the initial interview but is otherwise a good candidate, ignore the poor dress choice. See if he or she dresses more appropriately for the second interview. Do not immediately cross off a good candidate because of a poor initial appearance. Give your Gen Y recruit a chance to adapt once you have explained your company dress code.

Look Outside Traditional Parameters

Once you have created a value proposition, specific candidate profiles, and accurate, updated job descriptions, you are ready to recruit Gen Y in a new way.

Consider Gen Yers With Different Majors

You can greatly increase your pool of Gen Y candidates by looking outside traditional parameters. For instance, most companies hire college students who have majors that directly match their jobs. This is why in our scenario,

Jim, the recruiter for a marketing firm, was looking to hire marketing majors. But some companies find that English, history, anthropology, philosophy, and other "liberal arts" majors that have no direct job connections, turn out to be superior employees.

Gen Y is willing to explore types of jobs that don't match up to their backgrounds. If you can show them chances for growth and responsibility, they will consider something outside their apparent areas of interest. With the right training program, Gen Yers with different backgrounds can end up being a good fit for you. Remember, Gen Y is more willing than prior generations to explore different options instead of taking the expected path. They will investigate diverse settings to see what is offered and what they can learn. They also like challenges and learning new things.

Consider Gen Yers with Different Employment Backgrounds

Because of Gen Y's willingness to bide their time until they find the right job, you may find them in odd places. They look at many positions as temporary and don't mind working in jobs unrelated to their majors or their ultimate career interests. They might work as bank tellers, waitresses, bartenders, or clerks in a department store. Do not be put off by Gen Y candidates who have unusual or seemingly irrelevant work histories. They will take jobs that are not career matches until the right job comes along.

Be open to recruiting Gen Yers that you meet in daily encounters. Perhaps it is a bank teller who has the ability to connect with you as a customer, or a waiter who has great people skills, or a childcare worker who takes initiative. Give them your card, get their contact information, ask them about their goals, and try to introduce them to your organization. Offer them internships if they're still in school or bring them in part-time on a specific project. Always be recruiting!

KEY POINT

Everyone will go after the obvious stars. Be broader in your search to find the undiscovered stars.

Consider Nontraditional Work Hours

Over the past decade, many progressive companies have adjusted their recruiting to attract women who are looking for part-time jobs so that they can fulfill family obligations. We see this particularly with professional firms like accounting, advertising, and engineering companies. They offer flex-time or part-time jobs, usually with restricted pay and promotion opportunities. This could be a very successful way to attract Gen Y.

Scott Wood, president of Insurers Administrative Corporation, has found flexibility to be a key strategy to recruiting and retaining top talent. "I really needed to get past my own prejudices on this one," admitted Wood. "I grew up in an environment where work meant being seen by your boss, and working hard meant staying late.

"Over the last few years we have made significant strides in our efforts to retain top talent," said Wood. "One of our strategies has been to allow certain positions an opportunity to work remotely. This has greatly improved our retention. To be honest," said Wood, "if someone from my generation was in a coffee shop during work hours, we were most likely taking a coffee break. Now, if one of our employees is in a coffee shop during the day, most likely they are doing some important work."

Recruit Gen Y in Multiple Ways

In the days when older Baby Boomers were looking for jobs, they checked the classified ads in the newspapers, worked with college placement agencies, and mailed out lots of resumes. Younger Baby Boomers still worked with college placement agencies but also began to use networking to find a job. In 2004, a study of Gen Y employees found that the majority found their jobs through monstertrak. com, career fairs, and personal networking. Today, Gen Y still engages in networking but relies even more heavily on online tools such as CraigsList.org and monstertrak.com to find jobs.

Do Not Eliminate the Personal Touch

It is certainly important to utilize all of the Internet tools to recruit, but do not do so to the exclusion of personal recruiting. In our example, Jim was correct in using the Internet but was mistaken in eliminating job fair appearances and networking. Today, organizations have a tendency to concentrate more of their efforts on Internet-based recruiting. They still use networking, but fewer companies attend job fairs at colleges to recruit in person. Because networking and job fairs are more expensive in time, most companies tend to fall back on placing a few ads online and then trying to screen from among the many electronic resumes delivered to them.

As common sense would tell you, the easiest way to go — placing ads online — delivers the least-screened applicants. Although you will get more applicants, the process will actually require more time and follow-up to find the "golden" needles in the haystack of resumes. In fact, the more impersonal your recruiting procedures, the less effective they will tend to be in delivering quality, motivated applicants. Accordingly, it is important not to eliminate personal networking and the face-to-face recruiting at job fairs.

Gen Y expects a personal touch in the recruitment process to show that you're really interested in them. Despite the fact that they are tech savvy and comfortable with technology, Gen Y knows that email is impersonal when there is no prior relationship underlying it. In other words, email among their friends is one thing; email used by you to cultivate them for a job is another.

KEY POINT

High tech does not eliminate the value of the personal touch.

Recruit with Current Gen Y Employees

Gen Y expects recruiters who are good representatives of your company once the serious human recruitment part begins. You must have sharp people with excellent people skills working your job fair booth. Be sure your Boomers and Xers at the booth have an understanding of Gen Y's interests and needs.

It should also be mandatory to have a current Gen Y employee there. This will give you credibility as having a workplace that understands Gen Y needs. Remember, your current Gen Y employees are your best recruiters. They are living proof that your company is a great place for their generation to work. Existing Gen Y employees are your calling cards for future Gen Y employees. Also, bear in mind that like attracts like. Be sure your Gen Y staffer is representative of the kind of person you want to attract.

If your Gen Y candidate is on a serious short list, be sure that the people who recruited that candidate — junior and senior — are prepared to serve as part of the subsequent training team or as mentors. Once personal connections are made with individuals during the recruiting phase, they should not be severed when Gen Y is hired. Gen Y will feel like they have been abandoned!

Respond Quickly

When you utilize technology to recruit Gen Y, use it wisely. You will get significant numbers of applications by email if your job is posted on monstertrak, CraigsList, or other job websites. Be prepared to respond quickly. Have each job email on a separate autoresponder so that you can immediately acknowledge an application and tell each interested Gen Yer what to expect. When you receive a resume from Gen Y, you might send back a customized note like this:

> *Dear [personalized with their name],*
>
> *Thanks you for your application for our _____ job. As you might guess, we have received a lot of applications so it will take us a couple of days to get back to you with some preliminary feedback. I've enclosed a link to our website which has general information about us.*
>
> *Thanks again for your interest.*
>
> *Sincerely,*

Unlike the generations before them, Gen Y may not take the first job offered to them. However, the faster you are, the more you will set yourself apart from competitors. You will also build goodwill in your marketplace with fast, courteous, and informative responses. Gen Y talks to friends still at school, parents, teachers, and peers. They will spread the word about your quick and courteous response.

Another way to use technology wisely would be to develop a custom webpage for the job and application process. Show Gen Y you are as tech savvy as they are.

KEY POINT

Pay closer attention to the details of your recruiting efforts.

Coach's Corner

Don't Just Customize — Personalize

We have found that any correspondence that is perceived as rubber stamped and mass distributed can have a very negative effect. If the person receiving it finds it impersonal, it becomes meaningless.

Anything you can do to *personalize* your note will set you apart. Can you add a line that is only about them? When did they go to school…what are their interests?

We would advocate a personal, handwritten note as much as possible. Of course, we understand a handwritten note to smaller audiences, like basketball recruits, is much easier than sending notes to hundreds or even thousands of recruits. But I am convinced that a more personal message is most effective.

Gen Y talent does not care about company size, and personalization will make large and small organizations alike seem more equal.

New Recruiting Strategies for Gen Y

The billion-dollar giant, 3M, found that there was a shortage of sales talent in the 1990s. In response, they went to the source — colleges. It turned out that most marketing majors ended up in sales positions, but there were few sales courses in their curriculums. Even more, most of the students had a negative image of sales. Most of them thought it was persuading people to buy things they didn't want. They thought of the stereotypical pushy salesperson as the model of what selling was all about!

To deal with the negative image of sales and the lack of sales courses in college, 3M set up partnerships with a number of colleges such as DePaul University's Sales Leadership Program and supported their efforts to teach sales. 3M provided guest lecturers in courses and introduced a sales internship. It took years, but it changed the recruiting environment for 3M. 3M now has its pick of top students. They offer jobs to about 85% of their interns, and most accept. They hired 180 salespeople in 2006, and the number continues to grow.

Hewlett-Packard formed a similar partnership with high schools in the state of Washington. HP was looking for workers who were independent and could set their own goals, not the type of students traditionally emerging from high schools. They set up a long-term program with several local high schools to train students. Your company may not be able to invest the big bucks or create lengthy programs as 3M or Hewlett-Packard did, but you certainly can do a lot of new things to attract Gen Y.

Develop an Internship Program

A good way to both learn about GenY and have an edge in recruiting them is to increase your student intern programs. Internships provide an opportunity for "learning by doing" that is rarely found in classrooms and laboratories. This generation loves to have hands-on work experience and you'll find them to be eager workers in the right settings. Interns vary from free to paid. In either case, it's an inexpensive way to find and attract good workers and get work done at the same time. Both companies and interns get to look each other over in this process and many interns are offered regular jobs when they graduate.

For instance, Dr. Al Harrison, former long-time director of internship programs at UC Davis says:

> *Most companies are usually very happy with their interns, rating them highly, and 90%+ of interns consider their internships a good learning experience if they are given responsibility and work on real projects rather than just busy work. Both companies and interns get to look each other over in this process and many interns are offered regular jobs when they graduate.*

Most colleges and some high schools have internship programs designed to give students real-world experience in organizations big and small. Sometimes internship programs are coordinated through a central department at the school, but often companies can recruit interns directly through individual college departments or ads.

Internships are run in many different ways. If interns receive college credit for their work, the internship is generally clearly structured. Even if your interns are not receiving credit, it is worthwhile to follow a structured approach. This means that interns have an implicit or explicit contract with your organization. They are to be given meaningful work, regular feedback, and an overall evaluation at the end. When schools give credit, they generally do one site inspection of your organization that applies to all subsequent interns. Interns are generally required to write reports about their experiences and have faculty supervisors to help keep them on track.

Interns may be paid or unpaid, independent of their receiving academic credit. Internships give the students real job experience, a look at one possible career, and a change of pace from classroom learning. They give you a look at possible future employees and an enthusiastic workforce who can take on new projects or give a push to old ones. In addition, you get a chance to give back to the community and mentor young people. Dr. Harrison adds that "Many internship sponsors are at a point in life where they want to give back to their organization and the community and developing new talent is one way to do so." Even students who've done internships with other organizations can be worth hiring since they've had some real-world experience to apply.

Almost all internships are successful in the sense that the intern values the experience and learns something. "At least ninety percent of the internship reports that we get give the sponsors rave reviews" notes Harrison. A good internship program can further build your brand with Gen Y generally, and your interns' circles of influence in particular.

All in all, internship programs have very little downside, and considerable upside, if they are run well. Your existing Gen Y workers can even help supervise your internship program, giving them more responsibility and the students role models. (For a view of internships by one of our Gen Y interns, Alison Northrop, see Appendix B.)

Other Ways to Reach Gen Y

Be a Guest Lecturer

Is there a certain college where you want to recruit? Is there a young professional society in your area? Is there a trade school nearby? Offer your services as a guest lecturer or become an adjunct faculty member there. You can develop invaluable name recognition and make connections, not just with students but also with faculty and administrators. The latter are in a position to steer graduates toward your organization.

Sponsor Community Events

Gen Y is concerned about giving back to the community. More than any other generation, they support social causes and like to volunteer. Align your sponsorship of charitable and community activities with the social interests of the Gen Y candidates you are hoping to attract. Support events that draw your desired recruiting demographic. Get your organizations's name out there as being community conscious and involved. This is a great way to connect with Gen Y's entire circle of influence. Gen Y will get input from parents, peers, and friends, and these individuals may very well accompany them to the events.

Host a Seminar

Create leadership forums for possible candidates. Pro-vide some type of value-added learning opportunity for possible recruits. Your organization can partner with a college or trade school to conduct a seminar that allows you to see candidates in action. This will also provide the institution with a valuable program and help to establish a relationship with you.

Target Different Geographic Areas

The Gen Y workforce is more mobile than prior generations. You are not limited to recruiting only at the schools in the immediate vicinity of your organization's offices. Go where you think the best candidates are and be prepared to sell them on relocation.

Pursue the hometown candidates who live — or lived — near your offices as well. As discussed earlier, a high percentage of Gen Y plan on returning home to live with their parents after graduation. They may go to out-of-town schools yet fully intend to return home to work. Target the out-of-town schools that you know have large populations of students from your city. For example, the main campus of Penn State University is located in State College, in the center of Pennsylvania. However, 50% of their students are from Philadelphia. If your office is in Philadelphia, you should be recruiting at Penn State. Those students planning on returning home will be thrilled to interview with your "home-town company."

Recruit Gen Y's Circle of Influence

In this era of Gen Y hiring, you are no longer just recruiting individuals. You must attract Gen Y's circle of influence. These are all the people who can influence the decisions Gen Y makes with their comments, advice, and questions. Gen Y's circle of influence can include parents, friends, peers, siblings, teachers, and others. Make it your business to find out who Gen Y's influencers are. They can exert influence on Gen Y and be very persuasive when it comes to career decisions and job choices. Your reputation and image are very important to these influencers. Your goal is not to replace this circle of influence or somehow shut it out, but to partner with it to guide Gen Y to the best career choice.

> "Human beings are the only creatures on earth that allow their children to come back home."
> —BILL COSBY, *FATHERHOOD*

Gen Y's parents, in particular, have been more involved in their lives than earlier generations. In return, Gen Y can be heavily influenced by the input of their parents about their careers and about your job. It is not uncommon for a member of Generation Y to postpone making a decision until they discuss it with their family. We even know of a few cases where companies have encouraged parents to come to the applicant's final job interview.

Remember that the information you give Gen Y candidates to try to recruit them may very well be shared with others. Design it with this expanded group of people in mind and they may help sell your job to the candidate. If your organization has a yearly open house or company picnic, be sure to include Gen Y's family, friends, and circle of influence in the invitation. These goodwill open houses and picnics can create a sense of connectedness to companies and be an aid in recruiting. If you offer a tour to your Gen Y candidates as part of the recruiting process, it may be appropriate to offer to let them bring a parent or spouse along if they like.

Another way to reach out to Gen Y's circle of influence is to put them on your mailing list for newsletters and other company announcements.

Coach's Corner

Manage Your Wows

When I was an assistant at the University of Kentucky, the football recruiting coordinator, Tommy Limbaugh, taught us the valuable principle of "managing our wow." At the time, our players lived in Wildcat Lodge, a beautiful place right next to where we practiced. What we had been doing with recruits is when we would talk with them and their families on the phone, we would explain how great the Lodge was. Tommy Limbaugh said something very brilliant. He said we needed to manage our wow. He said the next time a recruit asks you where he would live if they came to UK, tell them the Wildcat Lodge and then quickly change the subject. Don't tell them anything about it. Tell them they'll get to see it on their visit.

What he was getting at was, if we described it with all kinds of gushing superlatives, we'd create expectations that couldn't meet these mythological standards we had created. So something that should have been a highlight that benefitted us actually became a downer. When we took his advice and said nothing about it, and they walked in and saw how unique it was, we gained a tremendous advantage. They were like, "Coach, you didn't tell me the Wildcat Lodge was this nice or that we'd get to live in place like this." By underplaying the lodge we increased our credibility and we managed our wow.

> **KEY POINT**
>
> **Manage your wows.**

Establish Realistic Expectations

There is a natural tendency to highlight the good points of your job and downplay or ignore negative ones. There is a good deal of research on the effect of expectations on subsequent adjustment to a new job. Most companies' approach to "selling" job applicants on their jobs actually has a *negative* effect on assimilation once the applicants are hired! Studies show that, sadly, the high point of your employees' interest in your jobs is usually *before* they've actually started them. That is, people's hopes and expectations about a new job are usually very positive. Once they start the new job, attitudes go down. This is particularly true for Gen Y.

As already mentioned, Gen Y has a shorter job horizon than longtime employees. They are looking at a point a year or two in the distance. Their commitment is limited because of their increased freedom and lack of familial responsibility. They are leasing the job, not buying it and they may or may not renew their lease. All humans have a tendency to avoid what is uncomfortable or painful — the "fight or flight" reflex. Gen Y's reflex time is a lot shorter.

Because they have so many options and a financial safety net, it is easier and more tempting for Gen Y to leave when things get tough or when the job disappoints them.

Fortunately, there is a way to overcome this typical problem. The secret to recruiting people and getting more of them to stay through difficulties they didn't anticipate or understand, is to give them very realistic — or even negative — expectations. That may sound odd, but look at it from the viewpoint of the new worker. Research shows that their attitudes are very positive *before* they start the job and go down from there. This is because they have unrealistic expectations. To a certain extent, they project their hopes and dreams onto your new job. Few jobs can live up to those kinds of expectations.

Perhaps raised expectations have affected you in a different context. For instance, someone has said they were going to tell you the funniest joke you've ever heard. Or wanted to take you to the best restaurant. Or promised that you were absolutely going to love someone they planned to introduce you to. When expectations are high, reality generally pales by comparison. Of course, you were disappointed by the joke, the restaurant, or the person because their value had been overinflated. This is exactly what happens with new jobs.

> **"Because realistic job previews bring about a greater alignment between expectations and reality, they can have a significant impact on the reduction of early turnover and can lead to substantial employee-replacement cost savings."**
> —John P. Wanous, *Organizational Entry: Recruitment, Selection, and Socialization of Newcomers*

Research shows that revealing negatives about a job to potential new hires can actually make the job *more* attractive and satisfying to them. This overly honest approach can do a number of things, depending on the personality involved. First, it prepares them with facts that can help them adapt or prepare for the challenges. Second, it keeps their expectations more realistic. Third, it can be a kind of reverse sell. When you say something negative, they may tend to see the opposite side. Fourth, it may challenge them. In other words, it makes them more interested in showing their capabilities if the situation is a challenge. Fifth, it builds your credibility as a good source of information. Instead of their believing you would lie to get them, you are bending over backwards to be honest with them. Sixth, when difficulties arise, it reminds them that you were honest with them about the challenge.

> **"None but the well-bred man knows how to confess a fault, or acknowledge himself in error."**
> —BEN FRANKLIN

Particularly with respect to Gen Y, the better you can explain possible negatives in the job, the better prepared they will be to handle the inevitable challenges or shortcomings of the job and the less likely they will be to bolt.

Will revealing the negatives scare too many prospects away? Actually, research shows that you don't lose many people this way. But think about it. If they are scared away by a few negative details, are they the kind of person you want working for you? They don't seem to have much fighting spirit, and they would be even more likely to quit when difficulties arose — thus costing you more. Probably they weren't that serious in the first place. A little judicious weeding of the applicant pool gives you more time and attention to focus on the serious candidates.

Try to become more aware of the expectations that your new hires bring to the job. Do these expectations fit the types of candidates you've decided to go after? Is your recruitment information one sided and overly positive? Make a preliminary list of all the bad things about the job from the point of view of a new worker. If you can't think of many, ask the people who have had similar jobs, or ask your newer employees, especially your current Gen Y employees.

Do any of the following issues fit your situation? If so, add them to your list.

- too much paperwork
- lack of team spirit
- time pressures
- unpaid overtime work
- disorganized work flow
- low initial pay
- not being in the loop
- cold calling
- dealing with angry customers
- outdated technology
- not enough training
- slow chances of advancement
- people don't appreciate good work
- heavy workload

Being honest, up-front, and realistic about your job is the best way to recruit Gen Y. They can be overly sensitive to surprise challenges and negative events, so give them a realistic picture of the job they are being recruited for. It is not perfect. No job is. But knowing the challenges and imperfections in advance will help them stay the course once they are on board.

KEY POINT

Creating realistic — or even negative — expectations can help you with recruits.

Enlist Existing Employees as Recruiters

Many companies get recruits who are friends, relatives, or acquaintances of current employees. Gen Y is particularly happy to bring their friends on board. Encourage your existing employees to constantly be on the lookout for new employees. Perhaps you can even offer a reward for finding a new employee who lasts a year or more. Your own employees are the best evidence of your company brand. If they're proud of where they work, they'll naturally talk it up and attract new recruits.

Stay Connected to "Second-Chance" Candidates

An often overlooked source of job candidates is the people you *don't* hire for a particular position. There can be at least three reasons why you don't hire them. You didn't offer them a job, you liked them but they weren't a good fit for the particular job, or they didn't pick you when you offered them a job.

How you treat non-hired job candidates can affect the reputation of your organization and future hiring. We suggest that you consider each job search a step in building a winning candidate pool over time. Take the first case. You didn't offer them a job, but if you handle it right, they will be flattered or at least have a very positive feeling about your organization. If you think they have ability, tell them why you didn't hire them — for example, another candidate had more relevant experience or credentials — and that you want to keep their name on file and keep in touch. The second case is very similar. You liked them but they didn't fit the *specific* job. Tell them you'd like to keep them in mind when a better-fitting job comes up. (This case also gives you a chance to encourage them to clarify what their perfect job would be.)

The last case is a bit more awkward for you, but actually can be made quite flattering for the candidate. You offer them the job but they turn you down. Rather than acting like you've been rejected, explore the facts further. If they don't like your company, it ends there. However, if they have been offered what appears to them to be a better job, you have another chance. We know that many companies disappoint Gen Y in new jobs. They tend to neglect newcomers once they are signed up. Keep in touch with these candidates. Your ongoing interest in them may start to look pretty good if their new job doesn't live up to expectations. Since most Gen Y change jobs in a year or two, you may have another shot at them. Then you will have the inside track.

Conclusion

You must have a specific candidate profile and accurate job description to best recruit any new employee, but especially Gen Y. Gen Y will pay attention to job details and can be alienated if the job they take with you does not match your description.

Expand your recruiting parameters to include different schools, different majors, different geographic areas, and different work histories. Gen Y is versatile and mobile. They are willing to work in fields that are different than their educational backgrounds and prior job experiences. Be aware of potential Gen Y employees who you may encounter in your day-to-day activities. Especially during tough times, many qualified Gen Yers are holding temporary jobs in different fields just biding their time for the right job to come along.

> "In response to deteriorating economic conditions world-wide, many...firms have scaled back their recruiting budgets and planned to recruit fewer entry-level [workers] for at least the next two years. Yet it is especially important in a down economy to hire the best, brightest, and most diverse [group]..."
>
> —*LEGAL MANAGEMENT*, FEBRUARY 2009

Use multiple methods to recruit Gen Y including the Internet, networking, job fairs, and current employees. But be careful not to lose the personal touch. When you use technology, use it wisely and efficiently. Show Gen Y you are as tech savvy as they are.

Enlist your current Gen Y employees in the recruitment process. They are the living proof that your organization is a good place for Gen Y to work.

Start to connect early with future Gen Y employees through internships, educational partnerships, and the sponsorship of community events. Remember, you are not just recruiting Gen Y, you're recruiting their whole circle of influence as well.

Be sure that you do not oversell your job or inadvertently cause candidates to have unrealistic expectations about it. Gen Y is inclined to leave uncomfortable or disappointing job situations instead of sticking around to resolve them. You can help prepare Gen Y to stay and handle challenging circumstances by letting them know what is coming.

Name: Kevlen
Age: 25
Location: Southeast

Kevlen's background:

- bachelor's of science, international business
- masters degree, international business
- 4-year varsity football letterman
- earned an athletic scholarship as a "walk-on"

Kevlen was a star athlete in high school and wanted to pursue a football career in college. While he had several schools offering scholarship opportunities, Kevlen wanted to make sure he was making the right academic choice.

"It is every players dream to play professionally," said Kevlen. "It was mine, too. However, I wanted to make sure there was a plan B, and that was a great education."

Kevlen decided to forgo the athletic scholarships and "walk-on" at a school that provided the best program in his desired field. "My parents fully supported my decisions to put academics first and football second," says Kevlen. He also quickly notes, "It is not as if I choose a football doormat. We did play in 3 bowl games while I was there."

Kevlen did win an athletic scholarship while there and graduated in 3.5 years. He went on to receive a Master's degree and is currently interviewing for several positions.

Kevlen feels he is a student of leadership and has seen the good, the bad, and the ugly during his football career. Kevlen believes the best leaders:

- are willing to push you to new heights

- use a blend of styles to 'coach' people to perform

- use positive reinforcement, as well as constructive criticism

- leave no doubt as to who is in charge

Chapter 13

Interviewing Gen Y

When Maureen, age 25, applied for the job she was really excited. Although she had a business degree, she had been working as a childcare provider for a year and this looked like the job she had been waiting for. She not only had the qualifications that fit the job description, she was inspired by the company philosophy. Maureen couldn't wait to meet people in the company and find out what else they were doing.

The company sent her a list of questions and asked her to submit her answers before her job interview. The questions confirmed her belief that this company was on her "wavelength." However, when she got to the interview, Patrick, the interviewer, acted distracted. He asked her a series of questions, but didn't seem to listen to her answers and didn't take a single note. It became obvious that he hadn't read the responses that she'd sent in ahead of time. Patrick couldn't understand why she had taken a job in childcare when her background was in sales, and when Maureen asked about the company philosophy and some of the interesting things the company was doing, Patrick said that wasn't his department. Maureen went away disappointed and made up her mind that if the company offered her a job, she wouldn't accept it.

What went wrong? Patrick did not have the right skills to interview. He did not give Maureen his full attention or really listen to what she was saying. Without taking notes, it is difficult to see how Patrick will be able to accurately summarize this interview or compare this candidate to others. He gave Maureen the impression that he wasn't interested in her and he did not pick up on the fact that she was excited about the company.

Patrick hadn't prepared properly for the interview by reviewing her answers and he wasn't able to give the most basic explanation of the programs and activities of the company. He also didn't seem to understand that, like many Gen Yers, Maureen had settled for a temporary job that was not in her field because she was waiting for the right job to come along. Patrick neither learned about Maureen nor promoted or sold his company to her, the two main tasks an interviewer is supposed to do. Instead, he took an excited applicant and turned her into a disappointed person who will spread the word to other Gen Yers about her negative experience with the company.

KEY POINT

An interviewer's job is to both learn about the applicants *and* sell the company.

Traditional Interviews Are *Not* Predictive of Job Success

Interviewing takes skill and preparation. Unless properly conducted, *most job interview ratings bear no relationship to how well someone will actually perform the job!* Whether you like or dislike a candidate has NO bearing on how well that candidate will do in your job. What this means is, if you were to interview 100 people and rate them on a scale from "loved them" to "hated them," then hired them all, your ratings would bear no relationship to how well they performed in your job!

Most interviews have no accuracy in predicting eventual job performance because:

- They are not structured.
- They are not systematic.
- They are not validated.
- Results are not properly documented.

To successfully attract the best and brightest of Gen Y — and those with the greatest likelihood of fitting into your organization — your interviewing strategy must include all of the above components.

Do Not Rely on Personal Impressions

Without structure or validation, the interviewer is simply acting upon overall personal impressions. Candidates will be judged on how articulate they are and their general social skills. There is a good deal of writing that says an impression is formed in the first 20 seconds. This certainly is not an accurate way to predict how well a candidate will do in a job. An impression based on physical attractiveness, confident posture, eye contact, the sound of a voice, how someone shakes hands, the style of dress, and so forth tells you a lot about how applicants come across when they're trying to make a good first impression, but little about how they will perform day to day in your job.

There are many examples of how first impressions can be misleading. Some people have learned how to make a good first impression. This has little to do with how they act once they get to know you or are working for you. Others won't make a good first impression but may be a great fit for your job. For instance, people who are good on the phone often are less comfortable in person. However, if you are hiring for a phone job what you want to know is how they are on the phone. Their interviews should probably be done on the telephone, and not in person. Others may be shy at first meeting and come across as aloof, but are warm and outgoing as they get to know you. While this type of individual is not suited for any job that involves meeting a lot of new people (sales or customer service, for example), there are plenty of other jobs that would fit them.

It's not surprising that traditional interviews have generally shown no validity. Since few companies actually test the accuracy of their interviews in a scientific manner, they think the interviewing process is predictive. Many candidates can perform the actual tasks of a job, so whomever you hire will usually work out adequately. Since you never see the other candidates you didn't hire, you have no idea if they would have been better or worse. Thus, the standard hiring situation is not set up to test its own effectiveness.

The Basics of Predictive Interviewing

There *is* a way to make your interviews more valid and reliable. You need to create a system and follow a series of steps like the following.

1. Train Your Interviewers!

The first step to conducting better interviews is to have better *interviewers*. Interviewing is a skill that can be taught. Some people may be naturally good interviewers, especially if they're interviewing for a job they supervise. They may be good at identifying candidates they wouldn't want to work with and those they would get along with. Some people have a knack for judging others. But the best rule of thumb is to pick interviewers who have excellent people skills, and carefully train them to use systematic and validated criteria.

The importance of having trained interviewers cannot be overstated. Gen Y can accept or reject a job based solely on the interviewer! As we saw in our example, Maureen was sold on the company until she met Patrick. His inattention to her and ignorance about the company were enough to scare her off, even though she had previously been excited about the job.

Interviewers must be able to balance talking and listening. They cannot spend too much time trying to sell the job to applicants. They must be able to ask questions and listen. Gen Y is particularly sensitive to this. They want to tell you about themselves. Besides, it is vitally important that you find out Gen Y's needs and goals as soon as possible. It will also impress Gen Y that you care about their personal visions. Interviewers must also have solid knowledge about the organization. In the above scenario, Patrick's ignorance about his own company was inexcusable and the biggest turn off for Maureen.

It is especially important that interviewers be aware of their own unconscious negative tendencies, things that could alienate Gen Y during the initial interview. Chapter 8 discussed personality profiling in detail. This analytical tool will give your interviewers "game film" to review. They may be unconsciously controlling the conversation, cutting off the candidate, bullying, or being too impatient. All of these behavioral tendencies can potentially cost you your Gen Y candidates. Fortunately, once a good interviewer is aware of these behaviors, he or she can control them.

Consultant's Corner

Train Your Interviewers

One of our international clients was experiencing a sudden lack of productivity from their new-hire salespeople. Historically, our client's new sales folks showed significant progress within 90 days of completing the new-hire training program. Over a nine-month period, there seemed to be a huge decrease in results produced by the new hires.

After some investigation, we realized the problem. The interviews were now being conducted by recently promoted sales managers. These managers, while anxious to take on a new responsibility, had no formal interview training.

We found that the interviewers were doing over *80%* of the talking during an interview. In short, the interviewers *liked* candidates who listened to their stories, not necessarily candidates who could actually sell!

After implementing a training program for the new managers, we found several who simply *could not* and *should not* be a part of the interview process. While they were very good sales managers, they were not very good interviewers.

Once properly trained, the remaining interviewers began to hire candidates who actually *exceeded* previous new-hire production.

---

2. Interviews Must Be Structured

To set up an effective interviewing system, you need a predictable, repeatable process that you can document and that anyone can be trained to use. The interviewer has a complicated task: selling the company and job, while trying to assess the candidate's strengths and potential fit. It's hard to do multiple things at once and best to have defined segments of the interview session devoted to each of your goals.

A good interview should be divided into several broad

areas and a good interviewer will walk through the details in each area. An unstructured interviewer will bounce around from area to area and lack continuity throughout the session.

In order to control and manage the interview process, the interviewer needs to consider the various areas of the candidate's life as "funnels" or personal life chapters. Information will start on top in a broad, general way and continue until it has narrowed down to more specific information. The funnels are as follows:

- personal background information
- evaluation of educational background
- activities and involvements
- work experience
- career goals and personal vision

Once the basic structure of the interview has been outlined, it must be carried out in a systematic and validated way.

3. Interviews Must Be Systematic

It is difficult enough to compare candidates when they are similar on all major criteria, but when you have an interview situation with many variables, the task is even harder. Be sure that your interviews:

- ask the same questions
- take place in the same setting
- take the same amount of time

Remove as many extraneous variables as possible. Have a list of questions that every candidate is asked. Naturally, the conversations will flow differently depending on how the candidates answer, how talkative they are, and so on. We're not suggesting you destroy a natural conversational feel. But be disciplined enough to keep control of the interview and stay on task by getting answers to the same questions.

4. Interviews Must Be Validated

Not only do your interviewers have to ask the same questions, they have to ask the *right* questions! Questions must be linked to the factors that are predictive of success on your job. As discussed in the prior chapter on recruiting, you must have a precise candidate profile and a current, accurate, job description. Review these carefully and prepare your questions accordingly. There is no substitute for preparation. In our scenario, Patrick was not prepared. He was unfamiliar with both Maureen's prior input and his company's activities.

In addition to job skills, be sure you have a solid list of the intangibles that you are looking for in a candidate, all tied to success on the job. Do not limit yourself to skills and talents that your new hire will need at the entry level. Think two to four levels above. What skills and talents will be needed by this employee in the future?

KEY POINT

"Normal" interviews are *not* accurate predictors of candidates' future job success!

Coach's Corner

Have a System and Ask the Right Questions

A scout from a professional team interviewed me about NBA prospects from the PAC 10. He was obviously using a questionnaire with answers on a scale of 1 to 10. I could tell that he was going to take my responses and compile them with everybody else's that he interviewed. It just seemed to me like the whole thing was flawed.

First of all, there were a lot of questions that I'd have no way of knowing the answer to. Second, what might have been an 8 to me would have been a 6 to someone else, although maybe we felt the exact same thing. There was no way to rate my experience and my ability to evaluate talent compared to someone else's. We were all going to be given equal weight in this process. It just seemed to me that the system they were using was so rigid that it would be difficult for them to come out with the right answer.

5. Results Must Be Properly Documented

Even the best-run interview will be a waste if the information secured from that interview is not properly documented. You must have a consistent way of recording answers and scoring candidates so that it is possible to make valid comparisons.

One way to make your interviews more objective and less subjective — and easier to compare across interviewers and candidates — is to make systematic notes on the answers of each applicant and on the interviewers' impressions. Let the applicant know that you will be making a few notes. Keep them brief and then expand them after the applicant has left.

To note answers easily and systematically, you need to have clear dimensions to rate. A good way to easily rate answers from job applicants is to build answer keys. This is a list of responses that you would expect for each question arranged in categories relevant to your job, such as "acceptable" and "unacceptable." As you interview people, you can add to the key if new answers come up. The interviewer's "impressions" should only be evaluations of things that can be objectively rated. This would include grooming, timeliness, good eye contact, and so on. Having a list of the types of answers makes it fast and easy to score answers across applicants and across interviewers.

You must also have a good record of the process as a whole: how many people you interviewed, the dates of the interviews, dates of decisions, when letters were sent and calls made, who said yes, who was rejected, and so forth.

Little Things Count When Interviewing Gen Y

It is important to pay attention to the little things when interviewing Gen Y. If Gen Y is traveling from out of town for the interview, consider providing them with a local weather update, having someone meet them at the airport, or making their hotel reservations for them. Once they arrive, the receptionist should greet them by name, offer them a cup of coffee (or Jolt cola!), and make them feel welcome and relaxed.

Consider having a "sponsor" for each candidate, someone who will escort the candidate through the interview agenda, give them the office tour, and be available to answer general questions. Give your sponsor a bio of the candidate in advance.

Whenever possible, individuals involved in recruiting the candidates should reconnect with them at some point before or after the interview. Of course, the interviewer should appear promptly to greet them.

The interview room should be neat and comfortable. Rather than using a sterile table and two hard chairs or your office with your desk as a barrier between you, you may want to use a room that feels friendlier and less formal. Remember, Gen Y is very attentive to subtle visual cues. What did the reception area say about your organization as the candidate sat there? What does your interview setting say?

YOU Need to Relax, Too!

Even if you are interviewing a series of candidates, you should try to project a relaxed feeling as if each individual were your only concern. Interviews that run like an assembly line can make you feel and act like a machine and are impersonal and unattractive to Gen Y. They like to be treated as individuals.

Gen Y candidates coming for an interview can be very nervous. Try to put them at ease. This will give them a positive impression of your organization. Provide an overview or context for the candidate by explaining how long the interview will last and what it will cover. Build a rapport with comments about their strengths or your personal similarities. ("I see we both went to State University. How was your experience there?") Ask if they had any trouble finding your office, or ask about unusual interests they list on their resumes.

Matching Visions

Start the interview with a few words about the company and the position. Find out which applicants have done their homework — read the material you sent them, visited your website, and so forth. Then ask your systematic, job-based questions.

At some point in the interview, it is critical that you ask your Gen Y candidates about their personal goals and vision. What are their expectations from this job? Where do they think it will take them? What do they want to accomplish with your company?

KEY POINT
When you find out what a Gen Yer's vision is, you will find out what he or she cares about and is really willing to work for.

As discussed earlier once you have identified the Gen Yer's personal vision, you must take the final step and link your vision for the organization with the Gen Yer's vision. This is a golden opportunity for your interviewer to show the

Gen Yer how unique your company is and how compatible it will be with his or her personal interests.

Follow Through

At the end of the interview, give all applicants a general idea of your decision timetable. Be sure that the time between interviews and decisions is not inordinately long. If you have a great Gen Y candidate you'd like to hire, act quickly! If you wait too long to make an offer, that talented individual will be snatched up by someone else.

It is important to contact all Gen Y candidates later, including the ones you don't hire. As discussed earlier, how you treat the job candidates you do not wish to hire, or the ones who turn you down, can affect the reputation of your organization. Gen Yers talk to each other. Tell them why you didn't hire them — another candidate had more experience, they didn't fit the specific job — and that you want to keep their name on file and keep in touch. They will be flattered or at least have a more positive feeling about your organization.

Evaluating Gen Y

Past Performance

It might be a challenge to pin down Gen Y's past performance because many of them will not have had prior jobs. The reason most companies are looking for someone with three to five years of experience is to save on training, and because past performance is often the best predictor of future job success. Knowing that someone has already performed a job that required the skills you need is a good predictor of the ability to demonstrate the same skill again in the future.

Some aspects of past performance will show on a resume. But these clues can be exaggerated or understated. Gen Y will probably not have much experience directly related to your situation. You'll have to design questions to uncover or clarify how their experiences in school and other areas might apply to your needs. For instance, a simple example would be indications of leadership from their activities in clubs, Greek organizations, and so on.

You may also find Gen Y candidates who have lots of experience but in fields unrelated to the job for which they are applying. Because of Gen Y's willingness to bide their time until they find the right job, they may have held some atypical jobs. They look at many positions as temporary and don't mind working in jobs unrelated to their majors or their ultimate career interests. Do not be put off by Gen Y candidates who have unusual or seemingly inappropriate work histories. Check to see if the skills or intangible traits involved in those jobs coincide with the skills and traits required in your available positions.

Attitudes

One of the hardest things to determine during an interview is whether your candidate has a can-do attitude. A can-do attitude is a combination of high self-esteem, persistence, optimism, aggressiveness, and many other factors. Some people are more likely to take the initiative and get things done despite obstacles. Others tend to give up when they hit barriers and wait for you to give them directions. Because Gen Y may overreact to initial difficulties in a job, you want to find someone who has a "can-do" attitude. This attitude may be hard to spot until you see it in action, but it can be shown by accomplishments in life, however subtle.

Designing questions that will really get at this important trait is hard. You can present candidates with situations where they have a choice between asking for advice versus trying something on their own. You don't want people who charge ahead without thinking, but a certain focused drive can be valuable. Peter Drucker said that all successful people are monomaniacs in some ways. To get at this can-do focus, you could set up situations where the candidates can at least take the initiative to gather more information before they ask for help. You can also ask them the traditional questions about situations where they have overcome obstacles.

Behavior-Based Questions Provide More Relevant Information

The top goal of a job interview should be to find out about the applicant's past experience relative to key knowledge, skills, and abilities needed for success in the job. Interview questions must be designed for this. As already discussed, many of your Gen Y applicants will not have had relevant job experience. If you don't have a candidate's record of performance in similar jobs, you need to ask questions that are performance oriented. Their answers can be based on their school experience, their volunteer work, their leisure activities, and so on.

You are in a better position to judge your applicants' abilities if they describe several specific instances where they had to deal with the types of issues the job entails. Simply ask applicants to describe the situation, what they did to address it, and what happened as a result.

This behavioral approach assumes that you have analyzed the job and know what key skills it requires. Be sure you know what qualities your applicants must have when you hire them. For example, people in customer service need to be comfortable answering questions, know how to use a database (with the information they need), have a friendly attitude, be patient, be able to handle angry customers, and so on. People in sales need to learn about your products or services, be comfortable talking with prospects, and be able to take rejection.

Once you have identified key skills for a job, you need to distinguish between those that applicants *must* have and those that they can learn on the job. It's often more important to hire people with the right attitudes than the right skills. Skills can be taught, but attitudes are tougher to change.

Look for Real Situational Information

You can see the benefit of asking questions that are behaviorally anchored. Traditional interview questions often ask applicants to rate their own abilities: "How good are you at working in a team?" Of course they'll give themselves a positive rating! Behavior-based questions force the applicant to be more specific and give examples. "Describe a time when you worked with a team at school and what you liked and disliked about it." By probing the details, you can learn more about how the applicants think and their underlying assumptions.

Behavior-based questions help you find out whether candidates have experience that can generalize to your job. A related approach is to use questions that describe a hypothetical work situation similar to those they will encounter in your job. These can help you understand how candidates think about the types of situations they will meet on the job.

There's No Substitute for Reality

Remember, however, that hypothetical examples are a weak substitute for actual behavioral responses. In one case, an applicant didn't have any work experience and was unable to come up with work examples. The interviewer then began to ask, "What would you do in that situation?" The applicant gave answers that fit what the organization was looking for.

To get at actual behavior, the interviewer changed the focus to volunteer work, or college projects that involved working with others. When they went over the same questions using *actual* behavior this time, the responses were different.

It's no secret that people will say things that make themselves look good. They will also say what they think you want to hear. When they report on their actual behavior, you have a somewhat better chance of learning what they will actually do and what they are actually like.

*Consultant's
Corner*

Behavior-Based Questions

We often work with our clients to help them develop a set of specific competencies required for each job. Once we have finalized the list, we are able to create specific behavior-based questions for each area.

Sample Competency Questions

RESULTS-DRIVEN: Achievement-oriented: Achieves and exceeds goals; pushes self and others for results.

Example: *Give me an example of a goal that you had set in the past and tell me about your success in reaching it.*

VERSATILE: Adjusts effectively to new work demands, processes, structures, and cultures.

Example: *Tell me about a time you had to handle multiple responsibilities.*

INFLUENTIAL: Makes an impact on people, events, and decisions; affects the thinking or actions of others by means of example or personality.

Example: *Describe a time when you affected other's decisions or thinking process.*

CUSTOMER-FOCUSED: Aware of customer needs; makes decisions with customer in mind; builds strong customer relationships.

Example: *Tell me about a situation when you had to deal with a very upset customer. What did you do? What was the result?*

Establish Realistic Expectations

As discussed at length in Chapter 12, you must avoid inflating Gen Y's expectations about the job. There is a natural tendency to highlight the good points of your job and downplay or ignore the negative ones during the initial interview. No matter how great your company is or how good the job is, there will be challenges, difficulties, and problems at some point, particularly early on. Gen Y needs to be prepared for these.

Be realistic about the negatives so that Gen Y is not painfully surprised when they discover that their "dream job" actually has some flaws. Remember Gen Y's fight-or-flight reflex time is a lot shorter. Because they have so many options and a financial safety net, it is easier and more tempting for Gen Y to leave when things get tough or when the job disappoints them. Being honest, up-front, and realistic about your job is the best way to prepare Gen Y for challenges and imperfections that will emerge. Your honesty will help them stay the course once they are on board.

Group Interviews

Today it is not unusual for a candidate to be interviewed by a group of people. The entire group can take part in the same interview, or several people can interview the candidate sequentially. A group interview can be quite stressful. We know of cases where interviews are deliberately stressful to see how a candidate handled it. If this is not your intention, you'll need to be careful how you set it up.

Another problem with multiple interviewers is a form of groupthink that can occur during the decision process. Research has found that often groups suppress dissent. Everyone goes along with what they *assume* the consensus to be.

In a group setting, sometimes a compromise candidate is selected. The compromise candidate is *acceptable* to everyone, but is no one's *favorite*. In this case, you may hire a safe person, but not the best person. Make sure someone likes them well enough to act as a mentor and sponsor. It is often better to hire a candidate who has clear strengths

---

Groupthink

Irving Janis at Yale developed the term "groupthink" to describe why no dissenting opinions were expressed about the Bay of Pigs invasion of Cuba during the Kennedy administration. He described it as a group's almost unconscious desire for uniformity leading to a lack of dissent and less reality testing. To avoid this, you need to encourage dissent or even appoint a devil's advocate. Once some disagreement is expressed, others feel freer to voice problems and take a more balanced approach in their analyses.

and weaknesses than a candidate without weaknesses but who will never be outstanding.

If multiple people are rating a candidate and one says that candidate is "a maybe" or "acceptable," we recommend that you take that as a no. You want higher ratings from key people or chances are you're not looking at an outstanding candidate.

Testing

Sometimes testing will be an appropriate part of the interview process. For some jobs, specific skills are an advantage. This means that you can use tests that reflect those skills. If you need people who can type fast on the computer, give them a typing test. If you want programmers in a certain computer language, have them code something for you.

Intelligence tests will give you an indication of intellectual potential. When combined with good grades in school, you will know if you're getting an under- or overachiever. You can also borrow a page from the AT&T job assessment approach. When they wanted to see if a candidate had leadership skills, they put him or her in a leaderless group task situation with other candidates and watched to see who emerged as the leader. If the job requires a lot of administrative work, set up an in-basket task and have him or her make decisions about a variety of items.

If the job is to do online research, use spreadsheets, or prepare reports, they could do the same thing as part of a job test. You know what you want your great new hires to

Contract-to-Hire

Contract-to-hire is becoming more popular and replacing probationary periods. You hire the Gen Y as an independent contractor. If they perform well, you offer a permanent job. If either of you doesn't like the situation, you can terminate at any time. Legally, you're in the clear, especially if you hire them through an employment agency. Gen Y can also like this setup because it allows them to take a good look at a job.

do. Try to test them on the actual skills they will need to use. You can sometimes test candidates as part of extended "interviews" as if they are working during a trial period. They can go out on a sales call, interview customers, shop the competition, or engage in other activities that fit their jobs. And, of course, a serious trial period is another way to test actual performance and learn whether a person's abilities fit your situation.

Role playing is another possibility. You may not be able to have a candidate deal with an angry customer or try to make a sale, but you can set up fairly realistic role plays for many situations.

A harder thing to test for is motivation. In fact, how motivated a new hire is may depend on how you treat them during the interview and during training. People can have all the skills and potential in the world, but they also need to be motivated to use them. Gen Y will be motivated by having an interesting job, compatible leadership, interesting peers, opportunities to learn, responsibility, and job ownership.

Conclusion

Liking someone in an interview has no bearing on how well they will do on the job. You cannot rely on the personal impressions you get from candidates because impressions are only a measure of how articulate candidates are and whether or not they have good social skills. In order to hire candidates who will actually be good workers for you, your interview process must be structured, systematic, and validated. You have to ask all candidates the same questions and you have to base them on a precise candidate profile and an accurate, up-to-date job description. The questions must be linked to the factors predictive of job success, including job skills and intangible traits like motivation and emotional intelligence. You must carefully document interview results in order to make valid comparisons.

It is imperative that your interviewers be trained and have good people skills. They can single-handedly make or break a candidate's experience with your company. Doing the "little things" when you interview Gen Y can make a big difference. They are sensitive to the personal touch. At some point during the interview, it is vital to ask about the Gen Yer's personal goals and vision. This is a great opportunity to link your goals and theirs. How you treat candidates before and after the interview can affect your overall reputation, particularly with Gen Y.

It is essential to help Gen Y acquire a realistic expectation of the job. Being honest and up-front, about potential negatives in the future job is the best way to prepare new hires for the challenges and imperfections that will come. Your thoroughnesss will help them stay the course once they are on board.

Name: Megan
Location: Northeast
Age: 23

Megan's background:

- graduated from a public university with a bachelor of science in communications

- Dean's List student

- during college secured several high profile internships

- very active in community service

Megan always knew she would attend college but the question was where. When her two brothers enrolled in the same school she would often visit them and grew very comfortable with the campus. When her time came to choose a college the choice was easy. "I was very familiar with the campus and the area. My brothers both had good experiences so it was a natural fit for me," said Megan.

"I wanted to major in something broad, like communications, so I would have a variety of options when I graduated," Megan explained. "The University is well respected for their program and I was able to experience several outstanding internships in radio, television, and event planning and promotions. All in all it was a great experience."

When Megan thinks about her future, much like how she chose her college, she is looking for a degree of comfort and stability. She sees no reason to be a job jumper. "Ten years from now I would really like to be with the same company. I don't want to job shop. If I can grow here and take on additional responsibility, why leave?" Megan asks.

There is one demotivator that would cause Megan to leave a job…negativity. She feels constructive criticism is essential to personal and professional growth, but constant negative feedback drains her energy. She witnessed this in her last job and realized the impact it had on her and her peers. In fact, she sites this issue as the biggest reason for the turnover her prior company experienced.

Megan thinks a good boss is someone who is:
- not a pushover
- willing to listen
- capable of having fun
- willing to help an employee when an issue arises
- a strong leader

Chapter 14

Onboarding Gen Y — Orientation and Training

Joe, age 24, was excited about his first day of work. The company looked good and he had liked the people he had met when he was recruited and interviewed. He had high hopes that the job would be challenging and a learning experience, but he didn't really know what to expect. When Joe reported for work, the day turned into a maze of faces, places, and random information. He filled out a lot of forms, met a lot of new people, and was assigned a desk. He spent most of the day watching a video about the company and reviewing several binders of product information. Although everyone was very nice, he never did see the people who had recruited or interviewed him. As the day progressed he felt more and more overwhelmed and less and less enthusiastic. He was exhausted by the end of the day. When his parents asked him how

259

the day went, Joe's dispirited response was: "What did I get myself into?"

What went wrong? Joe experienced a first day at work that would turn anyone off. It was impersonal, disorganized, and overwhelming. The company did not establish a personal connection that was welcoming. Joe met too many new people and the ones with whom he had developed a preliminary connection (through recruiting and interviewing) never reconnected with him. Watching a video about the company was no substitute for a personal tour and introduction. At his desk, Joe found a stack of paperwork to fill out and a pile of literature to review — no human connection there either. He was not asked about his goals, his job expectations, or even if he had any questions. He left at the end of the day with no idea of what was expected of him tomorrow. In fact, Joe was so discouraged that he may not show up tomorrow.

First Impressions Matter

The impressions Gen Y receives in the first few days will be powerful and hard to change. This is a unique "imprinting" period. As the old saying goes, you only get one chance to make a first impression. If you don't treat Gen Y right from the outset, you could fatally jeopardize the employment relationship.

Without enough personal contact, Gen Y will feel as if they are being processed. Rather than feeling like welcome newcomers, they will start out the job feeling like numbers or cogs in an impersonal machine. Overwhelming Gen Yers with paperwork and bureaucracy is demoralizing and de-motivating. First days that are hectic and confusing will leave Gen Yers exhausted — and they haven't even done any work yet. They will get through the days on adrenaline and then they'll crash. This is not the best way to make people feel welcome in new jobs. It can give any job an unpleasant, impersonal image.

Interview

Chris Martin
West Virginia University

Chris Martin is the Vice President for University Relations at West Virginia University.

Martin was named the West Virginia Professor of the Year, and a winner of the 1997-98 WVU Foundation Award for Outstanding Teaching. As dean, Martin established the nation's first online master's program in Integrated Marketing Communications. Martin speaks and consults nationally on writing, reporting, and mass communications.

With all of your communications background, what do you do differently today to get your message across?

Communicating with our current and prospective students is very different than 15 to 20 years ago. The marketing we do now is so customized, even personalized. Without this customization, Gen Y feels like they're not getting the attention they're entitled to and deserve.

Students now have a consumer mentality. We look at marketing now as "how do we get people to engage?" "Consumer" is not a dirty word anymore. Marketing is just building a conversation.

What differences have you seen between students in the mid-1980s and today's students?

Students in the late '80s and early '90s were more cynical, distrustful, and "lone wolf" types. They didn't always work well in groups. Today's students are joiners and they are more community oriented. It was harder in the '80s to get students to join classroom communities. Today it is much easier.

Students today are much more dependent and look to their parents for advice and help. In the '80s, college was a part of the letting-go process for parents. Today parents are there for every minute and every need.

Any advice you would offer leaders regarding communications?

Review all of your communications pieces and forums. Do they get Gen Y engaged? If not, it is time to re-address your materials and forums.

What differences have you seen in your interactions with Gen Y?

Gen Y wants, and some would agree, needs, attention. They do not want credit for something they didn't do, just recognition for things they did accomplish. In many ways, they want others to pay attention to them.

Many experienced managers view this as coddling. It isn't. It is listening to them and paying attention to them. Employers will lose people if they don't understand this new paradigm. Leaders need to identify the best and the brightest early on and give them time, attention, and feedback.

My advice to business leaders would be that Gen Y, more than any other group, works for meaning, not money. They want a sense that they are part of an important mission. Pay attention to…and recognize their contribution to the mission…regularly.

As you see students enter the work world, what differences do you see in their approach to their careers?

This is not a generation that will allow themselves to be put into a position where they have to make hard choices between their lives and their jobs. More than any group I have seen, Gen Y values family and friends equal to or more than career. Success is not as simple to them as getting ahead at work. It is more complex and requires balancing their entire lives.

I would tell leaders that their culture has to be such that you expect people to work hard and produce a good work product, but not at the sacrifice of their personal lives.

Any last points you think leaders should know?

Probably just two things. First, people should know that Gen Y expects to be coached. I think that is such a wonderful opportunity for leaders. Second, people need to know young folks don't trust leaders who do not show vulnerability. Leaders need to be honest and not afraid to show some vulnerability. The simplest way to do this is to ask for input and then listen. That simple act shows you don't think you know everything about everything.

The Basics

Orienting Gen Y

Both research and common sense support the fact that orientation has a direct impact on future productivity, performance, and job satisfaction. Typical orientations give new workers a tour of the facility, introduce them to a lot of people in a short time, make them sign a bunch of forms, and give them still more material to read later. This is exactly what happened in the above scenario with Joe, and it was disastrous. Companies try to do too much too soon. Joe was bombarded with information. It was too much to process and it left him feeling overwhelmed, not welcomed. Orientation can also be boring and repetitive for the people conducting it. This emotion will be conveyed to the new hires.

One of the secrets to a better orientation is not to try to do everything at once. Keep the feeling of being *processed* to a minimum. Fill out as many of the routine forms for new Gen Y employees as you can. Spread the required material over a period of time. Don't introduce them to everyone in a single day. Introduce the full details slowly.

We should also note that this recommendation of gradualism does not mean that Gen Y should not be given work immediately. If you have tasks that they can do, assign them. They like to work. Having a job to do gives them a focus outside themselves that can carry them through a lot of boring orientation. They want to contribute and be challenged. In the process of working, they will meet coworkers, learn new things, and understand procedures in a more natural context than through any orientation.

A Sample Orientation

The following are critical components of a successful Gen Y orientation program:

Critical Component #1: Welcome Gen Y

There should be some sort of official welcome for Gen Y on the first day of work. You need to create a warm human connection to the company. This is where many orientations go wrong. They are so busy conveying information that they forget to make the human connection. People relate to people. Something as simple as a warm smile with good eye contact and a positive, personal word will make a difference.

Meet Gen Y at the door on Day One and be sure they see all the familiar faces they already know. Employees who recruited them and interviewed them must make a point of meeting and greeting them again. Gen Y might actually feel abandoned if those familiar people do not check in. Unless there is an immediate personal connection, they will reach a quick conclusion that they don't matter to your company.

Really listen to what Gen Y is saying, particularly in those first days. Watch your unconscious negative behavioral tendencies. As discussed in Chapter 5, you may be too talkative, interrupt, or display other negative behaviors. Review your "game film' and control these negative tendencies.

Critical Component #2:
Understand Gen Y's Perspective

Finding Their Work Identity

During the early months of the job, Gen Yers are testing the reality of their careers. Their self-concept is still malleable so they're open to input from the job. They want to learn what the job can tell them about themselves. At this point, earlier generations were very concerned with acceptance by the organization. Gen Y is less worried about trying to please the organization. They will be looking for initial work assignments that are challenging and stimulating, and that complement their self-images.

Gen Y will also be exploring your company as a new reference group. They want to be part of the group, to understand the norms of the group and what is expected of them. There is a delicate balance here between the organization forcing new beliefs on Gen Y, and Gen Y's need to assimilate to the new group. If they feel pressured, they will resist. Gen Y doesn't want your organization to try to dominate their personalities, but they are willing to learn and change when they believe in the organization.

After a year or so on the job, Gen Y's emphasis will change from exploring themselves in the new role to looking to be part of something worthwhile and to achieving something to make their own mark. They will become assimilated and committed to your organization if they think they're making contributions and are being appreciated. They're still in the process of solidifying their career choices and developing their occupational self-images.

Overwhelmed by Information

It is important to understand how easily Gen Y can feel overwhelmed in the beginning. This is just a partial list of some of the new things they will be struggling to learn:

- position/job description
- manager/supervisor's name
- explanation of your company and philosophy
- list of your key people and their jobs

- co-workers' names
- company directory
- retirement/pension/ 401k arrangements
- pay, bonuses, and raises

- payroll procedures: when paid, deductions, etc.
- human resources issues
- union delegate and information if applicable
- recycling or environmental programs

- expense account procedures
- work and break times
- awards or incentive programs
- safety issues

- ombudsman or whistle-blowing procedures
- safety incident reporting procedures
- workers compensation claims
- layout of facility

- rules/procedures for using phone
- drug and alcohol policies and any testing
- conditions for termination (for example, at-will employment)
- quality management or other programs

- hours and how recorded (for example, flex or comp time)
- contacts for emergencies after hours
- sexual harassment policy
- parking
- travel procedures and policies
- lunch facilities
- locker rooms
- tools and equipment
- vacation policies
- sick leave policies

Not all jobs will involve all of the above, but most will include the majority of them. While this list seems detailed, there are many more items that have been left out, including where the bathrooms are! Also, many of the items have both physical and social components to learn. For example, a new employee has to learn what time lunch is, where the lunchroom is, how the cafeteria works and so forth. That's the easy part. The more stressful part is the frequently unspoken social aspects of the lunchroom — for example, whether certain groups have staked out certain tables or the etiquette of joining people already at a table.

There is a lot that will be novel to your new Gen Yers. Help them integrate and process it all. Be sensitive to the time it will naturally take for them to become oriented. Be as helpful and attentive as possible.

KEY POINT

Being a new employee can be overwhelming for anyone.

Critical Component #3:
Communicate Your Expectations

After you have listened to Gen Y's initial thoughts and impressions, and answered their immediate questions, use these early days to give Gen Y important messages of your own. You must communicate the following messages to Gen Y early and often:

Re-Sell Your Brand

While Gen Y needs job descriptions and technical information, this is also the time to tell Gen Y what your organization stands for and to enlist them to represent your standards. Gen Y can be motivated to excel when they believe in what you're doing. Re-sell your brand to new employees and tell them how they can contribute.

Re-Sell Your Vision

Take the time in your early discussions with your new Gen Y employees to tell them again what your company vision is. Ask them what their vision is and what their goals are. Show them how their vision and yours are linked. Reinforce your firm belief that they can achieve their goals by working with you in your organization.

Establish Your Leadership

One of the more intriguing discoveries we uncovered in our research is the fact that Gen Y *wants to be led*. They are looking for strong leaders and while Gen Y may push, the do not respect pushovers. It is important for leaders to set the standards early. What are your corporate values? Discuss these with your new hires. What are your cultural norms? Make sure these norms, things like being on time, follow up, respecting people's space, respecting peoples time and proper appearance are understood and are "non negotiable."

Expand Gen Y's Horizon

As we have discussed throughout this book, Gen Y has a different mindset about commitment to an organization because of their increased freedom and lack of familial responsibilities. They are looking for a one- to two-year work experience, not a long-term commitment. Your challenge is to stretch Gen Y's horizon, and the sooner you start doing that, the better. Help them identify and commit to a goal that is bigger than a one- to two-year commitment. As we will discuss below, you will want to engage them as soon as possible in projects that are longer term.

Coach's Corner

Setting Expectations

Starting any new program or project requires commitment if the desired change is to take hold. Setting the tone is critical. I firmly believe the messages leaders send in the early stages may be the most important communications of all.

I clearly recall my first team meeting at NC State. There was to be an announcement that morning about my appointment, and Todd Turner, the Athletic director, wanted to introduce me to the team first. He called a players' meeting at 7:30 in the morning before classes were to start.

When we arrived for the meeting, there were only a few players there by 7:30. We closed the door to the meeting room and began promptly at 7:30, even though many players hadn't arrived. Sure enough, shortly thereafter guys started knocking on the door. We answered the door and informed them the meeting had already started and they weren't allowed in. We finished the meeting and then let it be known that, as a team, we were in this together and being on time was critical.

The guys who were on time needed to get word to the others that since we all were not on time, we would all meet at 5:00 AM the next morning and run as a team. Let's just say the next morning we had a very challenging workout. Let's also say that we set the expectation: Punctuality is important.

As the spring semester came to an end, on more than one occasion, somebody from campus would bring it to our attention that they saw a basketball player running on campus to a study hall or class. They didn't want to be late.

It sure would have been easier to let the players into the room a little later. After all, it was our first meeting. However, it would not have set the expectation that it was important to be on time. We were serious, and everyone understood it.

Critical Component #4:
Assign Gen Y Meaningful Work

Get Gen Y involved with something worthwhile the first day. Too many companies use a routine approach and figure that they will give newcomers a chance to find their footing before putting too much on their plates. In fact, Gen Y needs to know they have something important to do on Day One. They should be able to go home and tell people, "I critiqued the company website" or something similar. It shouldn't be a major project that they are clearly not qualified for, but it can be support work linked to a larger, long-term project that they will be able to contribute to at a higher level later.

Let Gen Y be part of a team that is tackling something strategically important and also long-term. Is there something you have wanted to accomplish but have not had the time or resources to complete? Have you been thinking about conducting a customer survey, developing your newsletter, or other lengthy project? Introduce your Gen Yer to this meaningful assignment right away and get them interested in their new job on Day One. Give them something to look forward to on Day Two. As Hal Adler, president of the Great Place to Work Institute, says, "The most important anniversary for workers is the end of day one!"

Critical Component #5: Promise Feedback and Deliver It

Gen Y wants feedback and appreciation. This issue has been addressed in depth. Baby Boomer bosses may operate by the old rule that as long as they don't say anything, everything is fine — no news is good news. This will not work for Gen Y. To get a supportive message across, you have to send out three times the feedback that you think is necessary, and you have to say ten positive statements for every negative one. We're all oversensitive to negative feedback, but Gen Y on a new job is more so.

While daily feedback may sound like too much, Gen Y would like to be acknowledged every time they do something well. It's a little like saying thank you. If you automatically acknowledge a job well done, Gen Y will appreciate it and develop a bond with you and your organization.

As early as possible, sit down with your new Gen Y employee and agree upon a review schedule. Will you have a one-on-one every two weeks? Once a month? Every two months? If on Day One you set the date for a future performance management review, Gen Y will know that you are serious about monitoring their progress and listening to their ideas and concerns. Make the appointment and keep it.

Consultant's
Corner

Audit Your Material

There are many little adjustments you can make that can have a big impact. The first suggestion we always make to our clients is to audit your training materials.

A large insurance firm hired us to audit their onboarding process and to develop an aggressive retention strategy. It seemed as if there were one or two people quitting each new-hire class in the first week. In fact, their turnover rate was well over 80% for all new hires in the first year.

When we audited the new-hire training materials, we made several small adjustments that produced significant results. Previously, in the first hour on the job, every new hire received a 6-inch thick training manual for the next two week's training. These new employees were overwhelmed before they even started.

No matter how much material was covered during the training day, folks could not help but focus on what still needed to be done.

We suggested each day's section be handed out in the morning, prior to the start of training. This way, folks felt a sense of accomplishment at the end of the day, versus a sense of being overwhelmed.

The next thing we suggested was to go through the manuals and remove all redundant material. By simply streamlining the workbooks, it saved many wasted pages and pointless reading.

Finally, our client reformatted the workbooks to reflect their image and an updated brand. The fresh look was much more user-friendly and appealing to the learner.

It is natural for people to feel a sense of accomplishment when they successfully finish a project or task. This is also true with your initial training. By piecing out the material, you will allow your new employees to feel as if they are accomplishing something right away.

There is another major leadership benefit to this approach. As a leader, you will be sending a message of accountability and results versus one of unrealistic expectations. Subliminally you will be saying, "We get things done here," and not "You will always be fighting an uphill battle."

Critical Component #6:
Train the Way Gen Y Prefers to Be Trained

Most people who plan and deliver training are not specialists. They have to take care of training on top of their regular duties. Many of them are neither recognized nor rewarded for their training work. Even people with degrees in education are often not prepared to deliver training to adults in a work setting.

> **"There is probably nothing more essential...and more elusive...than great training for employees. Knowing how younger generations learn best will help you develop the next great leaders in your organizations."**
> —TRAININGTIME.COM

In prior years, companies did well enough with their training. Employees came and went and things got done. In the Gen Y era of hiring, a more systematic approach to training is necessary. It is important to treat your training program as a valuable asset. Your current Baby Boomer employees possess critical knowledge capital that can be passed on to Gen Y through great training programs. The type of job training your Gen Y employees need will vary depending on the job. Training will vary from informal — "watch how I do it" — to classroom. Many organizations get by without any real training. Newcomers simply learn by doing. Some organizations look at training as a costly necessity. They have to bring workers' skills up to a certain level to utilize them. Other organizations look at training as an investment. For instance, Motorola says that for every dollar they spend on training they get a return of ten times their money.

Five Reasons for Training

There are at least five related purposes for training:

1. The main purpose is to help workers deal with practical issues and problems — to do their jobs better. This basic purpose of training is intended to improve skills and knowledge in individuals.

2. The parallel reason for training, from the organizational side, is to help the organization survive, prosper, and change. Training also makes the organization stronger and more versatile. It helps individuals prepare for change as they train for future jobs or tasks.

3. In a related vein, training can simply be part of a growth plan for individuals — almost an end in itself.

4. Training can be used to look at broader issues that affect the organization, such as future scenario planning or brainstorming.

5. Finally, training can affect values and philosophies, which can create change in goals, policies, or beliefs. For instance, some organizations are "going green" in a sincere belief that this will affect the world and their companies for the better.

At another level, all the goals of training can be summarized as creating change for the better.

The Problem with Training

The problem with most training programs is that they follow models we learned in school. The teacher-to-student model is an authority lecturing to a beginner. It is a parent telling a child what to do. It is associated with powerlessness and boredom.

The problem with this child-teacher learning model is that it gets in the way of more useful role modeling and self-motivated learning approaches. You want people who think for themselves and ask questions, but this interferes with "covering the lesson" and slows down the teacher and the class.

For many decades school systems emphasized the importance of learning answers, not the importance of asking questions. These educational practices were useful in the old days for producing workers who could be cogs in an assembly line. But times have changed. You need employees who think for themselves, are self-motivated, and who challenge the standard way of doing things.

Hewlett-Packard says that they want workers who don't "come to work waiting for someone to tell [them] what to do today. Different people work in different ways to reach a common objective. We focus on people reaching a high level of success, not on how people accomplish their objectives."

The way that adults learn best is by doing. This involves all the senses, is more interesting, and is directly relevant. When training Gen Y employees, let them learn the basics in a self-paced manner such as a computer program. Then give them good role models and a safe environment to learn and make mistakes.

Learning Styles Overview

Of course it is obvious, but most training programs generally ignore it. Different learners prefer to learn and process information in different ways.

Reasons for Learning

People want to know *why* is this information important, and why do I need to know it. Some folks learn best when the information is timely and practical. These folks want to use the information immediately. Other learners are quite comfortable, and actually prefer to learn new information that may not be needed at the moment. As long as the information is new and interesting, immediate practical application is not a concern *for them.*

Learning Presentation

Some learners are uncomfortable with a free-flowing delivery of information. Here is where we see most subject matter experts stumble. There is a tendency for many experienced folks to "wing it" and fail to present the information in a logical order or format. Many of your Gen Y learners will be put off by this approach. Gen Y may well judge the presenter to be unprepared and uncaring.

Other learners actually prefer a more open structure. This allows them to organize the information the way they want. Once several pieces of information are presented, these learners start to decide what is relevant and what is not. Gen Y learners with this preference will be more tolerant of a free-flowing presentation.

Learning Involvement

Not surprisingly, learners prefer different ways to be involved in the learning process. Some learners prefer to be more active in the process while others prefer to be passive learners. Active learners prefer more discussion, breakouts, and variety. Passive learners prefer to work alone and have time to think and process the information being delivered.

Consultant's
Corner

Learning Styles

One of our clients was experiencing a significant (40+%) turnover rate of new employees *during* and *immediately following* the initial training period. We reviewed all of their materials and found that all of them were geared specifically for learners who preferred less structure and a more participative approach.

We conducted a survey of previous employees and found the majority (almost all) of the folks who left during or immediately following training preferred the opposite style. These folks were more structured and desired less group activity. Once we understood the issues, the training material was redesigned to engage both types of learners. Today, it is rare that anyone leaves the company during the initial training period.

Keep Focused

Your goal is to develop self-motivated, self-managing employees who seek out learning opportunities. This is how you will develop more experts within your firm. Of course, these learners tend to disrupt the status quo with their questions and with wanting to try new things.

Many training programs amount to giving the least training necessary in the shortest time so that a newcomer can get started on the job, along with instructions to a supervisor or co-worker to "answer their questions." Gen Y likes to learn by doing, and they like training. Try setting up your training program as an "opportunity" rather than a "requirement." In other words, after their basic training, allow them to continue learning new skills — even in advance of what their job requires. They will feel they have control and that they can grow as people.

If Gen Y can help with their own training, so much the better. For instance, if they're in a group, they can role play. If they're alone, they can keep notes on the training to critique it later. Keep them personally involved.

KEY POINT
Generation Y likes to be trained differently.

Cross-Training Gen Y

Cross-training involves giving an employee instruction in different departments and functions than the ones they are hired for. Gen Y are often interested in this because it is challenging and expands their learning. Cross-training gives the company the normal advantages of having workers familiar with a variety of jobs, and supports cross-fertilization of ideas. It also builds informal channels of communication. Some companies frown on this because people will go outside "official" channels. However, wise companies realize that allowing people to call directly to a friend in the shipping department can build overall company identity and help crucial work get done faster.

For Gen Y, cross-training allows them to feel more in the know. It gives them a more complete view of the company and helps them clarify their interests and skills. If you want fresh ideas in your organization, involving new workers immediately is the way to do it. Cross-training may occasionally cause newcomers to want to transfer to another department, but this is preferable to having an employee leave. You must be open to the idea that Gen Y might want to work in a different department; you would then get an employee who stays longer.

*Consultant's
Corner*

Process Documentation

All organizations, big or small, have a vast amount of knowledge capital to draw upon. Now consider the fact that every 8.5 seconds, someone turns age 55. Have you captured that knowledge capital — those best practices — that will soon be leaving your employ? Can you confidently answer these even tougher questions?

- Has your information technology department documented a plan for business continuity if all systems fail?

- If your payroll system crashed, do you have backup training and materials to process payroll promptly?

- If next month you must announce the elimination of an entire department, could your organization quickly fill the gaps?

- Better scenario — you are acquiring 300 employees in two months as a result of a planned acquisition....Do you have materials (procedures, guides for account receivable, inventory management, work orders, job costing, supply chain management, procurement, and so on) to onboard the new employees so they not only understand your culture, but how to fulfill their daily responsibilities?

- Your delivery teams have a proprietary process that they follow for all client projects — are materials readily available to ensure a consistent approach for all client delivery?

Interestingly enough, when we have worked with clients to document best practices for future employees, there has always been a huge side benefit. The experienced employees who served as experts expressed pride in knowing they would be helping the next generation succeed.

Teacher Training

Gen Y may also be attracted to "teacher training." This means giving them a chance to re-teach things they've learned to the next class of trainees. Teaching something is one of the best ways to learn it. Knowing you will be teaching the material in the future causes you to pay attention and ask key questions during training. Actually teaching forces you to organize the material in a logical way and helps you remember it.

Normally, new workers are not used for teaching. After all you have people with far more experience around. However, in many cases, the freshness that newcomers bring to a task will communicate more enthusiasm and interest than will a jaded expert. Other new workers may respond best to people who are closest to their own status. This can work well with Gen Y.

Conclusion

Remember that first impressions matter. When Gen Y new hires arrive, give them a warm welcome and something meaningful to do. Let Gen Yers know that you will be giving them feedback and answering their questions.

As soon as possible, find out what Gen Yers' goals and vision are and link them to those of your organization. Make sure your Gen Xer and Baby Boomer employees know that their success also depends upon the success of the new Gen Y teammates. Expand Gen Yers' horizons by introducing them to long-term, strategically important projects that they can be a part of at an entry level. Do not overwhelm them with information and endless paperwork.

Gen Yers' training should involve the latest technology and hands-on "learning by doing." Gen Yers will respond well to a variety of training methods including cross-training and teacher training. Excellent orientation and training programs geared to Gen Y will help them connect with your organization's vision, become productive sooner, fit in better with co-workers, and start the job with positive attitudes.

KEY POINT
A well thought out onboarding process is *crucial* for connecting a new employee to your organization.

Name: Joseph
Location: Midwest
Age: 30

Joseph's background:

- graduated from a private university with a double major in accounting and business

- varsity athlete and four-year starter

- won several academic and sports awards

- upon graduation became an auditor for the Department of Defense

Joseph joined the Department of Defense right out of college, and eight years later he is still there. He has had three different positions in that time and is currently considering his second relocation.

"I know Gen Y has the reputation for taking a job only as a stepping stone to look for the next thing," Joseph says. "In reality, I know I can further myself within my current situation. I don't need to jump around from organization to organization."

Joesph wants to advance his career, but he does not see the need to change for change's sake. As long as he is provided an opportunity to grow, he is content.

Joseph would consider making a change if an opportunity presented itself in an area he was passionate about. "I would consider a move to sports management, but I am not looking. I say considering because even that is not certain.

Family comes first, and my first decision would be based on what is best for my family." For Joe, his career is important, but family is the priority.

Joseph feels a good leader is someone who:

- listens to his team before jumping to a conclusion
- realizes that your title does not make you right all of the time
- helps his or her team get to the next level
- asks, "What can I do to help my staff get better and advance?"
- respects family situations
- is not a pushover
- challenges me and puts me in my place when I need it
- is willing to put his neck on the line for his team

Chapter 15

Tactics for Alignment: Integrating Gen Y

This and the next chapter follow from the previous ones, but they are organized a little differently. They are overviews of much of the book. They can also be used separately as an overview for employees or for training. They include thought starters for creating your recruitment and retention strategies. By developing these strategies you are taking the next step toward your organizational alignment. Also included are additional case studies of success strategies that can be applied by businesses.

Most companies that want to onboard new employees will focus on formal orientation programs. However, there are a number of other things you can do to help Gen Y, both before and after they come aboard.

You should begin to establish a welcoming connection with your Gen Y employees well before they show up on your doorstep for their first day of work.

Pre-Acceptance Communication

There will be a period of time after you have extended an offer but before Gen Y has accepted. Use this time to communicate with your candidate. Remember the role of their large circles of influence. Gen Yers may still be questioning some things, so make the communications interesting and accessible to the broader audience of influencers. Put them on your mailing list and, to every extent possible, personalize the information.

If you had summer interns who are now back in college, stay in touch with them. Keep them on your mailing list. Send them company updates. If they are great candidates and you are very interested in them, invite them to your company Christmas party.

The failure to communicate actually is a communication. It's the message: "We don't care about you!" This is not the message you want to give to Gen Y at any point in the recruiting or hiring process.

KEY POINT

Get a head start connecting with new employees before they come on board.

*Consultant's
Corner*

Early Signing Period

A tip we have shared with many of our clients is to take advantage of the "early signing period." If you have an impressive summer intern you want to hire after he or she graduates, do it now. Offer them a job predicated upon successful graduation. By being proactive, you may well eliminate your competition for this candidate. Once you make the offer and receive a commitment, be sure to constantly stay in touch with them while they're still in school.

Post-Acceptance Communication

Once a Gen Y candidate has accepted your offer, continue the communication. Again, silence speaks volumes. Every time you communicate is an opportunity to market your company brand and vision. Keep future employees abreast of company developments. Invite them to all company functions, parties, and picnics so they'll feel they're a part of the team.

As their first day approaches, think about the little things. Do they know how to get to your office, where to park, who their first contact will be? Confirm the day and time they are expected to be there. Give them a brief overview of the first day. If they are moving from out of town, be sure your HR department is helping them find a place to live. Just as you were attentive to the little things when you were interviewing, you need to maintain this concern for Gen Y.

Coach's Corner

Post-Acceptance Communication

While I was at North Carolina State, we recruited a young man, Engin Atsur, from Istanbul, Turkey. Engin committed and signed to play with us in the fall of his final year in high school. I, and one of our assistant coaches, Mark Phelps, went over to Istanbul in May. We spent 4 days together with Engin and his family touring the city, going out to dinner, and just hanging out so that we could get a better appreciation of where Engin was from, what his culture was like, and, most important, so that we could continue build our relationship.

Inevitably, people tend to feel more appreciated and more valued during the recruiting process when multiple schools are courting them than they do once they have signed on with one team. Perhaps we can't totally prevent those feelings, but we want to make sure that people always feel appreciated, valued, and deserving of our good will and attention, so we really believe that *the most important recruits we have are the players already on our team.* Even at that point, when Engin had signed and was already committed to NC State, we still went over and spent really good time with him and his family.

Prepare Your Current Employees for Gen Y

Are your current employees ready for the new Gen Y employees? As discussed in Chapter 2, Gen Y has been unfairly stereotyped. It is crucial that these stereotypes do not exist in your organization or in the hearts and minds of your employees. If your organization has a negative view of Gen Y, your new Gen Y hires will pick up on it, and it will hurt opportunities for team building.

It is incumbent upon you as a leader to check the pulse of your organization on this issue. How do your current employees feel about Gen Y? Have they bought into the stereotypes and misconceptions about Gen Y? What are their expectations for these future employees? Are they dreading working with them or looking forward to it? Do they understand why Gen Y is the way they are and what makes them "tick?" Do they understand the skills Gen Y brings with them to the company? And, most importantly, can they accept Gen Y's differences and work with them?

KEY POINT

Do whatever you need to do to eliminate prejudice before your new Gen Y employees arrive!

Knowledge Transfer

While you are orienting your existing employees to positively welcome Gen Y hires, you can also be laying the groundwork for another important job. You need to set up a formal knowledge transfer program that passes important information held by your most experienced workers to Gen X and Gen Y employees. If you don't act, valuable knowledge capital in your organization will be lost as people retire. Gen Yers will be particularly interest in receiving this knowledge. You can begin the transfer as you aid their assimilation.

Consultant's
Corner

A Knowledge Transfer Example

Recently we were hired by a multinational construction company to develop their internal training program. For the past several years senior management lost sight of mentoring and developing the next group of leaders. Ownership realized that, in a few years, they would not have enough "ready-now" project managers and superintendents.

The challenge was to create a program that fast-tracked a group of young succession candidates (the average age was 27). Our firm had the expertise to customize the leadership, supervisory, and communication skills necessary, but we are not construction experts.

In order to capture the construction knowledge needed, we turned to the internal subject matter experts (SMEs).

These folks all had 25 or more years of experience and at least 10 years of senior management experience. To a person, each of them understood the need to create this training program and the importance of passing along their knowledge capital.

We quickly realized that in spite of this intellectual understanding, the experienced managers had a difficult time accepting it emotionally. During our interviews, meetings, and conversations each of them wasted a great deal of time and energy complaining about "these kids." Everyone talked about "in my day we just went out there and did it; that's how you learn."

In addition to interviewing the managers, we also interviewed the high-potential succession candidates. If we were to succeed, we needed to know what made them tick. Here are some actual quotes from each of the groups:

Managers	*High Potential Candidates*
"If you want to be a superintendent, you need to realize you'll have to move every three years. In my day that was understood. To work here, you move; we had no choice. These kids are afraid to pick up and go."	"I don't want to be forced to move every few years. I will if I see an exciting opportunity. These guys had to move. I don't. What they don't understand is I'm constantly contacted by other local firms."
"I've been here 32 years and still don't control where I'll be next year. Your family just has to understand."	"I'll never give up control of my life and force my family to move just because they say so. I'll go to grad school if I have to."

"My family is settled here now, we just had grandkids. I come home every other week for a few days."

"I'll never put myself in the position of only seeing my family a few days a month."

While it was challenging, we were able to get the SMEs to realize the differences between the groups. Ultimately they stopped emoting and pressing their values on the succession candidates. As importantly, we were able to ensure there was no "emotional leakage" during the training program. Once the experienced managers stopped emoting and wasting time, they were able to connect better to the succession candidates. A very interesting side benefit occurred — several deep friendships and mentoring relationships developed naturally.

Results — Turnover is down dramatically and other high potential candidates from outside the firm are looking to be a part of their organization. Over 50% of the candidates did relocate and follow-up interviews confirmed it was because they felt they were given a choice. Finally, several of the SMEs have retired but continue to act as trainers and mentors in the program!

Knowledge transfer is one of the biggest issues most organizations will face as Baby Boomers begin to retire. We have seen many companies try to combat this by taking subject-matter experts and having them train new folks.

We believe this is a great strategy, with one key suggestion. Provide your subject-matter experts with some training on how to train. Most times people will train the way they like to be trained or the way they were trained, regardless of the audience's learning preference.

At a minimum, give your subject-matter experts information about learning styles. There are also many very good assessments your trainers can take to find out their own learning preferences. Similar to the personal profiles we discussed earlier, these learning-style assessments will help your folks adapt, once they know it is necessary.

KEY POINT
Your experienced employees have unique knowledge that needs to be passed on.

Job Shadowing

Job shadowing is an interesting method for both onboarding Gen Y and transferring expertise within your organization. It can be combined with a buddy system or a mentor approach, depending on the relative seniority of the people involved. For Gen Yers who are new on the job, it is an excellent way of having them try out a position, get cross-trained, and see career options.

As more and more Boomers retire, Gen Xers and Gen Yers need to take their place. Job shadowing is an excellent way to pass on knowledge from one generation to another. Sometimes companies don't want to make the investment of two people working on the same projects. For example, we know of a case where an experienced engineer was getting ready to retire and told the company that if they'd assign a young engineer to him, he'd train him to be his replacement. At his level, he was coordinating projects internationally and part of his success was in knowing people in different countries. If you don't show new people "where the bodies were buried," these interpersonal contacts are lost to the next generation. The company didn't want to invest in a young engineer for a few months. Sure enough, after a couple of years they had to hire the old engineer back as a high-priced consultant to show them what they needed to know about a couple of jobs.

Being a mentor or being job shadowed is flattering to your Baby Boomers, Gen Xers, and Gen Yers. It shows everyone that you value them for their expertise or projected expertise. If you have retiring people with skills and contacts, now is a perfect time to capture their knowledge for your organization while you train the next generation.

Ways to Help Gen Y Assimilate

Have a Plan

You must strategize before new hires arrive. Who are your ambassadors? Your mentors? Your buddies? How should they be interacting with new Gen Y employees? You must have people in place to help the new hires connect with the team.

Research shows that newcomers to groups tend to band together. When they are uncertain about the situation, they will bond with anyone who even seems to be in their same situation. Such newcomer bonding can make your new Gen Y workers feel more in control and safe in a strange environment — your company. However, the norms they develop may not be the norms you want.

Left to their own devices, new Gen Y employees will form a group with each other and they can develop an "us versus them" mentality. If one Gen Yer is dissatisfied, the rest may be disproportionately influenced. Your goal is to help new Gen Y hires form relationships with many employees so that the decision of one Gen Y hire will not automatically influence them all.

Be aware of how strong this effect can be and make sure that your new workers are influenced the way you want them to be. It's very important that you create programs that link newcomers to positive influences and role models. If you do these things before Gen Y arrives, you will have positioned your organization to effectively and successfully onboard Gen Y.

Utilize Your Internal Goodwill Ambassadors

Many groups like Chambers of Commerce utilize "ambassadors" to help them recruit and orient new members. Your ambassadors are analogous to what foreign ambassadors do — communicate for you to others. They can also be tasked to recruit Gen Y. For your ambassadors, you need friendly, outgoing people who want to spend some time with newcomers. While there can be overlap with people who become mentors later, ambassadors are particularly helpful during the early stages. A buddy system can be similar, but the buddies are often not trained or coordinated. Of course, Gen Yers can make excellent ambassadors for future Gen Y hires.

Mentors

It has been said that a mentor is someone who's hindsight becomes your foresight!

Research has shown that mentors can be very important for career success. Mentors are generally senior people who take a junior under their wing. While a mentor may be the mentee's formal boss, there are advantages to having someone serve as mentor who is more detached. Thus, the mentor can provide political advice, organizational information, and encouragement as an "objective" source. Mentoring often happens informally, on its own; however, companies should have a formal mentoring program to encourage this kind of practical training and role modeling. One thing that is sometimes overlooked is that multiple mentors can be useful. Some people can be helpful in some areas and others in quite different ones.

Have Gen Y Mentor YOU

Institute a reverse-mentoring program. Assign a Gen Yer to one of your Baby Boomer or Xer managers, or even to yourself. Allow the Gen Y employee to mentor you about their world, what's important, and how to connect with their generation.

Gen Y can give you a view of your organization, your customers, and your marketplace without the filters of

Reverse Mentoring

Jack Welch, author, past CEO of General Electric, and once the top-rated executive in America, pioneered reverse mentoring when he ordered hundreds of his top managers to create reverse-mentoring relationships with their newest employees. (At that time he was mainly interested in the new employees filling in their managers on technology.)

experience and preconceptions. Gen Y can give you a fresh perspective, and insights that you might never see on your own.

Buddy Systems

The buddy system is an old, worldwide, proven method of helping newcomers feel at home. It involves pairing a new worker with a coworker. Sometimes buddies happen naturally, but you'll want to set up a more official program to ensure that Gen Y gets the benefit of a friend to help them orient. You'll want to enlist buddies who represent the best of your organization and can serve as role models.

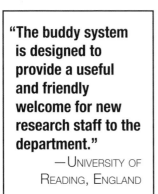

"The buddy system is designed to provide a useful and friendly welcome for new research staff to the department."

— UNIVERSITY OF READING, ENGLAND

A good buddy should be someone in close proximity to the newcomer so they can interact naturally. They should be patient "people persons" — individuals who have the knack of putting others at their ease and being nice.

A supervisor may not be able to deal immediately with every issue or question Gen Y raises. The newcomers may even feel hesitant about talking with their supervisors until they are more comfortable in their jobs. Buddies can handle many questions as they work with the newcomers. Buddies can communicate norms both directly and through their behavior. Buddies can also help Gen Yers fit in with the group and understand the realities of the job.

---

*Consultant's
Corner*

Conduct a Walk-Through

One thing we regularly do for our clients is a "walk-through" of their facilities. Oftentimes small changes can have a big impact on recruiting and retention. What we are looking for are the subtle messages the physical space sends.

- Where is customer parking?

- Where is executive parking?

- Where do new hires park?

- Who has the spaces closest to the door (or in the shade or undercover), and who has to park around back?

- Are new hires all in the same location or are they interacting with all of the employees?

It's not always the biggest adjustments that have the biggest impact.

Safety Training

Some specific types of training can be useful in the assimilation process as well for developing specific skills. For instance, new employees are more than twice as likely to have an accident as experienced workers. Lack of knowledge about procedures, and hesitation to ask for help, cause over 10% of new employees to be involved in some type of accident the first year on the job. The less time on the job, the more the danger. The first days, weeks, and months are the most critical times.

Gen Y workers will be at greater risk than seasoned workers. Sometimes it's because of the type of industry open to people without experience. High-risk jobs such as construction tend to create unfamiliar hazards for young workers. For instance, according to Canadian statistics, in the year 2000, young workers in Ontario construction were 24% more likely to be injured on the job than other age groups. According to *HR Magazine,* "New employees are involved in one in three workman's compensation accidents."

The other major risk factor for Gen Y is the lack of experience and training. New workers often try to create a good impression by working hard and fast. They can't recognize and assess hazards, and are reluctant to report unsafe conditions.

Safety training can be a good opportunity to establish rapport with Gen Y if it is presented for their benefit, not to reduce your insurance rates. According to research, when safety issues are included in new employee training programs, morale improves and the accident rate decreases. In other words, if you can show your concern for their well being during the training, they can learn something. Then you and they can be on the same side in terms of both wanting a safe working environment.

Customer Service Training

Like safety, customer service training is a good way to build rapport with Gen Y. Excellent customer service is something that every company wants. If you're willing to make great service a rallying point, Gen Y will be proud to get on board — if they know you're not doing it as a selfish, short-term marketing ploy. You have to be sincere in your support of such efforts.

Helping customers have a good experience makes workers feel good about their jobs and it makes their jobs more pleasant and easier. When workers go to bat for your customers, they help the customers, themselves, and the organization.

An extra benefit is that a good customer service program will include an aspect focusing on internal customers, which encourages employees to treat each other well.

Conclusion

There are many underutilized techniques to help assimilate newcomers. These include ambassadors, the buddy system, and mentoring Other regular training such as safety and customer service training can also help you connect new hires to your organization. It is vitally important that you nurture relationships between new Gen Y employees and soon-to-retire Baby Boomer employees. There must be a transfer of knowledge capital from your older employees to your younger ones. Job shadowing can also contribute to knowledge transfer while it orients and trains Gen Yers.

Chapter 16

Tactics for Alignment: Retaining Gen Y

According to PrincetonOne, a recruitment specialist, only 37% of Gen Y employees will stay in their jobs more than two years. Why? As we've already pointed out, Gen Y has the freedom to move from job to job because they are delaying the responsibilities of marriage and parenting and have a strong financial safety net in the form of parental support. They are also keenly aware of their other options and the demand for their services. If they do not like their jobs, it is easy for them to leave.

Case Study

Maurices

John Schroeder, senior vice president of Maurices, is a classic Baby Boomer in both age and experience. John has over 30 years of retail experience and has progressed from a part-time associate to a senior executive for the major fashion specialty store.

"I grew up in retail," said Schroeder. "My experience was 60- to 80-hour work weeks. A twelve-hour day was considered an easy day. As a Baby Boomer, that is what I thought needed to be done. If I was miserable, or my family time suffered, so be it. That is what was expected of us. Now I ask myself, 'Why would anyone want to do that?'"

What Schroeder and Maurices have concluded is that no one wants to work that schedule. At Maurices, no one does.

Maurices is a leading fashion retailer with nearly 600 stores around the country. Their target audience is "the savvy, fashion-conscious customer with a twenty-something attitude." In other words, their desired demographic is Gen Y.

The corporate values of Maurices are a *combination* of work, life balance, *and* results. In order to succeed at Maurices, it is critical to learn how to work efficiently, communicate effectively, and hold yourself and others accountable.

"Many of our successful store managers are from Generation Y," says Schroeder. "We have to constantly prove that we walk the talk. Gen Y is smart *and* brave enough to do something else if we are not living up to our values."

Maurices is a classic example of alignment. It all starts *before* a person is even hired, with the corporate values posted under the career section on the website. Maurices walks the walk by:

- providing new-hire training and ongoing training

- flexible (yet accountable) work schedules

- opportunities to develop their own personal vision and goals with senior management

- opportunities to develop other interests such as conducting training and mentoring others

- constant feedback and communication

- attitude surveys to monitor progress

- constant reinforcement of the vision (nearly 100% of the employees have a clear understanding of the corporate vision)

"We do not believe in any way that Gen Y are disloyal or job-jumpers," states Schroeder. "If a talented person leaves, it is because they were not getting something from us. The first thing we do is look in the mirror to see if it is our issue of leadership. When we can allow people to grow, be stimulated, and contribute meaningful results...and we take time to really listen to them...then we will have an employee for life."

The Costs of Turnover

As discussed in Chapter 2, losing an employee, any employee, is a tremendous financial loss. Estimates vary widely and depend on your industry, but it is extremely expensive to replace a worker. It can cost several thousand dollars to hire and train a new hourly employee, and much more to replace a manager. The estimates of turnover costs per employee, already given in Chapter 2, bear repeating:

- Construction $14,500
- Manufacturing $14,500
- Trade & Transportation $12,500

- Information $19,500
- Financial Activities $18,000
- Professional & Business $15,500
- Education & Health $14,000
- Leisure & Hospitality $7,000
- Other Services $12,750

In the case of Gen Y, it is doubly painful because your organization has already put a great deal of time, energy, and effort into attracting this person. In fact, you may have actually revamped your whole recruiting program specifically for Gen Y.

> "For a 40,000-employee company, total turnover costs would reach $80 million annually with a 15 percent turnover rate. The same firm with a 40 percent turnover rate would spend $214 million annually."
> — *THE TOTAL VIEW NEWSLETTER*

The need for Gen Y retention is particularly dire because as early as 2010 there will be a general labor shortage of seven to ten million workers. As your Baby Boomers retire and your Gen X employees move up, you will be fighting to attract *new* workers. You cannot afford to lose *any* of your existing employees.

Losing Gen Y employees also sends a powerful message to other Gen Yers that your company is not a good place to work. Remember, retention and recruiting go hand in hand. If you fail at one, you cannot succeed at the other.

> ### KEY POINT
> **In tough economic times, you need to attract and keep the best talent.**

Create a Retention Culture

As a leader, you need to create a culture for retaining Gen Y. You need to make it a priority and enlist the aid of your entire organization as you pursue this goal. A formal retention program can serve multiple purposes. First, it shows your organization that you are serious about keeping Gen Y. Second, it tells management that retention is a priority and they will be accountable if retention goals are not met. Third, it helps you develop a system for monitoring employee morale. Fourth, it tells Gen Y that they are valued. Fifth, it causes you to make changes in the organization and reward structure that will improve retention.

> ### KEY POINT
> **The culture that you design to attract and retain Gen Y will be appreciated by everyone, not just Gen Y.**

Retention Strategies

Strategic Planning for Retention

Even if you develop a culture that accepts Gen Y and promotes their full integration, you are still going to have more turnover today than we did with earlier generations. This is going to be a fact of life moving forward. It is critical that you and your team incorporate this reality into all of your strategic plans. It is a new cost of doing business.

To quote legendary football coach Vince Lombardi, "We're going to chase perfection in the hopes of catching excellence." As you develop your strategic plans, it will be critical for your team to understand and move proactively to the new paradigm Generation Y presents.

Items to consider for your strategic plan:

- recruiting and retention goal

- recruiting and retention owner

- sustainable business strategy

- resource allocation for:

  - onboarding

  - leadership development

  - change management

Give Gen Y Meaningful Work

The key to retaining Gen Y is to offer them work that is meaningful, and work that gives them responsibility and provides the opportunity for progression. Gen Y is not at all unique in wanting this kind of work.

Researcher Frederick Herzberg did studies on what motivates employees and influences them to commit to an organization. He developed a theory known as the Motivation-Hygiene Model. Herzberg found that there are two types of influences in the workplace, "positive motivators" and "hygiene factors." The "positive motivators" were primarily job qualities or components:

- the work itself
- challenge/achievement
- promotion prospects
- responsibility
- recognition

The "hygiene factors" were primarily monetary or other intangible benefits associated with the job or the work environment:

- pay and benefits
- company policy and administration
- relationships with co-workers
- physical environment
- supervision
- status
- job security

Herzberg found that the hygiene factors did not motivate people. In fact, these benefits were pretty much taken for granted in the Western world. Their presence in the workplace merely prevented employees from becoming *dissatisfied*. The factors that made a difference and led to worker commitment were the positive motivators. Herzberg also found that eliminating factors causing employee dissatisfaction did not make employees motivated.

KEY POINT
The only way to inspire people is to offer the positive motivators.

Gen Y will be motivated and stay committed only when their jobs have challenge, offer promotion prospects, and give them responsibility and recognition.

Consultant's Corner

Be Creative

As a leader, take some time to think about creative and non-traditional ways you can develop Gen Y. Your goal should be to create developmental opportunities that only you and your organization can provide. If you are successful, you will be branding yourself as an employer and leader of choice for Gen Y.

Ideas to consider:

- Do you sit on a board? Can you bring one of your succession candidates along at times to experience these executive meetings?

- Can you find a board for some of your Gen Y employees to join? If you are on the board too, all the better. In this situation, you will be peers.

- Do you know an author, business leader, politician, or similar professional who would agree to speak to your team? Consider creating a quarterly speakers' "Lunch & Learn" with contacts from your network. This would be something only you could provide.

It's Not Just About Money

Our research indicated that the top reasons for job dissatisfaction had nothing to do with money. The top two reasons for Gen Y's dissatisfaction were:

- lack of feedback or manager support
- work not challenging or meaningful enough

Unfortunately, when many organizations start losing people, they think money alone is the answer. We often see organizations try to address turnover by:

- increasing salaries
- enhancing tuition reimbursement
- adjusting vacation policies

These solutions ignore the actual sources of dissatisfaction. Many studies over the years have shown that managers often think workers want money and benefits when in reality they are looking for better communication, interesting work, and other nonmonetary benefits. Workers tend to take money for granted. Once they've accepted a salary, they are interested in other things.

"Many of our successful managers are valuable and desired by others," says John Schroeder of Maurices. "We believe if we provide the balance and challenge people need, our folks will stay because it is meaningful. We have had people leave in order to double their incomes and then want to return because the [other] environment was not supportive and challenging enough."

A high salary alone will not keep Gen Y in a job they don't care about or feel is part of their vision. Although tuition payments and more vacation benefits will certainly be attractive to Gen Y, they are no substitute if a job lacks substance or meaning. If Gen Y does not care about the work they are doing, they will use your tuition benefits to get another degree, then they will move on to the job they really want.

KEY POINT

Money does not create job satisfaction in Gen Y, nor does it buy loyalty!

Give Gen Y Work That Incorporates Their Vision

Make sure you understand what Gen Y really cares about and be sure it is incorporated into their jobs in some way. Make an effort to let Gen Yers shape their jobs. Give them more control over how they do the work, and let them become involved with projects that they find meaningful. Most important, find out if they believe the work they are doing advances their personal goals and vision.

Give Gen Y Challenges

Let Gen Yers work on projects where they can take responsibility. Encourage managers to delegate to Gen Yers and use checkpoints to track progress. Give Gen Yers help when needed. This will build their capabilities and free up their managers' time. Another approach is to create a slight mismatch between a Gen Yer's job skills and the job so that the Gen Yer has to stretch and grow. In other words, put Gen Yers in situations they've never dealt with before so they have the opportunity to learn and try new things.

Give Gen Y Long-Term, Strategically Meaningful Projects

As discussed earlier, Gen Y has a shorter job horizon than older employees. They are looking at a point one year in the distance or perhaps two. Help them commit to a goal that is more long term by enlisting them in lengthier projects. Is there something you have wanted to accomplish but have not had the time or resources to complete? Assign these tasks to your Gen Yers and be sure they understand the tasks' strategic importance.

If you are hiring an experienced Gen Y employee, do not be afraid to give him or her significant challenges right from the start. At Maurices, managers may be hired and given an underperforming store as the initial job assignment. This trial by fire has proven to be very successful. In one case, a store manager was hired (accepting a pay cut to join the culture) and assigned a below-average location. In less than two years, the store tripled in size and is now a top-5 location.

Coach's Corner

Be an Extreme Communicator

Today leaders have so many more opportunities to reinforce their message. Gen Yers are extreme communicators who are used to receiving and tuning out literally thousands of messages every day. For leaders to succeed, we must also become extreme communicators. While technology is an important tool, for example text messaging, I am not just referring to the obvious.

What I'm saying is, use every available means you have. Use a variety of methods to communicate your vision. Never miss an opportunity to sell your vision. Since Gen Yers are such extreme communicators, leaders need to communicate in different ways.

One example: Our team is doing a poor job rebounding, so how are we going to emphasize that and get the message across? To start, we're going to show a film of our not doing it the way we should. We're going to emphasize rebounding in practice. We're going to reward and penalize rebounding in practice. We are going to drill rebounding in practice. We're also going to wallpaper the locker room, with posters about rebounding. They go up to the sink to wash their hands and "Rebound" is written on the mirror in crayon.

We would then watch another film of the best team in college basketball rebounding. Now we showed how we're not doing it, plus we showed how this team does it. Then we'll pick the best individual rebounder in college or in the NBA and show a film. So we're working them on the court, we're penalizing and rewarding with it, we're emphasizing it, and we're using all available means to communicate the vision that we have to become a better rebounding team. Our players may even wake up and read a text message: "Did you rebound in your sleep last night?" We're going to get this message across: We have to rebound if we're going to be a good basketball team.

We will use all available means to communicate that message. Does it sound silly? Maybe. But it works.

Communicate, Communicate, Communicate

Keep Gen Y Informed

All employees want to know what is going on around them, but, as we've emphasized, Gen Y wants to know even more so. Keep your Gen Y employees in the loop. Schedule state-of-the-business meetings to keep your Gen Y talent aware of anything new in the company. Allow plenty of time for questions and answers. Consider other ways you can communicate. Perhaps there is a better way to reach your younger employees than the one you are now using.

And don't just communicate with your Gen Yers. Expand your communication to include Gen Y's circle of influence.

Place parents, appropriate sib—lings (spouses, if applicable), and all other influencers on your company newsletter mailing list, for example.

Provide Feedback

Gen Y needs and wants feedback. They are used to instant feedback. In our opening scenario, Christine was waiting for an annual review to give her Gen Y staff member feedback. This was too little, too late. Gen Y needs more.

> **What is the shortest word in the English language that contains the letters abcdef?**
>
> **Answer: *feedback*. Remember that feedback is one of the essential elements of good communication.**

Consultant's Corner

One-on-One Performance Management

An excellent tool for giving Gen Y employees feedback is the one-on-one review. Take the time to meet with your Gen Yers individually to discuss what they are doing and how they are doing it. Give them feedback on what they are doing right and wrong. Let them know how they can do things better. Give them the opportunity to ask questions. Gen Y wants to know where they stand. Remember to reinforce your *mutual* vision and ask them if they are making progress toward their personal goals.

Here is an overview of how to communicate with Gen Y:

Set up
- Once per month
- Set date and time two weeks in advance
- Informal setting
    - "No major problems" – setting for discussion can be informal
    - "Some problems" – office or more formal setting
- Be aware of employee's style
- Review employee's vision and goals

Substance
- Establish agenda
    - Any special projects?
    - Link to performance targets
- Prepare yourself to listen
    - Use open-ended questions to begin and dig deeper
    - Use close-ended questions to confirm
- Reach consensus/agreement on good performance and performance short of expectations
    - Agree on action/timing

Follow-up
- Short write-up is required, hopefully within 72 hours
- Use phrases like:
    - *I believe*   *You should*
    - *We agreed*   NOT *Don't ever*
    - *We said*   *You should have*

- Link write-up to the performance targets
- Reinforce current good performance
- Specifically state where "you've agreed" the performance is short of expectations
- Specifically state the action points "you've agreed" will occur
- Specifically state any actions the manager will take to help the employee reach his/her goals and expectations

Case Study

Henderson Brothers
Tom Grealish

Tom Grealish, President of Henderson Brothers, Inc., is focused on building a company recognized for excellence throughout the insurance industry. He believes the key to success is developing strategic plans that are *aligned* from top to bottom. In fact, for the past ten years he has even developed an annual personal strategic plan to guide his own development. This personal plan is also aligned to the larger corporate plan, which in turn is aligned to departmental plans.

Having been involved in many business leadership forums over the years, Grealish has heard all of the excuses leaders make for not creating, let alone aligning, strategic plans. "People will say, 'I'm too busy to create a strategic plan,'" said Grealish. "The fact is, I'm too busy *not* to create a strategic plan. I believe strategic planning is to continuous improvement as exercise is to fitness. One cannot be accomplished without the other."

At Henderson Brothers, the strategic plan begins with a vision and is carried all the way through to regular one-on-one meetings with every employee. Part of the vision statement refers to providing "heroic service." "You could build the entire platform on the word, heroic," Grealish says. "If you woke everyone up at 2:00 in the morning and asked 'What's the one thing you do at Henderson Brothers?" they'd say, 'Provide heroic service.'"

In order to assure alignment between his personal plan, corporate plan, and departmental plans, Grealish also has implemented regular one-on-one meetings for *every* employee with their managers. No one in his organization goes longer than 90 days (many people have monthly meetings) without a regularly scheduled session with their supervisor. "Strategic planning gives you a relentless scorecard to measure success," observes Grealish. "Our one-on-one process allows for regular, timely feedback on everyone's progress. If needed, we can quickly make adjustments and, maybe more important, give feedback, give recognition, and celebrate successes in real time."

"Most employees leave because they don't know they're valued in an organization, and they don't know where the organization is going," stated Grealish. "Our commitment to alignment and accountability means most people are invested in Henderson Brothers' strategic plan. People take ownership, everyone contributes, and even our newest Gen Y employees are connected to our long-term strategic success."

Grealish's Tips for Alignment

- *Words matter.* "Choose your vision and mission statement carefully. Make sure it is uniquely you and avoid a 'visions-R-us' approach."

- *Implement a regular one-on-one process.* "Annual appraisals are not enough. Our veteran employees appreciate the regular feedback and our newest employees almost demand it."

- *Train your supervisors.* "Many of our senior leaders never experienced a monthly meeting with their boss, so they didn't really know how to conduct a productive session. Give them some help."

- *Model the behavior.* "I still conduct monthly one-on-ones with my direct reports, and I am constantly aware that I am setting an example."

Face-to-Face Contact

Do not rely on electronic communications only. Gen Y prefers face-to-face communication. Do take advantage of email, cell phones, and texting, but the personal touch is still most meaningful to Gen Y. Further, talking to Gen Yers (or anyone) face-to-face can help eliminate misunderstandings. Sublte nuances of speech cannot be fully conveyed electronically with emoticons (little images like a smiling face or a person rolling on the floor laughing). Components of communication like inflection, tone, and facial expression are frequently needed to convey your message as you intended.

Explain the Why

On the day-to-day management level, don't just give orders, give the reasoning behind them. If you want your Gen Y employees to do something, tell them why in a way that lets them know the importance of the task to the company. Show them how their work will contribute to the bottom line and the big picture. They need to know they are making an impact, and details are also educational for them.

Make Your Office Inviting

A meeting in the boss's office is not perceived by Gen Y as punitive. It is seen as a great opportunity to interact and gain feedback. As discussed earlier, meetings in your office may seem counterintuitive to you. You may not have interacted with employees this way in the past. But you must adapt your style. Make your office inviting. Keep your door open. Track how often each Gen Y employee visits you. If it does not happen regularly, make changes so that it will.

Coach's Corner

Welcome Gen Y

When I was coaching at North Carolina State, I visited Jerry Wainwright's office at the University of North Carolina, Wilmington, where he was the head men's basketball coach.

When I walked into Jerry's office, I was immediately amazed at what I saw. This didn't look like any other office I had ever been in. Every nook and cranny, every wall space, was filled with a fun or interesting object. He had race cars, cartoon characters, sports figurines, stuffed animals, bobbleheads, and characters from the TV show

Family Guy cluttering his office and making it impossible to see it all at once.

Curious, I asked him what the purpose of all this stuff was. Why was his office decorated in this fashion? His reasoning was ingenious. He wanted his office to be inviting and welcoming to his players. He wanted to make it easy for them to want to go and see him. He wanted to encourage casual drop-bys.

We always talk about spending quality time with our children and families, but some of the best stuff happens when we're simply hanging out. It seems like when we're just hanging out spending time is the time when our kid takes his first steps. It's hard to plan for that. Jerry understood this, as he cultivated relationships with his players. That's why his office was decorated in this unique and brilliant fashion. And it worked.

Praise Gen Y

Employees of all ages are crying out for earned, genuine recognition. Many feel they are noticed only when they've made a mistake. Many organizations don't have a culture of rewarding employees. Others have complicated, ineffective, and expensive programs to motivate workers. Many assume that employees will be motivated by regular raises. Yet the best reward techniques are immediate and personal, particularly with respect to Gen Y. Better still, most of them are free. The reality is, it does not take much to reward employees, mainly just thoughtfulness. (For many examples, see Bob Nelson's book, *1001 Ways to Reward Employees.*)

Make Compliments Personal and Specific

Do not just say "Thank-you," or "Good job" — tie the praise to a specific project, idea, or accomplishment. This shows Gen Y that you actually know what they are working on and that you understand their personal role in the achievement or accomplishment.

Make Compliments Timely

Reinforcement is most effective when it is immediate. When a bonus is presented at the end of the quarter, employees have often forgotten what they are being rewarded for. Act promptly to praise achievements.

Our research reinforces the fact that an employee's favorite reward is an immediate, personal pat on the back. In other words, do not wait for a predetermined date nor do it as part of a planned program. In our case study at the beginning of the chapter, Christine (the boss) was very happy with her Gen Y's performance yet she was waiting to compliment him at his annual review. She should have been periodically praising him when he did something right.

KEY POINT
We all respond well to positive reinforcement, especially Gen Y.

*Consultant's
Corner*

Develop Communication Triggers

Adopt cues that will remind you to communicate with your Gen Y employees. Here are two simple techniques that will serve as reminders to communicate:

Three Pennies Tactic

Place three pennies in one of your pockets to start the day. During the course of the day, when you have sought out a Gen Y employee to interact with, move a penny from one pocket to another. Do not leave the building until you have moved all of the pennies.

Box of Cards

Buy a box of note cards and place them on your desk. Make it your goal to use one box of cards every month to write a thank you or other positive comment to an employee. Do not let a month go by without emptying the box.

Ask for Gen Y's Input and Really Listen!

Our research shows that the very best thing you can do to retain your Gen Y staff is to LISTEN to them. Hold impromptu meetings to learn about the progress of assignments. Schedule time in your weekly calendar to seek out Gen Y and ask for updates on what they are doing. Ask for their opinions on other subjects as well. Gen Y offers a fresh perspective and a new pair of eyes. They may be the ones who will ask the "Emperor's New Clothes" types of questions, particularly if your organization is subject to groupthink and there is a lack of questioning or exploring of options.

Promote open communication. Gen Y expects to be listened to. Don't react negatively if they bring up concerns or seem not to know their place; instead, encourage them to bring any issues to you. Repeat the open-door invitation often so they'll know you really do want to talk to them.

Communicate Carefully

As a leader, you are looked at differently. Realize that when you enter the workplace, people are paying attention to your actions, especially Gen Yers. Study your "game film" to be sure you are not missing small tendencies that may alienate your Gen Y workforce. Are you saying good morning? Are you ignoring people? Are you accessible? Do you smile?

Don't Send Workaholic Messages

Do not send email before 7:00 AM or after 6:00 PM. Program your system to release that email during regular business hours. When managers work late, they may send emails well into the night or very early in the morning. Your Gen Yer will interpret this as a sign that they are part of a workaholic environment that requires overly long days and late nights. Since life balance is critical to Gen Y, they may be alarmed by this. Demonstrating a good work ethic is fine, but insomniac emails send the wrong message.

> **KEY POINT**
>
> Not sending emails in the middle of the night is particularly important when you are recruiting a candidate.

Develop a Personal Relationship with Gen Y

Managers often think that their project management and other skills are the key to their jobs. However, building human connections with each worker is often more valuable than technical skills. Gen Y wants to be part of a group. They want to be treated as special by management. This is why informal management-by-walking-around, and spontaneous interaction, can be so valuable in an organization. Put another way, the reason Gen Y quits is often because they don't like their managers. Managers need to realize that they must create positive connections with their workers.

Take an Interest

Take time to understand what makes up Gen Y's world outside of work. Gen Y "works to live" not "lives to work." Their families, friends and leisure activities are important to them. The job can support their outside activities. Make it a point to understand the key circumstances of their lives that could effect a job change. Are their roommates moving out of town? Are they considering marriage?

Getting divorced? Is there some change in their world? Diplomatically stay on top of their circumstances without appearing to be nosy.

In our opening scenario, Christine did not know if her Gen Y employee was single, married, living at home, or had kids. He may have been quitting because he could not find daycare for his children or needed to be home with them. Maybe his roommate got transferred. Christine couldn't help him because she didn't understand his world. Some job departures are completely preventable if you know the circumstances and are willing to work with an employee.

Spend Time with Gen Y

Make time to take your Gen Yers to lunch or out for coffee, or just drop by their desk to "catch up." Connect with them in different settings. You do not always have to meet with them in your office. Plan for informal time.

Ask yourself if there are ways you can show an interest in your employees outside of their job-related duties. You are not looking to become one of their buddies but you are looking to connect with their outside world. It's as simple as commenting to them on the performance of their favorite sports team, or tearing out a review of a hiking trail from the local paper and giving it to your Gen Yer who hikes. What these (or similar) actions convey is that this person is important enough to you that you remembered a detail about his or her life and took the time to respond on a personal level.

Link Rewards to Performance

Do not simply give Gen Y an automatic raise based on time spent on the job. According to Dave Campeas, of the PrincetonOne staffing firm, the rewards most often used by employers were simply related to presence. That is, if you showed up regularly for a certain amount of time you would be rewarded, also known as "the annual raise." According to Campeas, employees place little value on such rewards. They want their managers to reward them for specific performance.

If at all possible, do not give raises on anniversary dates. Make sure you link them to production, not tenure. Gen Y wants to be rewarded for results. Do not send a message that time on the job alone equals rewards.

Inventory all of your rewards. Do you have event tickets, golf shirts, coffee cups, passes for a day off work with no questions asked, and other items? Do not just randomly pass them out. Make sure any reward you give is intentional and linked to something specific. (Do not give out tickets to tonight's game and expect to gain loyalty. The message you are really sending is "I couldn't find anyone else at the last minute.")

Reward effort as well as success. Sometimes good ideas just don't work out. You can award good efforts along the way, or do as some companies do and have an annual prize for the best idea that didn't pan out. The point is, if you only reward success, your staff will only promote safe ideas and you'll miss out on the more creative ones that may or may not work, but have a big upside potential.

Give Meaningful Raises

Instead of small percentage raises, consider giving a lump sum equal to the raise. For example, if someone is earning $45,000 a year and is going to receive a 4% raise, that would translate into a lump sum of $1,800. Receiving a lump sum might have a bigger impact on your employee than an hourly increase that amounts to less than $1 per hour.

Offer Alternative Rewards

In addition to, or in lieu of, financial raises, you may want to give free-time opportunities. You can offer days off, additional vacation time, travel vouchers, and so forth instead of dollar raises. Gen Y highly values free time and often will place greater value on vacation days than on financial compensation.

Offer Gen Y Flexible Working Conditions

Flexible Hours

Try to be flexible with Gen Y's hours. Consider offering them flex time, comp time, telecommuting, job sharing, or part-time work. Most Gen Y employees will use only the flex time and comp time, but they will appreciate your flexibility on the other options. Gen Y likes to be in control. When they feel in control, they are calmer and are more likely to give their best.

Flexible Staffing

Flexible staffing is an idea that is little used. Think of it as giving you a larger workforce without much extra cost. From Gen Y's perspective you offer them the opportunity to balance work and life as they prefer. Some Gen Y may prefer four-day 32-hour weeks. Or four-day 40-hour weeks. If you have multiple people who work less than 40 hours, or are slightly overstaffed, many Gen Yers will be able to work as much or as little as they like. At the same time, you'll have people to fill in when you lose a person and you'll have more people to welcome and train newcomers.

Flexible Locations

Offer Gen Y a variety of work locations if at all possible. Can your Gen Y employees work from a coffee shop? Can they work from home? Even if this is not possible 40 hours per week, is it possible for some amount of time? Be flexible on site as well. Vary the locations of meetings. Put variety into the day-to-day work world. Do not have conferences in the same place, at the same time, with the same agenda.

KEY POINT
Flexibility costs you little and buys you a lot.

Case Study

Accurate Home Care

Amy Nelson, founder of Accurate Home Care, is an entrepreneur. In 1999, after volunteering in an emergency room, Amy became interested in the medical field. In 2002, at the age of 18, she decided to "listen to the calling" and start her own company. Today, Accurate Home Care employs over 1000 people and serves hundreds of clients.

Amy realized the home care industry needed to focus better on respecting the needs of everyone associated with the industry. Her goal was to build an organization dedicated to her clients, employees, and community.

As a member of Gen Y and the president of her own multi-million dollar company, Amy has some advice for Gen X and Baby Boomer leaders.

What do you think is the biggest prejudice Boomers and Xers have against Gen Y?

I believe the other generations start off with an assumption that Gen Y is lazy and lacks ambition. Folks believe we think everything needs to be on our schedule. For example, I would rather start my day a bit later, say 9:00 AM. I'll work until 10:00 PM if needed. More traditional managers think the work day must be a 7:30 AM-5:30 PM type of thing.

It is important to be open-minded about flexibility. I know it is not always possible to have flex hours, but it is possible sometimes. Managers should not assume flexibility equals laziness.

What mistakes do you see experienced supervisors make in regard to Gen Y?

Gen Y has tons of drive, ideas, and energy. People need to accept that, even embrace it. Too often I see people try to squash it, instead of nurture it. Don't look at a Gen Yer like, "What would you know?" Instead, ask for their ideas and try them — they just might work.

For me, personally, I was honestly intimidated by the challenge of starting my own firm. Many people tried to squash my ambition. The key is to never give up.

You were running your own business, so your quitting wasn't an issue. Why do you think so many Gen Y folks do leave challenges?

I don't think they do leave challenges as much as Xers and Boomers think. They may well leave right after a hurdle has been cleared, but I don't think my generation is a bunch of quitters.

When a Boomer manager does try to squash a Yer's energy, or doesn't listen to their ideas, it can be a motivator for us. I think we Gen Yers will persevere through the challenge, overcome it, and feel vindicated. We will prove our point…then we may leave.

Managers need to coach constructively, not push "Do it the way I did it." Gen Y will prove a point and then take that experience elsewhere.

Do you have any other observations about the generations you would like to share?

My only observation is, I think Baby Boomers and Gen Xers want to start their day earlier and Gen Y prefers to start later. I don't have any data; that's just my observation.

What advice would you offer Generation X and Baby Boomer leaders?

Stand your ground. What I mean is, if you have *truly* considered Gen Y's input, and reviewed your policies and procedures to fix outdated items, then don't compromise the culture by saying yes to every request.

Gen Y is like everyone; we will push our boundaries to see where the line really is. My advice to leaders is…lead. Gen Y wants, needs, and even expects to be led. If you compromise your culture, you will lose the respect of your Gen Y employees, even though you gave in to their requests. The truth is, if you cave in too often, you will lose your Gen Y employees, not retain them.

The best example I have is our desire to be flexible. So far, I have never told an employee no when they have asked to take a day off, leave early, or whatever. I am happy to say it has never been abused. We have made it culturally inappropriate to take advantage of our flexibility. Because we constantly held our ground about work hours in the beginning, everyone respects our policies. In fact, the rest of the team would address anyone who is trying to abuse our culture long before it would even come to a manager's attention.

Any final thoughts?

At the end of the day, everyone wants to feel they're contributing. If you really listen to folks, and address the issues, people will feel more than safe to contribute. They will feel powerful.

Do Not Assume Gen Y Is Satisfied

Just because your Gen Yers are working hard and seem to be enjoying their work, do not assume they are satisfied or are planning to stay with your organization for the long term. And by all means don't assume that your Gen Y employees are happy just because they don't complain! No news does not mean good news. Do not be unpleasantly surprised like Christine in our opening story. She mistakenly equated a lack of complaints with satisfaction. Your Gen Y employee may just be biding his or her time until a better opportunity comes along.

Take the initiative to find out what your Gen Y employees are really thinking. Good leaders know the attitudes of their workforce. Remember, satisfaction can simply mean a lack of dissatisfaction. It can also mean everything's okay until something better comes along. You want loyalty and commitment, not simply compliance.

Keep Recruiting and Selling Gen Y

Constantly recruit your current Gen Yers. It is exciting to be recruited. Continue to tell them how special they are and how their talents will be very beneficial to the organization. Your Gen Yers don't stop being special once they're onboard. Constantly re-sell your mutual vision.

How you handle the early days will have a lot to do with retention. The old joke about people choosing between Heaven and Hell can be applied to recruiting workers. When a person visits Hell there's a great party going on with lots of food and great music. When they visit Heaven it's very nice but somewhat boring. So they choose Hell. But when they arrive, it's horrible — hellish. The newcomer asks the devil why everything was so great yesterday for his visit and so terrible now. We all know the punch line: "Yesterday we were recruiting you, today you're an employee!"

Does your organization tend to recruit people hard and then take them for granted after they're hired? If you don't keep selling Gen Y, you'll lose them. In the past marketplace, with more good applicants than jobs, you could be careless about how you treated newcomers and just see who stuck. But in today's marketplace, the opposite is true.

First impressions are powerful and difficult to change. During the first few months on a job, new Gen Yers are developing a picture of your workplace, while at the same time coworkers and bosses are forming impressions of them. Little things can be very important at this point. You should have your friendlier workers contact Gen Yers in the first few days.

Gen Yers' initial work assignments are crucial, too. Lots of research shows primacy effects: The first things we are exposed to are more memorable and have a bigger impact. This includes impression formation. Put your best foot forward to help Gen Yers get a positive impression of their new workplace. Give them the most important work that you can at that early stage. They need to be challenged and excited, to feel they are part of something worthwhile. This impression will be a lasting one and, if it is positive, will contribute to retention.

Keep Training and Educating Gen Y

Offer Gen Yers as much training and cross-training as they'll take. As long as they're learning, they'll stay interested in their jobs.

"Even in difficult times, keep training and investing in people," says John Schroeder of Maurices. "In challenging times it is even more important to show that your values will not be compromised." Be sure to include technology training on the latest gadgets. Gen Yers may then also be useful as formal or informal tech trainers of others, once they have mastered a new technology.

Give Gen Y Something to Believe In and Be Part Of

Gen Y wants to be part of an organization that stands for something and represents values they share. Gen Y will gain some of their personal identities through association with your organization. Be sure it is an organization Gen Y can be proud of. Select people who fit your corporate culture, who share your values. This means that you have to be clear on what your organization stands for and communicate it to all job candidates. Let Gen Y know they were selected by you because they fit your culture. This may increase their desire to fit in and stay.

Strengthen Your Internal Brand

Your brand building inside the company should reflect your company's philosophy and mission and be something with which Gen Y can identify. People like to identify with winners. That's why sports fans come out of the woodwork when a team is winning. Gen Y wants to contribute to a winning organization. Let Gen Y know that your organization is committed to winning, even if the current situation may not be completely healthy. Gen Y wants to contribute to the overall success in a significant way.

Be Socially Responsible

Gen Y would like to see you actively contributing to the community, and you can enlist them to spearhead your efforts. This brands you in the community and with Gen Y. Young workers "are seeking companies that contribute to the community through volunteer work," according to Tom Grealish of Henderson Brothers. Align your community service obligations with your Gen Y employees.

Make Your Workplace Positive

Show respect for employees as people. Personal insults and bad temper have no place in management. Focus on treating employees well. You need positive people who want to help each other and don't get involved in petty politics. This is what Gen Y expects and wants in a workplace — a friendly atmosphere and support.

A good work environment can make a lot of difference in retaining Gen Y. If your teams are particularly friendly or unfriendly, that can attract or drive away Gen Y. Remember that they have always enjoyed being part of a group. For instance, much of their youthful dating was in groups, not couples. A friendly, convivial atmosphere will help keep them happy. Research by the Gallup organization suggests that it's helpful if employees have good friends or even best friends at work. If most of their friends are at work, they prefer to be with them. But one sarcastic individual, bully, slacker, or other negative type can turn them off about your workplace.

Just as employees tend to treat customers the way they are treated, it is often overlooked that they tend to treat each other the way you treat them. You can improve group dynamics in your workplace by treating your employees well. Happy Gen Y employees are indispensable for recruiting new Gen Y employees.

Encourage Fun

Gen Y responds well to fun. Whether it's casual Fridays, free pizza some days, games with prizes, or other rewards, find a way to encourage fun in the workplace. Recognize and celebrate success as important goals are achieved. Create organizational traditions. Have a 4th of July picnic. Match employees' volunteerism at charities with money. Have an annual awards dinner. Celebrate tax freedom day or do something just plain wacky.

Treat Employees Like Volunteers

Max Depree, author of books such as *Leadership Is an Art,* was famous for running a happy workplace at the Herman Miller furniture company. His secret was that he treated his employees as if they were volunteers. Think about doing "the little things." Make a list of what you can do to make your employees' lives easier. Are your Gen Y employees traveling? Can you have something waiting in their hotel room upon their arrival? Can you give them a rental car upgrade? Some of your airline miles? Little things matter!

Retaining Gen Y Is Everyone's Job!

It is not just your problem or your responsibility to retain Gen Y. It is everyone's job and a mission that must be operationalized. The entire organization benefits when a good Gen Y employee stays, and it suffers when a talented Gen Yer leaves.

Be Sure Managers and Supervisors Are in Alignment

Ensure that all of your managers and supervisors are in full alignment with the strategy to retain Gen Y. Most managers feel that Gen Y turnover is HR's problem. The reality is, it is everyone's problem. Managers are usually directly involved when an employee is unhappy. People quit managers more than they quit companies. Hold your managers accountable when Gen Y quits. Make retention part of their annual appraisal/performance management. Give managers and supervisors bonuses for high retention rates. Penalize them if they have high rates of attrition. Institute a policy of chargebacks. Link turnover to a manager's profit-and-loss statement. Charge the department for the cost of replacing employees.

KEY POINT
Employees quit managers more often than they quit a company!

Referral Bonuses

Offer generous referral bonuses for additional Gen Y employees. Find out who their friends are and if they are interested in working for your organization. Pay one half of the bonus upon hire and the other half on the newer employee's first anniversary. Make it financially beneficial to bring in new Gen Yers.

"Goodbye" Is Not "Goodbye"

If good Gen Y employees do leave, find out why. Conduct a real exit interview. Enlist their help. Ask them what it was about their job or your organization that they didn't like. Ask them how you could do things better. Tell them that you hope they'll consider coming back if the new job doesn't work out.

Conclusion

It costs a company thousands — actually tens of thousands of dollars — to hire, lose, and replace a worker. As your Baby Boomers retire, it will become increasingly expensive and damaging for you to lose your current Gen Y employees. Generation Y can be dedicated, long-term employees if you give them jobs that have meaning, provide the opportunity for advancement, and give them responsibility.

Once you have given them a job they care about, you must communicate frequently with them to determine how the job is going and whether they are on track to achieve their goals. You must also give them frequent feedback and regular opportunities for input. Develop a personal relationship with them. Make sure your workplace is Gen Y friendly. Understanding and being sensitive to the needs of these workers will be the key factor in retaining them. If you want them to care about your company, show them that you care about them.

Gen Y might take a job with your organization with every intention of leaving after a year or so. But if they get involved with meaningful work, receive reinforcement, and are in a positive work environment, they may feel connected to your organization in a way they never anticipated and stay longer than they ever thought they would. That is your goal.

KEY POINT

Working with Gen Y can make you a better leader.

You now have a fuller understanding and awareness of the opportunities and challenges presented by Gen Y. They are different and they are not going to change. You are going to have to revolutionize your organization to attract, hire, and retain them. You are going to have to reach out to them as never before and treat them differently every step of the way. You are going to have to adapt jobs to them, have an ongoing dialogue with them, and generally modify and adjust your behavior toward them. And you will have to operationalize these changes and be sure your people and programs are in alignment on this mission.

Make no mistake about it, successfully attracting and hiring Gen Y over the next decade is going to take a lot of work. In a sense, it's going to be like turning a ship in icy waters. You're the captain. You see the icebergs. You know what's at stake. If you don't do something, a disastrous collision is inevitable. You need to act quickly. You need to enlist the aid of all deck hands. You need to issue orders that must be obeyed from the top all the way down the chain of command. Your passengers are depending on you. Your ship is depending on you. It's going to be difficult. It's going to take time, but it must be done.

You have no choice. You are facing the icebergs of an imminent labor shortage as 77.5 million Baby Boomers retire. Gen Xers cannot make up the difference. Your Baby Boomer employees are retiring and Gen Y employees are their indispensable replacements. They are your future. Fortunately, it can be a great future if you adapt to it.

Chapter 17

Now It's Up to You

Early in this book we talked about the leadership challenge facing you today. Gen Y is here now...and they have rewritten the rules. We've shown you how to benefit from these new rules to improve your leadership and your organization.

As a leader, will you fight change or embrace it? Will you drive your culture to new heights, or will the weight of your prejudices sink your chances? Will you really seek to understand before seeking to be understood? Will you find new and creative ways to recruit and work with talent, or will you hold fast to the historically successful tactics of the 20th century?

> **"Those who don't use what they know are no better off than those who know nothing."**
> — PARAPHRASE OF AN OLD PROVERB

Don't Fight the Last War

Tactics from the past tend to hang on despite important changes having occurred. For instance, many of the Civil War military leaders, from both the North and the South, were trained at West Point where everyone studied military strategy. The model for tactics, later used by both Union and Confederate generals, was Napoleon.

The Napoleonic Wars, which ended in 1815, saw the design and implementation of the most advanced battle tactics in history — *to that point.*

Nearly every general in the Civil War developed their battle strategies based upon these "Rules of Engagement." There was one significant flaw, however. In the 46 years between wars, technology had advanced dramatically. Specifically, the inaccuracy of the musket in Napoleon's day gave way to the extremely accurate rifle and artillery of the Civil War. Every military leader of the day failed to grasp this significant change. This failure to adapt is the single biggest reason the Civil War claimed so many casualties.

Unfortunately, every general held firm to the "tried and true" strategies that had worked in the past. While technology changed, the battle tactics did not.

As a leader, it is your *responsibility* to challenge conventional thinking. If your competition *cannot* see the changes that are occurring, this will become your strategic advantage. Bold leadership is required to seize this opportunity, adapt your organization's culture, and become an employer of choice.

Coach's Corner

Embrace Change

The 3-point line was universally implemented for the 1986–1987 college basketball season. Many coaches were adamantly against this rule change. Some of those who did not favor the change almost obstinately refused to implement it in their game planning and preparation. Others struggled to know for sure how to use the 3-point line to their advantage.

On the other hand, Coach Pitino immediately embraced the rule change and declared to his team that he wanted them, as a goal, to attempt at least 25 3-pointers per game. He ingeniously incorporated the 3-point shot in his offense, eventually revolutionizing how coaches across the country would approach offensive basketball. Because he was way out in front and accepted and embraced the change, our Providence College team that year took advantage of the 3-point line like few others. In fact, during Big East conference play we made more 3-pointers than our opponents even attempted. Largely for this reason our Providence College team became the Cinderella of college basketball and advanced to the 1987 Final Four...still considered one of the most amazing turnarounds in recent college basketball history.

KEY POINT
To stay competitive, you must be willing to change and improve your leadership skills.

Look to the Future

Challenge yourself on what a "classic leader" is today. Like the Civil War generals, just because something is the accepted practice and everyone has been taught the same strategies and tactics doesn't mean you should ignore the changes going on around you. There will be a significant competitive advantage to those leaders who not only adapt the quickest, but also to those who get their own leaders (generals) to do the same. Gen Y *wants to be led* and are looking for the right leaders.

We realize the myths about Gen Y can be hard to ignore. When an incident occurs that reminds us of, or reinforces, our prejudices, it is oftentimes easy to revert back to our Baby Boomer/Gen X "high ground," looking down on Gen Y.

Gen Y, like previous generations, will test boundaries. They may even position this test as a demand. A statement like, "I want to be promoted within six months," may really mean, "I want to advance here as quickly as possible." Don't take their "demands" negatively. Give them the benefit of the doubt; ask questions. Listen.

5 Myths About Gen Y
Myth 1 Slackers/Lazy
Myth 2 Need instant gratification
Myth 3 Disloyal/"Job Jumpers"
Myth 4 Self-centered/Selfish
Myth 5 Pampered/Spoiled

"I think managers have a real opportunity to guide Gen Y in the area of communications," observes Chuck Fowler, president of Fairmount Minerals. "Gen Y is used to communicating in different formats, like text messaging and email. They may not always present their communications as we would like. This is a great opportunity, not an overwhelming negative."

Amy Nelson, Gen Yer and president of Accurate Home Care, warns business leaders about overreacting. "Gen Y wants leadership, not capitulation or overreaction. Do not give in to unreasonable demands and do not overreact to possibly poorly phrased requests. Remember, as talented as Gen Y may be, we are still learning. If we phrase something inappropriately, ask clarifying questions. Help us learn and get better."

As a leader, if you find yourself starting to believe the negative myths about Gen Y again, take time to re-center yourself. Your organization is watching. Manage your film clips.

---

*Consultant's
Corner*

What Your Environment Conveys

When our consultants are on site, one of the things we look for is the cartoons people have posted in their work spaces. Many times these are there to send a message. For example, are there Dilbert™ cartoons posted about unproductive meetings, annual appraisals, promotions, or other office challenges? We want to be aware of these subtle messages.

The reason these cartoons resonate with workers is because they take an issue and blow it out of proportion. By exaggerating a point and playing into humorous stereotypical situations, the reader gets a chuckle and can send a powerful, subtle message.

Lately we are seeing more and more of these messages about Gen Y. From email to the funny papers, more writers are taking aim at the stereotypical Gen Yer.

As a leader, keep your antennae up and watch for these signs. While harmless on the surface, these 'jokes' can undermine your efforts. Find out why these jokes are resonating with your employees and make sure you and your folks are not having your Gen Y prejudice buttons pushed.

In Chapters 4 and 5 we discussed Gen Y's 6 new skills and the 8 new realities.

Gen Y's 6 Superior Skills

1. Gen Y is tech savvy.

2. Gen Y is diverse.

3. Gen Y understands the global marketplace.

4. Gen Yers have good self-esteem and are independent.

5. Gen Y has a sense of security and is ambitious.

6. Gen Y has life experience in the marketplace.

Your Only Constant Is Change

Our challenge to you as Boomer and Xer leaders and managers is to constantly be aware and expand these lists. Look for even subtle changes along the way. Take the time to really understand your Gen Y employees' superior skills as a whole and then individually. Recognize and reward their skills with your praise and with challenging work assignments. Be sure your Gen Y (and all employees) know you are aware of — and value — their strengths.

It's Still Awareness

The 8 New Realities are a living list, and subtle changes will be occurring constantly. Keep your eyes and ears open about these changes. Remember, these are unwritten rules.

8 New Realities About Gen Y

1. Gen Y is delaying marriage and parenthood.
2. There is no stigma attached to moving back home.
3. When Gen Y quits, the problem is you!
4. Gen Y "leases" a job, not "buys."
5. Multiple jobs are a badge of honor.
6. Your leadership is constantly being evaluated.
7. Their circle of influence is also watching.
8. The extended family is coming back for Gen Y.

It is challenging enough to lead when the rules are written. Awareness. Awareness. Awareness.

"One of the biggest challenges for leaders can be making the time to spend with Gen Y," says Tom Grealish, president of Henderson Brothers. "While a challenge, I find it to be a selfish benefit on my part...I gain so much from these interactions. It is a pleasure to see how motivated folks are when truly challenged. Also, I get to learn what makes Gen Y tick and the subtle changes that are constantly taking place."

Be a World-Class Performer

1. Use performance feedback or "game film."
2. Turn unconscious, negative tendencies into conscious, positive choices.
3. Practice energy management.
4. Realize that what is required for improvement may be counterintuitive.
5. Develop a tactical and measurable action plan.
6. Have a *clear* vision.

As a leader, increasing your awareness is critical. The three levels every leader must address are:

1. Awareness of the fundamentals

2. Awareness of personal leadership tendencies and their impact

3. Awareness of cultural/organizational tendencies and their impact

We're All Learning

Over the course of writing this book we have been constantly challenged about our own prejudices toward Gen Y. We both understand that no matter how hard we work at it, some prejudices will pop up from time to time. It is a leader's responsibility to be aware when this is happening.

Deal With Your Own Reaction First

An example of our prejudices for the both of us came from our alma mater (Carnegie Mellon University). Several years ago our school built a gorgeous university center for the students. The building is state of the art, with restaurants, fitness facilities, lecture halls...you name it. It is truly a wonderful building providing first-class resources for the students.

We laugh now as we recall our initial reaction: "We didn't need this place when we were students here. Why spend all of this money and waste resources?" The truth is, we would have loved to have a facility like that. Our initial and very natural reaction, if we are to be honest, was one of jealousy.

If a leader is not self-aware, this initial natural reaction will never be challenged and will become the prevailing opinion. Even though this initial feeling is natural, it needs to be managed and addressed. What we had back in the day is irrelevant to the current campus environment. What is relevant is what the university needs *now* to be competitive and provide a world-class education.

The above case is a micro example of emotional push back and the natural resistance to change. As a leader, it is your job to manage this push back on a macro level. Merely dismissing a very real emotional response will not be productive.

KEY POINT

Accept emotional reactions as real, but keep the pressure on for change.

In Chapters 10 and 11 we discussed change management and creating organizational alignment. A solid change management strategy, with ongoing, candid communications will help eliminate the initial negative emotional responses. A leader who realizes the importance of attracting and retaining Gen Y must also be able to convince the organization and create sustainable change.

Creating Alignment

Every organization, like every team, is different. Each has a unique culture, talent mix, and history that sets it apart. It is a leader's job to blend the unique aspects of the organization into winning teams. There are no "magic bullet" answers for anything, especially developing a winning strategy to attract and retain Gen Y.

Alignment

Awareness

Understanding

Develop Your Roadmap

This book gives you a roadmap to follow and many tactics you can implement in your game plan. Creating your desired culture will take time. Set a bold vision and do not waiver. Be patient and persistent.

Communicate your plan across the organization and develop as many ambassadors as you can. Reward your "teamers" and watch the "fence sitters" follow. Post a scoreboard of some sort measuring your retention goals. Better yet, make attracting and retaining top talent a key indicator of success in your performance management system. Reward your supervisors, managers, and leaders for their ability to develop and retain talented people.

Over the course of writing this book we have experienced a full conversion and have gone from supporters of, to advocates for, Gen Y. There are so many things Gen Y has figured out. And for much of what they haven't figured out, Gen Y looks to us Baby Boomers and Gen Xers for help, guidance, and leadership.

Gen Y has always looked to Gen X and Baby Boomers. In many ways that is why they have so much figured out. They learned from us. It is now up to us to take this opportunity to develop our leadership legacy. It's an exciting challenge that we look forward to. How about you?

A Final Thought

We close this book by asking you, as a leader...how will history judge your leadership? Fifty years from now, long after you are gone, will old men and women gather and speak about your leadership legacy? Will this group of great grandparents tell how you helped mold them and were instrumental in their careers and their lives? What will your legacy be?

Appendix A

45 Key Competencies to Look for in a Job Candidate

Strategy Competencies

1. **Strategic** — thinks "big picture"; commits to a course of action to accomplish long-range goals; is forward thinking and adept at seeing future outcomes and results

2. **Entrepreneurial** — thinks outside the box; takes risks; invests time and thoughts to possibilities

3. **Competitive** — aware of the playing field; spirited; aggressive; driven to win

4. **Brave** — displays courage in difficult, ambiguous, and high risk situations

5. **Conflict-Comfortable** — manages tension filled situations; views conflict as an opportunity; builds consensus

6. **Innovative** — generates new ideas and solutions from self and others

7. **Negotiator** — able to find common ground; wins while preserving relationships; can be both assertive and diplomatic

8. **Change Agent** — initiates and promotes new approaches and transformations to reach a higher level of performance

9. **Decision Maker** — uses sound judgment to provide an accurate and prompt solution or course of action

10. **Communicator** — proactively conveys a clear, convincing, and timely message; possesses strong verbal, written, and presentation skills

Execution Competencies

1. **Accountable** — follows through in all areas; accepts and delivers on responsibilities; requires others to follow through on commitments

2. **Analytical** — logical, systematic, and methodical in working through a plan or problem; provides solid research on which to base decisions; establishes process for workflow

3. **Technically Competent** — possesses and maintains the functional and technical knowledge and skills to successfully perform job

4. **Quality Conscious** — delivers accuracy and precision in work products; mindful of technical requirements, rules, and standards

5. **Perspective** — able to put ideas into context to help others anticipate impact and future needs

6. **Time-Wise** — prioritizes; respects others' time; adheres to schedules and agendas

7. **Objective** — places personal emotions, beliefs or preferences aside to address issues

8. **Committed** — sticks with the program from beginning to end; does not waiver from an established plan or process

9. **Results-Driven** — achievement-oriented; achieves and exceeds goals; pushes self and others for results

10. **Creative** — generates unique and original ideas and concepts; finds new avenues around challenges and obstacles

11. **Business Savvy** — possesses business and organizational know-how; understands how to accomplish tasks through formal channels and informal networks

12. **Versatile** — adjusts effectively to new work demands, processes, structures, and cultures

13. **Avid Learner** — seeks new information and perspectives; is curious; finds new and better ways of doing things

14. **Problem Solver** — uses data and logic to quickly find solutions to difficult challenges

Relationship Competencies

1. **People Reader** — can quickly determine style, strengths and limitations of others in order to develop stronger relationships and better business outcomes

2. **Influential** — makes an impact on people, events, and decisions; affects the thinking or actions of others by means of example or personality

3. **Trustworthy** — credible and ethical; interacts in a manner to allow others to believe and have confidence in one's intentions

4. **Optimistic** — sees the glass half full; is persistent against the odds; makes the workplace positive

5. **Networked** — possesses a multitude of contacts, acquaintances, and resources; is popular and connected to newly released and vital information

6. **Straightforward** — candid, authentic, and sincere in approach; without hidden agendas

7. **Customer-Focused** — aware of customer needs; makes decisions with customer in mind; builds strong customer relationships

8. **Empathetic** — able to identify with and understand another person's feelings and challenges; is considerate of others

9. **Self-Aware** — possesses knowledge of personal strengths, weaknesses, opportunities, and threats; is aware of one's own image and effect on others

10. **Active Listener** — focuses attention on hearing what others say without interruption; is able to repeat and confirm what the other person has said even in a disagreement

11. **Hospitable** — welcoming, friendly, and accommodating; makes others comfortable

12. **Adaptable** — has awareness of others' communication styles and changes approach when warranted

Talent Development Competencies

1. **Inspirational** — leads through vision and values; motivates others to higher levels of performance

2. **Empowering** — gives others the authority to act and make decisions

3. **Open to Feedback** — willing to receive thoughts, ideas, and opposing opinions to enhance style or reconsider position

4. **Collaborative** — works effectively with others to accomplish goals

5. **Resourceful** — knows how to get what is needed; manages time and workloads for maximum efficiency

6. **Delegator** — effectively assigns work and responsibility; supports and provides feedback on performance

7. **Coach** — equips individuals with the tools, knowledge, and opportunities to develop their skills and improve performance

8. **Team Builder** — builds cohesive teams and strategic partnerships

9. **Informing** — open and generous in providing the relevant and necessary information to help others succeed

Appendix B

A Gen Yer's View of Internship Programs

by

Alison Northrop

An internship program is one of the most successful ways of finding the best of Generation Y. An intern is a temporary employee, generally a college student, who wishes to learn about a certain field. Hiring an intern is beneficial for your company, the student, and your community. The idea of internships is growing increasingly popular among students and employers; however, too many programs have been thrown together in a haphazard fashion. To maximize the potential of the program, employers should be intentional, having goals and a plan like the one set out below.

Building Your Pool of Prospects

There are many reasons why hiring interns is a good idea. First and foremost, it can help you with your future employment needs. Jared Sadowski of Henderson Brothers likens it to the "farm system" in baseball. You pick the best candidates to be interns, and then see how they do during an approximately four-month time period. You can see if they fit into the organization's culture, whether they are hard workers, and if they produce satisfactory results.

When a job opening becomes available at your organization, you will already have a good candidate base from which to choose. It is an investment for your Human Resources department, because instead of spending hours sorting through resumes, they have a group of people that they already know and who already know your company.

Along the same vein, by hiring interns, you will establish a relationship with colleges and college students. As students discuss where they worked, your organization's name will be mentioned, and if you have facilitated the internship successfully, it will be talked about in a positive manner. This can only lead to a better reputation on campus, which means more and better applicants for internships and jobs.

You will also develop a relationship with colleges' Career Centers, which will help you in future hiring. This will give you easier access to the many resources that are available at universities, should you need them. If you are not interested in hiring any new employees in the near future, think of your interns and their friends as potential future clients. Everyone wants to work with people they know and trust, and the internship will be a good foundation.

A Low-Cost Option

Another basic reason to hire interns is to get work done. They are a cheap way to hire a talented workforce. Face it, interns are a steal! You're paying them barely above minimum wage and in a few months or years, they will graduate and demand a hefty salary. They are usually very productive workers, too, because they employ the latest technology and they like to get their work done as efficiently as possible so they can go have fun. You can assign them tasks that have been on the back burner for a while and you've been meaning to get done. They can also assist overloaded and stressed employees.

Recruiting Prospects

Now that you know why to have an internship program, you must figure out how to run it successfully. It starts with finding the best candidates through effective advertising. First, write a job description. Be very specific about what they'll be doing, what kind of candidate you want, and the position's pay. Include some background about your company. You want this job description to be shown to as many people as possible, but you want to only receive resumes from truly qualified candidates, so make the job description as narrow as possible.

Second, get the word out, and get it out early. The best candidates start looking for internships around four months before the starting date. Tell your employees that you're looking to hire an intern. Give them the job description and ask for referrals. Contact the Career Centers at local colleges and universities. Send them the job description and ask for it to be emailed to students and posted on the Career Center website. Finally, you can post the job description on the Internet, specifically with websites such as collegegrad. com, monster.com, or collegerecruiter.com.

Selecting Interns

The next step is the selection process, and this works much like hiring a regular employee. Treat it with the seriousness of normal hiring. You're looking for employees for not just a few months, but for full-time positions in two or three years. Depending on the number of responses you receive, you may need an initial screen, like GPA. The exact numbers vary depending on your situation, because some companies hire one intern, others, 20. Email all potential candidates and ask for an interview. This could be face-to-face or on the phone, depending on the situation. Get a general feel for the candidate and make sure he or she fully understands the position. Narrow the field and bring back a smaller percentage for a second round, preferably in person. Decide who would best fit your organization and offer them the position. Once you have it filled, send out letters to those you decided not to hire.

Running a Program

Map out the basic structure of your program according to the following:

- Hire the intern for a set time period of about four months. Summer is the best time to have an intern, but you can also employ them in either the fall or spring semester, generally for fewer hours. Create an agreement for a certain number of weeks they will work and their hours.

- On their first day, provide the intern with some basic training and information about your organization. This includes everything from your department's vision to how to use the telephone. Let them know the written and unwritten rules.

- The intern will need an office space that is similar to regular employees. Provide them with a desk, chair, computer, and phone in a cubicle or an office. Ensure that they have a designated space to call their own.

- Pay should be a bit higher than minimum wage. Ask around in your industry to determine the appropriate pay. Also allow for the intern to have a small expense account. Furthermore, many students do internships to earn college credit. Check with them and their school so you can do everything possible to facilitate their credit-earning. [Authors' note: some interns are "paid" only with their college credits.]

- Assign each intern a supervisor/mentor. This should be the person to whom they report. The mentor will guide an intern's learning process by assigning tasks, checking up on them, evaluating their progress, and being available for questions. All the tasks that employees want the intern to do should go through their mentor.

- Require the intern to set goals about two or three weeks into the internship, once they see what your organization has to offer. They should compile a list of about five things they hope to accomplish during their time at your organization. These goals should concern the intern's professional development and learning, and must be measurable. Along with each goal, there should be a brief statement of how the goal will be achieved and a due date. The mentor will review the goals and help the intern accomplish them.

- Perform regular evaluations, both of how the intern is performing and how the internship is meeting his or her needs. The intern and mentor should schedule a lunch each month to discuss these topics in a candid manner. At the end of the internship, the intern and the mentor should each fill out a written evaluation. Use these to discuss the intern's development, ways to improve the internship program, and also as a way to remember the intern when they're interviewing for a job or asking you for a reference.

- Include the intern in all company meetings and parties. Make them feel like a wanted part of the organization. Celebrate their arrival and departure.

Institute these basic formulas, and then tweak them according to each intern's needs. Remember to be flexible because, if the internship is during the school year, schooling must be the student's top priority, and if it is during the summer, it's their vacation and they're going to want to have some fun.

What Interns Can Accomplish

What is your intern going to do all day? That depends on your needs and situation, but here are some suggestions:

- Make the job project-oriented with defined goals and deadlines.
- You may want to assign one intern per department or have them work together on a larger, team-based project.
- Keep them busy. It should be a mixture of fun and tedious work, not just all the work that everyone else doesn't want to do.

- Provide them with learning opportunities.
- Allow the day-to-day work to morph according to their tastes and strengths.
- They should not perform solely secretarial duties unless that was specifically in the job description.
- They want to make valuable contributions to the organization, so allow them to tackle big projects.

Interns are young and filled with college knowledge, so allow them to bring energy into your organization. Encourage innovation and creativity. They may seem young, especially if you hire freshmen or sophomores, but don't treat them like children. They have chosen to do an internship instead of a summer at the pool or working fast food, so you should encourage them to pursue their career goals. Give them opportunities to prove themselves in small tasks, and then give them more responsibility.

Summary

Having an effective internship program will help your organization by creating a candidate pool for future hiring, getting work done, establishing a relationship with colleges, bringing in new spunk, and many other reasons. If you are intentional about the process and follow a plan like the one outlined above, then both your interns and your organization will benefit from the relationship.

References

Alessandra, A.J., O'Connor, T., Alessandra, M.J. (1996). *The platinum rule: Discover the four basic business personalities — and how they can lead you to success.* New York: Warner Books.

Bar-On, R. & Parker, J.D.A. (Eds.). (2000). *Handbook of emotional intelligence.* San Francisco: Jossey-Bass.

Bradberry, T. & Greaves, J. (2005). *The emotional intelligence quick book.* New York: Simon & Schuster.

Caruso, D.R., & Salovey, P. (2004). *The emotionally intelligent manager.* San Francisco: Jossey-Bass.

Chester, E. (2005). *Getting them to give a damn: How to get your front line to care about your bottom line.* New York: Kaplan Business.

El-Shamy, Susan. (2004). *How to design and deliver training for the new and emerging generations.* New York: Pfeiffer.

Emmerling, R.J. & Goleman, D. (2003). *Emotional intel–ligence: Issues and common misunderstandings. issues in emotional intelligence* [On-line serial], 1(1). Available at http://www.eiconsortium.org.

Goleman, D. (1995). *Emotional intelligence.* New York: Bantam.

Janis, I. (1972). *Victims of groupthink: A psychological study of foreign-policy decisions and fiasco.* Boston: Houghton-Mifflin.

Mathews, G., Zeidner, M., & Roberts, R. D. (2002). *Emotional intelligence: Science and myth.* Cambridge, MA: MIT Press.

Mayer, J.D., Salovey, P., & Caruso, D.R., & Sitarenios, G. (2003). Measuring and modeling emotional intelligence with the MSCEIT V 2.0. *Emotion, 3,* 97–105.

Nelson, B. (1994). *1001 ways to reward employees.* New York: Workman Publishing Company.

Petrides, K. & Furnham, A. (2000). Gender differences in measured and self-estimated trait emotional intelligence. *Sex Roles, 42,* 449–461.

Salovey, P., & Mayer, J.D. (1990). Emotional intelligence. *Imagination, Cognition, and Personality, 9,* 185–211.

Wanous J.P. (1980). *Organizational entry: Recruitment selection and socialization of newcomers.* Reading MA: Addison-Wesley.

Index